Quote
UNQUOTE

D1419285

VOLUME 2:
inspirational
quotes FOR
meaningful
moments

Compiled by:

Erin Trimble

designing
with
dw
utilities

DW Utilities is a brand-new
line of books that have
been designed as reference
tools for the scrapbook and
paper artist. Brought to you
by the minds behind the
famous "Designing With"
series, the DW Utilities
books will inspire fresh
ideas and infuse new
life into your projects.
Watch your local scrapbook
store for upcoming titles.

Dedicated to my mom, Ann Mabee,
who reminds me, "remember who you are,"
and to my late grandma, Doris Bowler,
whose silly quote I will always remember:
"I love you to my heart,
I love you to my liver.
If I had you in my mouth,
I would spit you in the river."

Quotes are nothing but inspiration for the uninspired.

— RICHARD KEMPH

Let's face it. We've all had moments of "uninspiration". Some of us have these moments more often than others, and while we may lack inspiration, we no longer have to agonize over what to say.

In fact, Ralph Waldo Emerson quipped,

"Next to the originator of a good sentence is the first quoter of it."

If you're stuck trying to think of striking words, take advantage of these enlightening remarks and let another's words work for you.

Chosen for scrapbookers, card makers, journal keepers, artists and word gurus, the quotes in **Quote, Unquote: Volume 2** will inspire and delight you while aiding your quest to express your feelings in a most meaningful way.

In **Quote, Unquote: Volume 2**, we focus on life's meaningful moments—happy or heartbreaking, merry or miserable, exciting or everyday, luxurious or lackluster—because as Ralph Waldo Emerson once again observed, "By necessity, by proclivity, and by delight, we all quote."

Our life is frittered away by detail...
Simplify, simplify.
— HENRY DAVID THOREAU

Simplicity is making the journey of this life with just baggage enough.
— CHARLES DUDLEY WARNER

It has been a long axiom of mine that the **little things** are infinitely the **most important**.
— A. CONAN DOYLE

Nothing is more *simple* **than greatness;** indeed, **to be** *simple* **is to be great**.
— RALPH WALDO EMERSON

The ability to simplify means to **eliminate the unnecessary** so that the necessary may speak.
— HANS HOFMANN

The **sculptor** produces the **beautiful statue** by chipping away such parts of the **marble** block as are not needed — it is a process of **elimination**.
— ELBERT HUBBARD

5

Simplicity, carried to an extreme, becomes elegance. — JON FRANKLIN

Little by little does the trick. — AESOP

It's the little moments that make life **big.** — UNKNOWN

A gentle word, like summer rain,
May soothe some heart
and banish pain.
What joy or sadness often springs
From just the simple little things.
— WILLA HOEY

Simplicity is the ultimate sophistication. — LEONARDO DA VINCI

HOW MANY THINGS ARE THERE WHICH **I DO NOT WANT.** — SOCRATES

Who is rich?
He who rejoices in his portion.
— THE TALMUD

I would sooner live in a **cottage** and wonder at everything than live in a **castle** and wonder at nothing.

— JOAN WINMILL BROWN

It's the simple joys, the simple pleasures the heart remembers and dearly treasures.

— HADIN MARSHALL

Little drops of water,
little grains of sand,
Make the mighty ocean,
and the pleasant land:
So the minutes, humble though they be,
Make the mighty ages of eternity.
Little deeds of kindness,
little words of love,
Help to make earth happy,
like Heaven up above.

— JULIA CARNEY

Life is a great bundle of little things.

— OLIVER WENDELL HOLMES

Where do we find **peace**?
Peace is in the rosy softness
of a new **dawn** breaking.
It's the sound of the **wind**
across a **mountain** peak,
It's the **waves** breaking as
they splash upon the **beach**,
The quiet and mystical **beauty**
of a **snowflake** drifting
silently downward
to a land blanketed in **white**.
Peace is the elusive kingdom
of the **soul** which God
alone in his **love** does hold.

— UNKNOWN

If there is to be any peace,
it will come through being,
not having. — HENRY MILLER

Peace starts with a smile.

— MOTHER TERESA

PEACE IS THE EVENING STAR OF THE
SOUL, AS VIRTUE IS ITS SUN: AND THE
TWO ARE NEVER FAR APART.
— CHARLES CALEB COLTON

We seek peace, knowing that peace is the
climate of freedom. — DWIGHT D. EISENHOWER

There is no way to peace;
peace is the way.

— A.J. MUSTE

If we have no peace,
it is because we have
forgotten that we belong
to each other.

— MOTHER TERESA

PEACE IS NOT SOMETHING
YOU WISH FOR;
IT'S SOMETHING YOU **MAKE**,
SOMETHING YOU **DO**,
SOMETHING YOU **ARE**,
AND SOMETHING YOU **GIVE AWAY**.

— ROBERT FULGHUM

For it isn't enough to *talk* about peace.
One must *believe* in it.
And it isn't enough to *believe* in it.
One must *work* at it.

— ELEANOR ROOSEVELT

You can't shake hands
with a clenched fist.

— GANDHI

The **peace** is won by accompanying
God into the battle. — EIVIND JOSEF BERGGRAV

Peace within makes
beauty without.

— ENGLISH PROVERB

Peace is rarely denied
to the peaceful.

— FRIEDRICH VON SCHILLER

9

...peace be with thee.
— PSALMS 122:8

Peace is not the product of a victory or a command. It has no finishing line, no final deadline, no fixed definition of achievement. **Peace is** a never-ending process, the work of many decisions. — OSCAN ARIAS

nature

*In summer,
the song
sings itself.*
— WILLIAM CARLOS WILLIAMS

In all things of **nature** there is something of the marvelous.
— ARISTOTLE

We still do not know **one thousandth** of one percent of what **nature** has revealed to us.

— ALBERT EINSTEIN

To lie sometimes on the grass under trees on a summer's day, listening to the murmur of the water, or watching the clouds float across the sky, is by no means a waste of time.

— SIR JOHN LUBBOCK

Young and **old** come forth to play on a **sunshine** holiday.

— JOHN MILTON

The rich fire of the orange sunset gloriously announces the coming night.

— SUSAN S. FLORENCE

Nature is the art of God.

— RALPH WALDO EMERSON

Sounds of the wind or
sounds of the sea
make me happy just to be.

— JUNE POLIS

The **sun** does not shine for
a few trees and flowers,
but for the wide world's **joy.**

— HENRY WARD BEECHER

THE AIR IS LIKE A **BUTTERFLY**
WITH FRAIL BLUE WINGS.
THE **HAPPY EARTH** LOOKS
AT THE SKY AND SINGS.

— JOYCE KILMER

The kiss of the sun for pardon,
The song of the birds for mirth,
One is nearer God's heart in a garden
Than anywhere else on earth.

— DOROTHY F. GURNEY

**One touch of nature makes
the whole world kin.**

— SHAKESPEARE

Climb the mountains and get their good tidings.
**Nature's peace will flow into
you as sunshine flows into trees.**
The winds will blow their own freshness into you...
**While cares will drop
off like autumn leaves.**

— JOHN MUIR

TO ME A **LUSH** CARPET OF PINE
NEEDLES OR SPONGY GRASS
IS MORE **WELCOME** THAN THE MOST
LUXURIOUS PERSIAN RUG.

— HELEN KELLER

Spring is when you feel like whistling even with a shoe full of slush.

— UNKNOWN

Delicious autumn! My very soul is
wedded to it, and if I were a bird
I would fly about the earth
seeking the successive autumns.

— GEORGE ELIOT

SUMMER AFTERNOON,

SUMMER AFTERNOON; to me

those have always been the two

MOST BEAUTIFUL WORDS in the

English language.   — HENRY JAMES

The poetry of the earth
is never dead.

— JOHN KEATS

Each flower is a soul opening out to nature. — GERARD DE NERVAL

Look deep, **deep into nature**, and then you will understand everything better.

— ALBERT EINSTEIN

Adopt the pace of nature: her secret is patience.

— RALPH WALDO EMERSON

The bluebird carries the *sky* on his back.

— HENRY DAVID THOREAU

And forget not that the earth delights to feel your bare feet and the winds long to play with your hair.

— KAHLIL GIBRAN

Next time a sunrise steals your breath or a meadow of flowers leaves you speechless, remain that way. Say nothing, and listen as heaven whispers, "Do you like it? I did it just for you."

— MAX LUCADO

Snowy, Flowy, Blowy,
Showery, Flowery, Bowery,
Hoppy, Croppy, Droppy,
Breezy, Sneezy, Freezy.

— GEORGE ELLIS, "THE TWELVE MONTHS"

How cunningly nature hides every wrinkle of her inconceivable antiquity under roses and violets and morning dew!

— RALPH WALDO EMERSON

I wandered lonely as a cloud
That floats on high o'er vales and hills,
When all at once I saw a crowd,
A host, of golden daffodils;
Beside the lake beneath the trees,
Fluttering and dancing in the breeze.

— WILLIAM WORDSWORTH

> **Animals are such agreeable friends – they ask no questions; they pass no criticisms.**
>
> — GEORGE ELIOT

There is no psychiatrist in the world like a puppy licking your face.

— BERN WILLIAMS

If there is one spot of sun spilling onto the floor, a cat will find it and soak it up.

— JEAN ASPER MCINTOSH

DOGS come when they're called; CATS take a message and get back to you later.

— MARY BLY

Our perfect companions never have fewer than four feet.

— COLETTE

If there were to be a universal sound depicting peace, I would surely vote for the purr.

— BARBARA L. DIAMOND

THERE IS SOMETHING ABOUT THE **PRESENCE OF A CAT** THAT SEEMS TO TAKE THE BITE OUT OF BEING ALONE.
— LOUIS J. CAMUTI

Old dogs, like old shoes, are comfortable. They might be a bit out of shape and a little worn around the edges, but they fit well.
— BONNIE WILCOX

Every puppy should have a boy.
— ERMA BOMBECK

Whoever said you can't buy **happiness** forgot about **little puppies.**
— GENE HILL

THE **DOG** IS THE **GOD** OF **FROLIC.**
— HENRY WARD BEECHER

A *dog* **wags its tail with its** *heart.*
— MARTIN BUXBAUM

17

Every child is an artist.

The problem is how to remain an artist once he grows up.

— PABLO PICASSO

The object of **art** *is to give life shape.*

— JEAN ANOUILH

ART is the most intense mode of INDIVIDUALISM that the world has known.

— OSCAR WILDE

Every *artist* dips his *brush* in his own soul, and *paints* his own *nature* into his *pictures*.

— HENRY WARD BEECHER

The **art** of a people is a true **mirror** of their **minds**.

— JAWAHARLAL NEHRU

Art is a collaboration between God and the artist, and the less the artist does the better.

— ANDRE GIDE

Art is not a handicraft, it is the transmission of *feeling* the artist has experienced.

— TOLSTOY

Great *art* picks up where nature ends.

— MARC CHAGALL

Anyone who says you can't **see a thought** simply doesn't know art.

— WYNETKA ANN REYNOLDS

BEING AN ARTIST MEANS ceasing to take seriously that very serious person we are when we are not an artist.

— JOSE ORTEGA Y GASSET

Painting is just another way of keeping a diary.

— PABLO PICASSO

Art is the only way to run away without leaving home.

— TWYLA THARP

Painting is silent poetry.

— PLUTARCH

19

CREATIVITY is inventing, experimenting, growing, taking risks, breaking rules, making mistakes, and having FUN.

— MARY LOU COOK

Creativity: Take the obvious, add a cupful of brains, a generous pinch of imagination, a bucketful of courage and daring, stir well and bring to a boil.

— BERNARD M. BARUCH

Originality is not doing something no one else has done, but doing what has been done countless times with **new life, new breath.**

— MARIE CHAPIAN

Creativity **is a celebration of one's** *grandeur,* **one's sense of making anything possible.**

— JOSEPH ZINKER

It is better to fail in originality than to succeed in imitation.

— HERMAN MELVILLE

Creativity is allowing yourself to make mistakes. ART is knowing which ones to keep.

— SCOTT ADAMS

The whole life lies in the verb *seeing*.

— TEILHARD DE CHARDIN

The courage to *imagine* is our greatest resource, adding color and suspense to all our life. — DANIEL BOORSTIN

The creation of a thousand forests is in one acorn.

— RALPH WALDO EMERSON

Be daring, be different, be impractical. Be anything that will assert imaginative vision against the play-it-safers, the creatures of common-place, the slaves of the ordinary.

— SIR CECIL BEATON

Creativity is a continual surprise.
— RAY BRADBURY

Learn the craft of knowing how to open your heart and to turn on your creativity. **THERE'S A LIGHT INSIDE OF YOU.**
— JUDITH JAMISON

If you are seeking creative ideas, go out walking. Angels whisper to a man when he goes for a walk.
— RAYMOND INMAN

True *creativity* often starts where language ends.
— ARTHUR KOESTLER

Creativity is a type of learning process where the teacher and pupil are located in the same individual.
— ARTHUR KOESTLER

dancing

Kids: they dance before they learn there is anything that isn't music.

— WILLIAM STAFFORD

The dancer's body is simply the luminous manifestation of the soul.

— ISADORA DUNCAN

Dancers are the athletes of God.

— ALBERT EINSTEIN

Movement never lies. It is a barometer telling the state of the soul's weather.

— MARTHA GRAHAM

Dancing can reveal all the mystery that music conceals.

— CHARLES BAUDELAIRE

Dancing **is the poetry of the foot.**

— JOHN DRYDEN

It takes an ATHLETE to dance
but an ARTIST to be a dancer.
— SHANNA LAFLEUR

Dancers are instruments, like a piano the choreographer plays.
— GEORGE BALANCHINE

Dancing is like dreaming with your feet!
— CONSTANZE

Remember, Ginger Rogers did everything Fred Astaire did, but backwards and in high heels.
— FAITH WHITTLESEY

Dancing with the feet is one thing, but dancing with the heart is another.
— UNKNOWN

Dance till the stars come down from the rafters Dance, Dance, Dance till you drop.
— W.H. AUDEN

You can dance anywhere, even if only in your heart.
— UNKNOWN

Anyone who says sunshine brings happiness has never danced in the rain. — UNKNOWN

The dance is a poem of which each movement is a word.

— MATA HARI

DRAW A CRAZY **PICTURE**,
WRITE A NUTTY **POEM**,
SING A MUMBLE-GUMBLE **SONG**,
WHISTLE THROUGH YOUR **COMB**.
DO A LOONY-GOONY **DANCE**
'CROSS THE KITCHEN **FLOOR**,
PUT SOMETHING SILLY IN THE WORLD
THAT AIN'T BEEN THERE BEFORE.

— SHEL SILVERSTEIN

Dancing is the body made poetic.
— ERNST BACON

The body says what words cannot.

— MARTHA GRAHAM

O body swayed to music,
O brightening glance,
How can we know the
dancer from the dance?

— W.B. YEATS

D A N C E
is the landscape of man's soul.

— MARTHA GRAHAM

I get up, I walk,
I fall down. Meanwhile,
I keep dancing.

— HITTEL

writing

WRITING IS NOTHING MORE
THAN A GUIDED DREAM.
— JORGE LUIS BORGES

There is nothing to writing.
All you do is sit down at a
typewriter and open a vein.
— WALTER SMITH

A word is **dead**
When it is said,
Some say.
I say it just
Begins to **live**
That day.
— EMILY DICKINSON

Find your own quiet
center of life and write
from that to the world.
— SARAH ORNE JEWETT

Writing is a marathon of the spirit.
DON'T GIVE UP. — STUART COHEN

FILL YOUR PAPER WITH THE
BREATHINGS OF YOUR HEART.
— WILLIAM WORDSWORTH

I love writing.
I love the *swirl* and
swing of words as
they tangle with human emotions.
— JAMES MICHENER

Don't tell me the moon is shining;
show me the glint of
light on broken glass.

— ANTON CHEKHOV

Poetry we will call musical thought.

— CARLYLE

But words are things, and a small drop of **INK**, falling like dew upon a thought, produces that which makes thousands, perhaps millions **THINK**.

— LORD BYRON

READING ALL THE GOOD BOOKS IS LIKE A CONVERSATION WITH THE FINEST MEN OF PAST CENTURIES.

— RENÉ DESCARTES

Literature is my utopia.

— HELEN KELLER

A home without books is like a body without a soul.

— MARCUS TULLIUS CICERO

BOOKS are the TREASURED WEALTH of the WORLD and the fit INHERITANCE of GENERATIONS and NATIONS.

— HENRY DAVID THOREAU

books

Make thy books thy companions.
Let thy cases and shelves be thy
pleasure grounds and gardens.

— JUDAH IBN TIBBON

To add a library to a house
is to give that house a soul.

— CICERO

*I go into my library and
all history unrolls before me.*

— ALEXANDER SMITH

A real book is not one that
we read, but one that reads us.

— W.H. AUDEN

The dearest ones of time,
the strongest friends of soul — **books**.

— EMILY DICKINSON

When I want to read
a good book, I write one.

— BENJAMIN DISRAELI

**A book should serve as the axe
for the frozen sea within us.**

— FRANZ KAFKA

I conceive that a knowledge
of books is the basis on which
all other knowledge rests.

— GEORGE WASHINGTON

Books are the food of youth, the delight of old age;
the ornament of prosperity, the refuge and comfort of
adversity; a delight at home, and no hindrance abroad;
companions by night, in traveling, in the country.

— MARCUS TULLIUS CICERO

Book : A garden carried in a pocket.
— ARABIAN PROVERB

Libraries are not made; they grow.
— AUGUSTINE BIRRELL

The true university these days is a collection of books.
—THOMAS CARLYLE

Books are the perfect Time Machine.
By the simple act of opening a book you can, in an instant, be travelling up a jungle river without once being bitten by mosquitoes, or you can almost die of thirst in the desert while holding a cold drink in your hand, or dine in the finest restaurants and never have to worry about paying the bill, or ride the wild country of our western frontier and never worry about losing your scalp to a raiding party.
— LOUIS L'AMOUR

A book is good company. It is full of conversation without loquacity. It comes to your longing with full instruction, but pursues you never.
— HENRY WARD BEECHER

Books are the bees which carry the quickening pollen from one to another mind.
— JAMES RUSSELL LOWELL

An hour spent in the library is worth a month in the laboratory.
— ANONYMOUS

I have always come to life after coming to books.
— JORGE LUIS BORGES

29

It is a great thing to start life with a small number of really good books which are your very own.

— SIR ARTHUR CONAN DOYLE

There is more **treasure** in books than in all the pirate's loot on Treasure Island and at the bottom of the Spanish Main... and best of all, you can enjoy these **riches** every day of your life. — WALT DISNEY

BOOKS are companions, teachers, magicians, bankers of the treasures of the mind. Books are humanity in print.

— BARBARA W. TUCHMAN

People say that life is the thing, but I prefer reading.

— LOGAN PEARSALL SMITH

The **empires of the future** are the empires of the mind.

— WINSTON CHURCHILL

The possible's slow fuse is lit by the imagination.

— EMILY DICKINSON

music

Music washes from the soul the *dust* of everyday life.

— AUERBACH

Music is the art of THINKING with sounds.

— JULES COMBARIEU

After **silence**, that which comes nearest to expressing the inexpressible is music.

— ALDOUS HUXLEY

A painter paints pictures on canvas. But musicians paint their pictures on silence.

— LEOPOLE STOKOWSKI

Music is what *feelings* sound like.

— UNKNOWN

Music is an **outburst** of the soul.
— FREDERICK DELIUS

Music is moonlight in
the gloomy night of life.
— JEAN PAUL RICHTER

*When words leave off,
music begins.*
— HEINRICH HEINE

music is the
medicine
of the
breaking **heart.**
— LEIGH HUNT

**Music is well said to be the
speech of** *angels.*
— THOMAS CARLYLE

The infant is music itself.
— HAZRAT INAYAT KHAN

Architecture is frozen music.
— GOETHE

Music is **LOVE** in
search of a word.
— SIDNEY LANIER

Music, the greatest good that mortals know,
And all of heaven we have here below.
— JOSEPH ADDISON

SO SHE POURED OUT THE LIQUID MUSIC OF HER VOICE TO QUENCH THE THIRST OF HIS SPIRIT.
— NATHANIAL HAWTHORNE

success

The **road to success** is not a path you find but a trail you blaze.
— ROBERT BRAULT

Get someone else to blow your horn and the sound will carry twice as far.
— WILL ROGERS

The SECRET OF SUCCESS is to do the common things uncommonly well.
— JOHN D. ROCKEFELLER, JR.

If you find it in your heart to care for somebody else, you will have succeeded. — MAYA ANGELOU

A man who wants to lead
the orchestra must turn
his back on the crowd.
The real moment of success
is not the moment
apparent to the crowd.

— GEORGE BERNARD SHAW

A fellow who does things that count, doesn't usually stop to count them.

— UNKNOWN

If at first you don't **succeed**, do it like your **mother** told you.

— UNKNOWN

Success is not the result
of spontaneous combustion.
**YOU MUST SET
YOURSELF ON FIRE.**
— REGGIE LEACH

*To freely bloom —
that is my
definition of
success.* — GERRY SPENCE

Recipe for success:

Study while others are sleeping; work while others are loafing; prepare while others are playing; and dream while others are wishing.

— WILLIAM A. WARD

YOU'RE NOT A FAILURE if you don't make it. **YOU'RE A SUCCESS** because you tried.

— SUSAN JEFFERS

Success is peace of mind which is a direct result of self-satisfaction in knowing you did your best to become the best you are capable of becoming.

— JOHN WOODEN

The more you *praise* and *celebrate* your LIFE, the more there is in LIFE to *celebrate*.

— OPRAH WINFREY

Whenever I hear, "It can't be done," I know I'm close to SUCCESS.

— MICHAEL FLATLEY

You always pass failure on the way to success.

— MICKEY ROONEY

Success is the ability to go from one failure to another with no loss of enthusiasm.

— WINSTON CHURCHILL

Do what you do better than anyone else that is doing it and you'll always be a success.

— FLORENCE LITTAUER

I WISH, I CAN, I WILL— these are the three trumpet notes to victory.

— UNKNOWN

The only place you find success before work is in the dictionary.

— MAY V. SMITH

If someone can stand on my shoulders and take their dream to a higher level, maybe that's success, too.

— STEVE POTTER

Success is failure turned inside out.

— FRANK TYGER

the journey

It is good to have an end to journey towards; BUT IT IS THE JOURNEY THAT MATTERS IN THE END.

— URSULA K. LE GUIN

How we spend our days is, of course, how we spend our lives.

— ANNIE DILLARD

Traveling is almost like talking with men of other centuries.

— RENÉ DESCARTES

One's destination is never a place, but a new way of seeing things.

— HENRY MILLER

37

A good traveler has no fixed plans and is not intent on arriving.

— LAO TZU

Let your MEMORY be your TRAVEL BAG.

— ALEXANDER SOLZHENITSYN

Stop worrying about the potholes in the road and celebrate the journey.

— FITZHUGH MULLAN

The world is a *book* **and those who do not** *travel* **read only a page.**

— ST. AUGUSTINE

It is not down in any map; true places never are.

— HERMAN MELVILLE

The most important trip you may take in life is meeting people halfway.

— HENRY BOYE

The **REWARDS OF THE JOURNEY**
far outweigh the risk
of leaving the harbor. — UNKNOWN

The *journey* is
greater than the inn.

— JOHN WOODEN

Sometime in your life

you will go on a journey.

It will be the longest

journey you have ever taken.

IT IS THE JOURNEY

TO FIND YOURSELF.

— KATHERINE SHARP

A journey is best
measured in
FRIENDS,
rather than miles.

— TIM CAHILL

I never travel without my
diary. One should always
have something sensational
to read in the train.
— OSCAR WILDE

> In Africa, to go on SAFARI—the Swahili word for journey—is to leave the comfort of civilization to **venture into the wilderness**. Each time you listen to your authentic self, you do the same. **Remind yourself** on this often.
>
> — SARAH BAN BREATHNACH

Make voyages!
Attempt them!
There's nothing else.

— TENNESSEE WILLIAMS

To travel hopefully is a BETTER THING than to arrive.

— ROBERT LOUIS STEVENSON

TRUE PILGRIMAGE CHANGES LIVES
whether we go halfway around the world, or out to our own backyard.

— MARTIN PALMER

I am not the same, having seen the moon shine on the other side of the world.

— MARY ANNE RADMACHER-HERSHEY

Quotes to Keep

Quotes to Keep

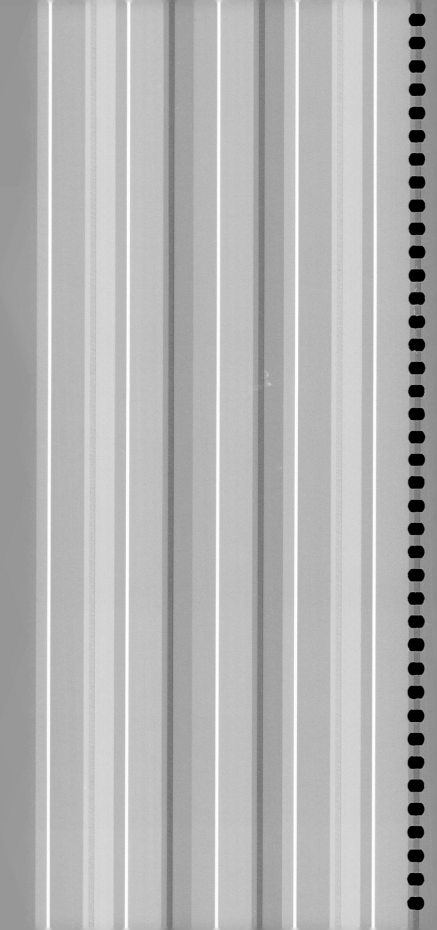

Dreams are renewable. No matter what our age or condition, there are still untapped possibilities within us and new beauty waiting to be born. — DR. DALE TURNER

Within your HEART, keep one still, secret spot where DREAMS may go.

— LOUISE DRISCOLL

My eyes are an ocean in which my dreams are reflected.

— ANNA M. UHLICH

Throw your dreams into space like a kite, and you do not know what it will bring back,
a new life,
a new friend,
a new love,
a new country. — ANAIS NIN

Dreams are the touchstones of our character.

— HENRY DAVID THOREAU

Whatever you can do or dream you can, begin it; Boldness has genius, power and magic in it.

— GOETHE

I know nothing with any certainty, but the sight of stars makes me dream.

— VINCENT VAN GOGH

Thinking is the work of intellect, dreaming is pleasure.

— VICTOR HUGO

Yes, you can be a **dreamer** and a **doer** too, if you **remove** one word from your **vocabulary: Impossible.** — UNKNOWN

I think we **dream** so we don't have to be apart so long. If we're in each other's dreams, we can be together all the time.

— BILL WATTERSON, CALVIN & HOBBES

When I dream, I am ageless.

— ELIZABETH COATSWORTH

KEEP **TRUE** TO THE **DREAMS** OF YOUR **YOUTH.**

— FRIEDRICH VON SCHILLER

Like dreams, small creeks grow into mighty rivers.

— UNKNOWN

Be careful what you set your heart on, for it will surely be yours.

— RALPH WALDO EMERSON

Dreams are the soul's pantry. Keep it well stocked and your soul will never hunger.
— SHIRLEY FEENEY, *LAVERNE & SHIRLEY*

Dreams are journeys that take one far from familiar shores, strengthening the heart, empowering the soul.
— UNKNOWN

A dream is **woven** from thin air and nothing,
Embroidered with wishes and everything,
Then **filled** with the padding of **hope** and **delight**.
— JAMES W. KING

A rock pile ceases to be a rock pile the moment a single man contemplates it, bearing within him the image of a cathedral.
— ANTOINE DE SAINT-EXUPÉRY

Give me my robe, put on my crown; I have Immortal longings in me.
— SHAKESPEARE

Dreams come a size too **BIG** so we can grow into them.
— JOSIE BISSETT

To accomplish great things, we must not only act, but also dream, not only plan, but also believe.
— ANATOLE FRANCE

Dreams are only **thoughts** you didn't have **time** to **think** about during the **day**.

— UNKNOWN

A dream is a microscope through which we look at the hidden occurrences in our soul.

— UNKNOWN

If there were *dreams* to sell,
Merry and sad to tell,
And the crier rung his bell,
What would you buy?

— THOMAS LOVELL BEDDOES

What is worse than having no sight is being able to see but having no vision.

— HELEN KELLER

LIMITATION IS A CREATION OF THE MIND.

— KY HURST

Follow your bliss.

— JAMES CAMPBELL

Dreams are true while they last,
and do we not live in dreams?

— ALFRED TENNYSON

It's easier to go down a mountain than up,
but the view is always best from the top.

— UNKNOWN

HOLD FAST TO DREAMS,
for if dreams die,
life is a broken-winged
bird that cannot fly.

— LANGSTON HUGHES

One person working
toward a dream is worth
99 people just working.

— LANI KRAUS

**Each of us has a fire in our hearts for something.
It's our goal in life to find it and keep it lit.**

— MARY LOU RETTON

The only way to discover the
limits of the possible is to go beyond
them to the *impossible.*

— ARTHUR C. CLARKE

The golden
opportunity you are
seeking
is in yourself.

— MARY ENGELBREIT

*Follow your desire
as long as you live.*

— PTAH-HOTEP

When your heart is in your dream,
no request is too extreme.

— JIMINY CRICKET

Set out each day believing in your dreams. Know without a doubt that you were made for amazing things.

— JOSH HINDS

All that we see or seem is but a dream within a dream.

— EDGAR ALLAN POE

There are **no rules** of architecture for a castle in the clouds.

— G.K. CHESTERTON

I **dream** for a living.

— STEVEN SPIELBERG

Far away there in the SUNSHINE are my HIGHEST aspirations. I may not REACH them, but I can look up and see their beauty, BELIEVE in them, and try to FOLLOW where they LEAD.

— LOUISA MAY ALCOTT

LAUNCHING A DREAM IS LIKE THE MIND TAKING A BREATH OF FRESH AIR... LIKE A SURPRISE GIFT ALWAYS WAITING TO BE OPENED... LIKE A **JOURNEY** TO A **FAVORITE** PLACE.

— UNKNOWN

IN THE ARITHMETIC OF LOVE,
ONE PLUS ONE EQUALS EVERYTHING,
AND TWO MINUS ONE EQUALS NOTHING.
— NINON DE L'ENCLOS

In family life, love is the oil
that eases friction, the cement
that binds closer together, and
the music that brings harmony.
— EVA BURROWS

Give all to love; Obey thy heart.
— RALPH WALDO EMERSON

To LOVE for the sake of being loved is human, but to LOVE for the sake of loving is angelic.
— ALPHONSE DE LAMARTINE

Love is the only flower that grows and blossoms without the aid of seasons.
— KAHLIL GIBRAN

Dregs of love as sweet as the first sip warm our precious numbered days.
— HUGH MILLER

I need so much the quiet of your
LOVE after the day's loud strife.
— CHARLES HANSON TOWNE

The *heart* can do anything.
— MOLIERE

Come live with me, and be my love;
And we will all the pleasures prove
That valleys, groves, hills, and fields,
Woods or steepy mountain yields.

— CHRISTOPHER MARLOWE

FAMILIAR ACTS ARE BEAUTIFUL THROUGH LOVE.
— PERCY BYSSHE SHELLEY

I saw Eternity the other night
Like a great ring of
pure and endless light.

— HENRY VAUGHAN

Where there
is **great** love
there are **always**
miracles.
— WILLA CATHER

Your *Love* is my light,
sun of all my mornings,
fire of all my nights.

— UNKNOWN

LOVE is like a BEAUTIFUL FLOWER
which I may not touch, but whose
FRAGRANCE makes the garden a place
of DELIGHT just the same.

— HELEN KELLER

The way to love anything is to realize that it might be lost.
— GILBERT K. CHESTERTON

To love is to place our happiness in the happiness of another. — GOTTFRIED WILHELM VON LEIBNITZ

Love is a symbol of eternity. It wipes out all sense of **time**, destroying all memory of a beginning and all fear of an end.
— UNKNOWN

WITHOUT LOVE, WE ARE BIRDS WITH BROKEN WINGS.
— FROM *TUESDAYS WITH MORRIE*

When you *love* someone, all your saved-up wishes start coming out.
— ELIZABETH BOWEN

LOVE is a canvas furnished by NATURE and embroidered by IMAGINATION.
— VOLTAIRE

I love you more than yesterday, less than tomorrow.
— EDMOND ROSTAND

Love is a game that two can play and both win.
— EVA GABOR

LOVE IS a fruit in season at all times, and within reach of every hand.
— MOTHER TERESA

LOVE IS the permission to be.
— UNKNOWN

LOVE IS a great beautifier.
— LOUISA MAY ALCOTT

LOVE IS friendship set to music.
— UNKNOWN

Real love stories never have endings.
— RICHARD BACH

LOVE IS the greatest refreshment in life.
— PABLO PICASSO

LOVE IS the irresistible desire to be desired irresistibly.
— LOUIS GINSBERG

LOVE IS the master key which opens the gates of happiness.
— OLIVER WENDELL HOLMES

It is at the edge of a petal that LOVE waits. — WILLIAM CARLOS WILLIAMS

The heart that loves is *always* young. — PETER USTINOV

Being deeply **LOVED** by someone gives you **strength**; loving someone **DEEPLY** gives you **courage**. — LAO TZU

Dive deep, O mind, dive deep in the ocean of God's beauty! If you descend to the uttermost depths, there you will find the gem of love. — BENGALI HYMN

There's nothing half so *sweet* in life as love's young dream. — CLEMENT C. MOORE

To love and be loved is to feel the sun from both sides. — DAVID VISCOTT

Love builds bridges where there are none. — R.H. DELANEY

I PRIZE THY LOVE MORE THAN WHOLE MINES OF GOLD.

— ANNE BRADSTREET

Are we not like *two* volumes of *one book*?

— MARCELINE DESBORDES-VALMORE

And what's romance? Usually, a nice little tale where you have **EVERYTHING AS YOU LIKE IT**, where rain never wets your jacket and gnats never bite your nose and it's always **DAISY-TIME**.

— D.H. LAWRENCE

LOVE looks not with the eyes, but with the mind;
And therefore is winged Cupid painted blind. — SHAKESPEARE

For it was not into my ear you whispered, but into my HEART. It was not my lips you kissed, but my SOUL.

— JUDY GARLAND

Stop looking for Prince Charming. Cinderella's already got him.

— ILENE BECKERMAN

LOVE is such a big word, it really should have more letters.

— KOBI YAMADA

Spread your love everywhere you go.

— MOTHER TERESA

Last thing I remember I was living all alone—
No one on my front porch;
no one on the phone.
Miracles can happen—
one did when I found you
And now all of a sudden,
the miracles are two.

— CHARLES R. STEWART

I am seeking,

I am striving,

I am in it with

all my heart.

— VINCENT VAN GOGH

Love is something eternal...
The aspect may change but
not the essence.

— VINCENT VAN GOGH

The more you invest in a marriage, the more valuable it becomes.
— AMY GRANT

My heart is ever at your service.
— SHAKESPEARE

Once in a while, right in the middle of an ordinary life, **LOVE** gives us a **fairy tale.**
— ANONYMOUS

A *kiss* is a lovely trick designed by nature to stop speech when words become superfluous.

— INGRID BERGMAN

The sound of a kiss is not so loud as that of a cannon, but its echo lasts a great deal longer.

— OLIVER WENDELL HOLMES

A **KISS** CAN BE A COMMA, A QUESTION MARK OR AN EXCLAMATION POINT. THAT'S **BASIC SPELLING** THAT EVERY **WOMAN** OUGHT TO KNOW. — MISTINGUETT

A kiss, when all is said, what is it? ...a rosy dot placed on the "i" in loving; 'tis a secret told to the mouth instead of the ear.

— EDMOND ROSTAND

Soul meets soul on lover's lips.

— PERCY BYSSHE SHELLEY

I wasn't kissing her, I was whispering in her mouth.

— CHICO MARX

People who throw kisses are mighty hopelessly lazy.

— BOB HOPE

Kisses are like grains of gold or silver found **upon the ground**, of no value themselves, but *precious* as showing that **a mine is near**.

— GEORGE VILLIERS

A **KISS** is the anatomical juxtaposition of two orbicular muscles in a state of contraction.

— CARY GRANT, QUOTING DR. HENRY GIBBONS

The moment eternal—
Just that and no more—
When **ecstasy's** utmost
we **clutch** at the core,
While cheeks burn,
arms open, eyes shut,
and **lips meet!**

— ROBERT BROWNING

The sunlight clasps the earth
And the moonbeams kiss the sea:
What are all these kissings worth
If thou kiss not me?

— PERCY BYSSHE SHELLEY

I FEEL **WORTHY** OF EVERY **KISS I LAID UPON YOU** FOR IN EACH OF THEM WENT PART OF **MY HEART.**

— ALBERTO CARLOS CAMPOS

Is not a *kiss* the very autograph of love? — HENRY FINK

I can express no kinder sign of love, than this kind kiss.

— SHAKESPEARE

kiss

With a kiss let us set out for an unknown world.
— ALFRED DE MUSSETT

THEN I DID THE **SIMPLEST THING** IN THE WORLD. I LEANED DOWN... AND **KISSED** HIM. AND THE WORLD CRACKED OPEN.
— AGNES DE MILLE

If love is the best thing in life, then the best part of love is the kiss. — THOMAS MANN

...We kiss. And it **feels like** we have just shrugged off the world.
— JIM SHAHIN

How delicious is the winning of a kiss at Love's beginning.
— THOMAS CAMPBELL

Kisses: Words which cannot be written.
— NICOLE LOUISE DIVINO

A legal kiss is never as good as a stolen one.
— GUY DE MAUPASSANT

It is the PASSION that is in a KISS that gives to it its SWEETNESS; it is the AFFECTION in a KISS that SANCTIFIES it. — CHRISTIAN NESTELL BOVEE

Kisses are the messengers of love.
— DANISH PROVERB

happiness

Shall I give you my recipe for happiness? ... I find everything wonderful and nothing miraculous.
— NORMAN DOUGLAS

Happiness does not consist in things themselves but in the relish we have of them....
— FRANCOIS, DUC DE LA ROCHEFOUCAULD

Always remember to forget the things that made you SAD, but never forget to remember the things that made you GLAD.
— VICTOR BORGE

Happiness is a **butterfly**, which when pursued, is just out of grasp. But if you sit down quietly, may alight upon you.
— NATHANIEL HAWTHORNE

Happiness is itself a kind of gratitude.
— JOSEPH W. KRUTCH

Be happy in the moment, that's enough.
Each moment is all we need, not more.
— MOTHER TERESA

To live happily is an inward power of the soul.
— MARCUS AURELIUS

To be without some of the things you want is an indispensable part of happiness.
— BERTRAND RUSSELL

To fill the hour, and leave no crevice...
that is happiness.
— RALPH WALDO EMERSON

He who leaves his house in search of happiness pursues a shadow.
— UNKNOWN

Happiness does not depend on outward things, but on the way we see them.
— LEO TOLSTOY

HAPPINESS grows at our own firesides, and is not to be picked in stranger's gardens.
— DOUGLAS JERROLD

Happiness is not perfected until it is shared.
— JANE PORTER

If you always do what interests YOU, at least one person is pleased.
— KATHARINE HEPBURN

61

HAPPINESS is like those palaces in fairy tales ...
we must fight in order to obtain it.
— ALEXANDER DUMAS

The *secret* of *happiness*
is to make others believe
they are the cause of it.
— AL BATT

Learn HOW
to *feel* joy.
— SENECA

CHERISH ALL YOUR
HAPPY MOMENTS:
THEY MAKE A FINE
CUSHION FOR OLD AGE.
— CHRISTOPHER MORLEY

Nothing that once made you HAPPY is ever lost.
A golden thread of PLEASURE runs through your *life*.
You just need to REDISCOVER this *thread* before the
JOY OF LIVING completely *unravels*.
— SARAH BAN BREATHNACH

If you want to
be happy, BE.
— LEO TOLSTOY

Wherever you go, no matter
what the weather, always
bring your OWN SUNSHINE.
— ANTHONY J. D'ANGELO

HAPPINESS is when what you THINK, what you SAY, and what you DO are in harmony.

— GANDHI

A JOY that's shared is a JOY made double.

— ENGLISH PROVERB

The HAPPINESS OF LIFE is made up of minute fractions— the little, soon-forgotten charities of a kiss or smile, a kind look, a heart-felt compliment, and the countless infinitesimals of pleasurable and genial feeling.

— SAMUEL TAYLOR COLERIDGE

Scatter seeds of kindness everywhere you go;
Scatter bits of courtesy—watch them grow and grow.
Gather buds of friendship, keep them till full blown;
You will find more happiness than you have ever known.

— AMY R. RAABE

A multitude of small delights constitute happiness.

— CHARLES BAUDELAIRE

WHEN YOU DIG ANOTHER OUT
OF THEIR TROUBLES, YOU FIND
A PLACE TO **BURY YOUR OWN.**
— ANONYMOUS

That man is **happiest** who
lives from day to day and
asks no more, garnering the
simple goodness of life.
— EURIPIDES

It was only a sunny SMILE,

And little it cost in the GIVING.

But like MORNING LIGHT,

it scattered the night,

And made it the DAY WORTH LIVING.
— ANONYMOUS

Success is getting what you want;
happiness is wanting what you get.
— ANONYMOUS

A smile is a whisper of a laugh. — UNKNOWN

HAPPINESS is the
intoxication produced by
the **moment** of poise
between a **satisfactory**
past and an immediate
future, **rich** with promise.
— ELLA MAILLARC

64

In the BOOK OF LIFE, the answers aren't in the back.

— CHARLIE BROWN

Every day brings a chance for you to draw in a breath, kick off your shoes, and step out and dance—to live free of regret and filled with as much joy, fun, and laughter as you can stand.

— OPRAH WINFREY

Color in a picture is like *enthusiasm* in LIFE.

— VINCENT VAN GOGH

We either make ourselves happy or miserable. The amount of work is the same.

— CARLOS CASTANEDA

I never lose sight of the fact that just BEING is fun.

— KATHARINE HEPBURN

Do something today which the world may talk of hereafter.

— ADMIRAL COLLINGWOOD

ALL *know the way.* **FEW** *actually walk it.*

— BODHIDHARMA

Wheresoever you go, go with all your heart.

— CONFUCIUS

To **ENJOY** the flavor of life, take **BIG BITES**.

— ROBERT HEINLEIN

If you can't do GREAT things,

do small things in a GREAT way.

Don't wait for GREAT opportunities.

Seize common, everyday ones

and make them GREAT.

— NAPOLEON HILL

Life's a *voyage* that's homeward bound.

— HERMAN MELVILLE

Don't go through life, GROW through life.

— ERIC BUTTERWORTH

Be glad of life, because it gives you the chance to love and to work and to play and to look up at the stars.

— HENRY VAN DYKE

We must always have old memories and young hopes.

— FORTUNE COOKIE

LIFE is short;
LIVE it up.

— NIKITA S. KHRUSHCHEV

There is no wealth but life.
— JOHN RUSKIN

LIFE is not a "brief candle".
It is a splendid torch that I want to make
burn as brightly as possible before
handing it on to future generations.
— GEORGE BERNARD SHAW

A life recorded is twice
precious, first the
experience itself and
then the memory of it
full and sweet when we
read it again later.
— UNKNOWN

*Life is a handful
of short stories,
pretending to be a novel.*
— UNKNOWN

MY life is MY
MESSAGE. — GHANDI

The end of life is to be like God, and the soul
following God will be like him.
— SOCRATES

Don't be afraid
your life will end;
be afraid that it
will never begin.

— GRACE HANSEN

Life isn't a matter of milestones but of moments.

— ROSE FITZGERALD KENNEDY

Life brings simple pleasures to us every day. It's up to us to make them wonderful memories.

— CATHY ALLEN

THERE'S ABSOLUTELY NO REASON FOR BEING RUSHED ALONG WITH THE RUSH.

— ROBERT FROST

SOMETIMES **LIFE OFFERS** MOMENTS OF ABSOLUTE **PERFECTION** AND WRAPS US IN HEAVENLY DUST.

— PHILIPPE DJIAN

IT'S NOT ENOUGH TO BE *good* IF YOU HAVE THE ABILITY TO BE *better.* IT IS NOT ENOUGH TO BE VERY *good* IF YOU HAVE THE ABILITY TO BE *great.*

— ALBERTA LEE COX

LIFE is a succession of moments. To LIVE each one is to succeed.

— CORITA KENT

Every man's life is a fairy tale written by God's fingers.
— HANS CHRISTIAN ANDERSEN

What a **circus act** we WOMEN perform **every day of our lives**. It puts the trapeze artist to shame. LOOK AT US. We run a tight rope daily, balancing a pile of books on the head. Baby-carriage, parasol, kitchen chair, **still under control**. STEADY NOW!
— ANNE MORROW LINDBERGH

I don't want life to imitate art.
I want life to be art.
— FISCHER

Don't hurry. Don't worry. And be sure to smell the flowers along the way.
— HAGEN

LIFE is a journey, not a guided tour.
— UNKNOWN

If you are not living on the edge, you are taking up too much room.
— AFRICAN PROVERB

Life is something that happens when you can't get to sleep.
— FRAN LEBOWITZ

...the powerful play goes on, and you will contribute a verse.

— WALT WHITMAN

ENJOY YOURSELF. It is later than you think.

— CHINESE PROVERB

Start every day off with a *smile* and get it over with.

— W.C. FIELDS

Only those who will RISK going TOO FAR can possibly FIND OUT how far one can go.

— T.S. ELIOT

Our life *is what our thoughts make it.* — MARCUS AURELIUS

LIFE presents each of us with **challenges** that eat at us like thorns, briars, slivers, or a crown of thorns... And yet there is also **exquisite beauty** and **fragrance** to be found in life — and a **crown of glory**.

— JAMES E. FAUST

The secret of happiness is to count your blessings — not your birthdays.

— ANONYMOUS

Blessed are the joymakers.

— NATHANIEL PARKER WILLIS

Let your life lightly **dance** on the **edges of time** like **dew** on the tip of a leaf.

— RABINDRANATH TAGORE

Oh, the wild joys of living!

— ROBERT BROWNING

Hit the ball over the fence and you can take your time going around the bases.

— JOHN W. ROPER

The purpose of life is LIFE.

— KARL LANGERFELD

Enjoy life—there are no re-runs.

— SHIRL LOWERY

Every day give yourself a good mental shampoo.

— SARA JORDAN

71

Life is God's novel. Let him write it.

— ISAAC BASHEVIS SINGER

Expect nothing;
live frugally on surprise.

— ALICE WALKER

Live out of your **imagination** not your history.

— STEPHEN R. COVEY

WHAT IS LIFE? IT IS THE FLASH OF A FIREFLY IN THE NIGHT. IT IS THE BREATH OF A BUFFALO IN THE WINTERTIME. IT IS THE LITTLE SHADOW THAT RUNS ACROSS THE GRASS AND LOSES ITSELF IN THE SUNSET.

— CROWFOOT

Live to shed joys on others.

— HENRY WARD BEECHER

I don't want to get to the **end of my life** and find that I just lived the **length** of it. I want to have lived the **width** of it as well.

— DIANE ACKERMAN

Life is full of surprises.
Open them slowly.

— JACKIE MUTCHESON

Sooner or later we all discover that the **IMPORTANT** moments in life are not the advertised ones, not the birthdays, the graduations, the weddings, not the great goals achieved. The real **MILESTONES** are less prepossessing. They come to the door of memory.

— SUSAN B. ANTHONY

Do not be too timid and squeamish about your actions. All life is an experiment.

— RALPH WALDO EMERSON

Heroes take journeys, confront dragons, and discover the treasure of their true selves.

— CAROL PEARSON

Heroism... is endurance for one moment more.

— GEORGE KENNAN

We are the hero of our own story.

— MARY MCCARTHY

It is extraordinary how extraordinary the ORDINARY PERSON is.

— GEORGE F. WILL

A hero is no braver than an ordinary man, but he is braver five minutes longer.

— RALPH WALDO EMERSON

Nurture your minds with great thoughts. To believe in the heroic makes heroes.

— BENJAMIN DISRAELI

We can't all be heroes because somebody has to sit on the curb and clap as they go by.

— WILL ROGERS

BE BRAVE.
Even if you're not, pretend to be.
No one can tell the difference.

— H. JACKSON BROWN

A hero is simply someone who rises above his or her own human weaknesses, for an hour, a day, a year, to do something stirring.

— BETTY DERAMUS

I believe it is the nature of people to be heroes, given the chance.

— JAMES A. AUTRY

SOME PEOPLE **QUIETLY** MAKE A DIFFERENCE IN OUR LIVES, AND **WILL ALWAYS BE HEROES** UNAWARE.

— FLAVIA

HEROES are people who **RISE** to the occasion and **SLIP** quietly away.

— TOM BROKAW

I base most of my fashion sense on what doesn't itch.

— GILDA RADNER

When in doubt, wear RED.

— BILL BLASS

High heels were invented by a woman who had been **kissed** on the forehead.

— CHRISTOPHER MORLEY

Of all the things you wear, your expression is the most important.

— JANET LANE

Fashion *can be* bought. Style *one must* possess.

— EDNA WOOLMAN CHASE

> *The apparel oft proclaims the man.*
> — SHAKESPEARE

It is charming to totter into vogue.
— HORACE WALPOLE

STYLE is the hallmark of a temperament stamped upon the material at hand.
— ANDRE MAUROIS

Only great minds can afford a simple style.
— STENDHAL

MY ADVICE TO YOUNG FILM-MAKERS IS THIS: DON'T FOLLOW TRENDS, **START THEM!**
— FRANK CAPRA

Style is the dress of thoughts.
— LORD CHESTERFIELD

Fashion is architecture:
it is a matter of proportions.
— COCO CHANEL

Style isn't always just a look, it's a feeling.
— KRISTINE IRVING

Style isn't about fashion, it's about what *makes your heart sing.*
— TRACEE ELLIS ROSS

Wear pink and make the boys wink.
— LILLY PULITZER

Quotes to Keep

Quotes to Keep

To Do List

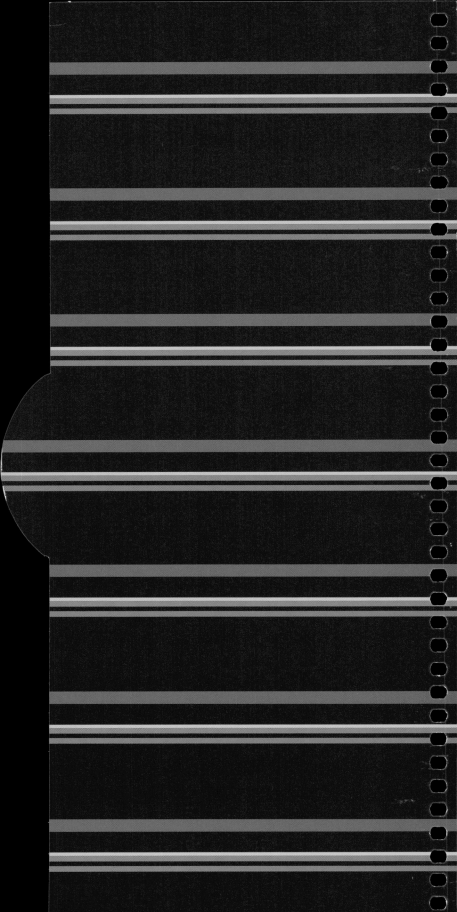

> "Decide what your **priorities** are and how much time you'll spend on them. If you don't someone else will.
> — HARVEY MACKAY

START by doing what's necessary, then what's *possible* and **SUDDENLY YOU** are doing the *impossible.*
— SAINT FRANCIS OF ASSIS

Always do more than is required of you. — GEORGE S. PATTON

If you do not change direction, you may end up where you are heading.
— LAO-TZU

Go for long walks,
indulge in hot baths.
Question your assumptions,
be kind to yourself,
live for the moment,
loosen up, scream,
curse the world,
count your blessings,
**just let go,
just be.**"
— CAROL SHIELDS

Do first what only you can do.

— DAISY HEPBURN

LIVE with intention.

Walk to the **EDGE**.

LISTEN hard.

Practice **WELLNESS**.

PLAY with abandon.

LAUGH.

CHOOSE with no regret.

Continue to **LEARN**.

APPRECIATE your friends.

Do what you **LOVE**.

LOVE as if this is all there is.

— MARY ANNE RADMACHER

FOR A WEB BEGUN, GOD SENDS THREAD.

— ITALIAN PROVERB

Shoot for the moon. Even if you miss, you'll land among the stars.

— LES BROWN

If opportunity doesn't knock, BUILD A DOOR.

— MILTON BERLE

Ideas are like stars — you will not succeed in touching them with your hands, but like the seafaring man on the desert of waters, you choose them as your guides, and, following them, you reach your destiny. — CARL SCHURZ

In life, as in football, you won't go far unless you know where the goalposts are.
— ARNOLD H. GLASGOW

Goals are stars to steer by, not sticks to beat yourself with.
— BARBARA B. SMITH

Do not attempt to do a thing unless YOU are **SURE** of yourself; but do not relinquish it simply because someone else is **NOT SURE** of you.
— STEWART E. WHITE

ACT AS IF **YOU ARE** AND **YOU WILL** BECOME SUCH.
— LEO TOLSTOY

Positive *anything* is better than negative *nothing.*
— ELBERT HUBBARD

Stick to a task, 'Til it sticks to you. Beginners are many, Enders are few.
— ANONYMOUS

Set goals and follow through on them.
You TRANSFORM YOURSELF from one of
life's spectators into a real participant.
— LOU HOLTZ

If you don't know where you're going,
any road will get you there. — LEWIS CARROLL

You get credit for
what you finish,
not what you start.
— UNKNOWN

The **great thing** in
this WORLD is not so
much where we are,
but in what **direction**
we are *moving*.
— OLIVER WENDELL HOLMES

To accomplish great things we must not
only plan but also believe.
— ANATOLE FRANCE

FAITH moves mountains,
but you have to keep pushing
while you are praying.
— MASON COOLEY

A good beginning makes
a good ending.
— ENGLISH PROVERB

*Your diamonds are not in far
distant mountains or in yonder seas;
they are in your own backyard,
if you but dig for them.*
— RUSSELL H. CONWELL

Every man is the architect of his OWN fortune.
— APPIUS CLAUDIUS

As long as you're going to be thinking anyway, think **big**.
— DONALD TRUMP

A dream is just a **dream**. A **goal** is a dream with a plan and a deadline.
— HARVEY MACKAY

purpose

KNOWING WHERE YOU'RE GOING IS **ALL YOU NEED** TO GET THERE.
— CARL FREDRICK

A goal properly set is halfway reached.
— ZIG ZIGLAR

83

People with goals succeed
because they know where
they are going...
It's as simple as that.

— EARL NIGHTINGALE

The beginning is the most important part of the work.

— PLATO

When we are **motivated** by goals that have deep meaning, **by dreams** that need completion, **by pure love** that needs expressing, then we truly **live life**.

— GREG ANDERSON

They know enough who know how to learn.

— HENRY BROOKS ADAMS

It is what you learn after you know it all that counts.

— JOHN WOODEN

Education is not a preparation for life; education is life itself.

— JOHN DEWEY

Learning is not attained by chance, it must be sought for with ardor and attended to with DILIGENCE. — ABIGAIL ADAMS

The wisest mind has something yet to learn.
— GEORGE SANTAYANA

EVERY PERSON YOU MEET KNOWS SOMETHING YOU DON'T; LEARN FROM THEM.
— H. JACKSON BROWN

EDUCATION is not filling a bucket but lighting a fire.
— WILLIAM BUTLER YEATS

Education is hanging around until you've caught on.
— ROBERT FROST

Learning is a treasure that will follow its owner everywhere.
— CHINESE PROVERB

YOUR BRAIN BECOMES A MIND WHEN IT'S FORTIFIED WITH KNOWLEDGE.
— UNKNOWN

You'll never have any MENTAL MUSCLE if you don't have any heavy stuff to pick up.

— DIANE LANE

To learn it, DO IT!

— ROGER SCHANK

Everyone is a genius at least once a year. The real geniuses simply have their bright ideas closer together.

— GEORGE CHRISTOPHER LICHTENBERG

Try to learn something about everything and everything about something.

— T.H. HUXLEY

I AM LEARNING **ALL THE TIME.** THE TOMBSTONE WILL **BE MY DIPLOMA.**

— EARTHA KITT

A **mind** once *expanded* by a **new idea** **never** returns to its **original** dimensions.

— OLIVER WENDELL HOLMES

When the student is ready, the master appears.

— BUDDHIST PROVERB

The whole purpose of education is to turn mirrors into windows.

— SYDNEY J. HARRIS

MAY **YOUR MIND** FOREVER SPARKLE LIKE A STAR, **YOUR HEART** REMAIN PURE AS NEW FALLEN SNOW, AND **YOUR SPIRIT** FOREVER SENSE THE WONDERMENT OF A CHILD.

— MARY SUMMER RAIN

Take fast hold of instruction; let her not go: keep her; for she is thy life.

— PROVERBS 4:13

Happy is the man that findeth wisdom, and the man that getteth understanding.

— PROVERBS 3:13

As knowledge increases, wonder deepens.

— CHARLES MORGAN

Total absence of **humor** renders life impossible.

— COLETTE

You can't deny LAUGHTER; when it comes, it plops down in your favorite chair and stays as long as it wants.

— STEPHEN KING

A man isn't poor if he can still laugh.

— RAYMOND HITCHCOCK

Laughter is the sun that drives winter from the human face.

— VICTOR HUGO

A man without **mirth** is like a wagon without springs; he is jolted disagreeably by every pebble in the road.

— HENRY WARD BEECHER

A good time for *laughing* is when you can.

— JESSAMYN WEST

The most wasted day of all is that on which we have not laughed.
— CHAMFORT

There is nothing sillier than a silly LAUGH.
— CATULLUS

LAUGHTER IS INNER JOGGING.
— NORMAN COUSINS

THE BEST BLUSH TO USE IS LAUGHTER:
IT PUTS ROSES IN YOUR CHEEKS AND IN YOUR SOUL.
— LINDA KNIGHT

HUMOR IS THE GREAT THING, THE SAVING THING. THE MINUTE IT CROPS UP, ALL OUR IRRITATION AND RESENTMENTS SLIP AWAY, AND A SUNNY SPIRIT TAKES THEIR PLACE.
— MARK TWAIN

At the height of **laughter**, the **universe** is flung into a **kaleidoscope** of **new** possibilities.
— JEAN HOUSTON

Even if there is **nothing** to **laugh** about, **laugh** on credit.
— UNKNOWN

Laughter is an instant vacation.

— MILTON BERLE

A HEARTY **LAUGH** GIVES ONE A DRY CLEANING, WHILE A GOOD CRY IS A WET WASH.

— PUZANT KEVORK THOMAJAN

A laugh is a *smile* that bursts.

— MARY H. WALDRIP

The only way to get through life is to **LAUGH YOUR WAY** through it. You either have to laugh or cry. I prefer to **LAUGH.** Crying gives me a headache.

— MARJORIE PAY HINCKLEY

Laughter is the sensation of feeling good all over and showing it principally in one place.

— JOSH BILLINGS

Imagination was given to us to compensate for **what we are not;** a sense of **humor** was given to us to console us for **what we are**.

— MACK MCGINNIS

Shared laughter is like throwing open the shutters in a gloomy room and letting in fresh air and sunshine.
— LILA GREEN

A GOOD LAUGH is *sunshine* **in a house.**
— WILLIAM THACKERAY

FUN is fundamental.
— DOUG HALL

A light heart lives long.
— SHAKESPEARE

Life isn't just the front page — it's the comics, too. — JIM ALTHOFF

Oh, the laugh of a child, so wild and so free, Is the merriest sound in the world for me!
— ISABEL ATHELWOOD

A *merry* **heart doeth good like a medicine.**
— PROVERBS 17:22

Gratitude is the fairest blossom which springs from the soul.
— HENRY WARD BEECHER

GRATITUDE unlocks the fullness of life. It turns what we have into enough, and more. It turns denial into acceptance, chaos to order, confusion to clarity. It can turn a meal into a feast, a house into a home, a stranger into a friend. GRATITUDE makes sense of our past, brings peace for today, and creates a vision for tomorrow.
— MELODY BEATTIE

Gratitude is the most exquisite form of courtesy.
— JACQUES MARITAIN

Seeds of discouragement will not grow in the THANKFUL heart.
— UNKNOWN

Gratitude is the memory of the heart.
— MASSIEU

If the only prayer you ever say in your life is THANK YOU, it will be enough.
— MEISTER ECKART

One single grateful thought raised to Heaven is the most perfect prayer.

— G.E. LESSING

There shall be eternal summer in the grateful heart.

— CELIA THAXTER

A joyful spirit is evidence of a grateful heart.

— MAYA ANGELOU

WE ALL HAVE ANGELS GUIDING US...THEY LOOK AFTER US. THEY HEAL US, TOUCH US, COMFORT US WITH INVISIBLE WARM HANDS...WHAT WILL BRING THEIR HELP? ASKING. GIVING THANKS.

— SOPHY BURNHAM

Every time we remember to say 'Thank you', we experience nothing less than heaven on Earth.

— SARAH BAN BREATHNACH

It isn't what you have in your pocket that makes you thankful, but what you have in your heart...

— HADLEY GOAD

GRATITUDE can transform common days into thanksgivings, turn routine jobs into JOY, and change ordinary opportunities into BLESSINGS.

— WILLIAM ARTHUR WARD

93

He who forgets the language of GRATITUDE can never be on speaking terms with happiness.

— C. NEIL STRAIT

To **speak gratitude** is courteous and pleasant, to **enact gratitude** is generous and noble, but to **live gratitude** is to touch Heaven.

— JOHANNES A. GAERTNER

Blessings brighten when we count them.

— MALTBIE D. BABCOCK

GRATITUDE.
More aware of what you have than what you don't.
Recognizing the treasure in the simple—
a child's hug,
fertile soil,
a golden sunset.
Relishing in the comfort of the common.

— MAX LUCADO

HE WHO RECEIVES A BENEFIT
WITH **GRATITUDE** REPAYS THE FIRST
INSTALLMENT ON HIS DEBT.
— LUCIUS ANNAEUS SENECA

Gratitude is the sign of noble souls.
— AESOP

Flowers of gratitude bloom forever in the heart.
— ANONYMOUS

The unthankful heart...
discovers no mercies;
but let the **thankful heart**
sweep through the day and,
as the magnet finds the iron,
so it will find, in every hour,
some heavenly blessings!
— HENRY WARD BEECHER

GRATITUDE EXPRESSED TO OTHERS
IS A BALM OF SWEETNESS THAT
MAKES LIFE MORE PLEASANT.
— EVA ARRINGTON

If there is no wind, **row.**

— LATIN PROVERB

It's a simple formula;
do your best and somebody might like it.

— DOROTHY BAKER

*It is the time you have
wasted for your rose that
makes your rose so important.*

— ANTOINE DE SAINT-EXUPÉRY

Opportunity is missed by most people because it is dressed in overalls and looks like **work.**

— THOMAS EDISON

It is better to **wear out** than to **rust out.**

— RICHARD CUMBERLAND

There is **no** substitute for hard work.

— THOMAS EDISON

Work is the best narcotic!

— MAURICE MOLNAR

WORK and PLAY are words used to describe the same thing under differing conditions.

— MARK TWAIN

Find a job you love and you'll add 5 days to every week.

— H. JACKSON BROWN, JR.

LUCK IS NOT CHANCE
IT'S TOIL —
FORTUNE'S EXPENSIVE SMILE
IS EARNED.

— EMILY DICKINSON

We should all do what, in the long run, gives us joy, even if it is only picking grapes or sorting laundry.

— E. B. WHITE

The reward of a thing well done is to have done it.

— RALPH WALDO EMERSON

97

I know of no more encouraging fact than the unquestionable ability of man to elevate his life by a conscious endeavor.

— HENRY DAVID THOREAU

Every job is a **self-portrait** *of the person who does it. Autograph your work* **with excellence.**

— UNKNOWN

Hard work has made it easy.
That is my **SECRET.**
That is why **I WIN.**

— NADIA COMANECI

You cannot plough a field by turning it over in your mind.

— IRISH PROVERB

Pleasure in the job puts *perfection* in the *work.*

— ARISTOTLE

LET US REALIZE THAT THE PRIVILEGE TO WORK IS A GIFT, THAT POWER TO WORK IS A BLESSING, THAT LOVE OF WORK IS SUCCESS.

— DAVID O. MCKAY

WHATEVER YOU DO, DO IT WITH ALL YOUR MIGHT. WORK AT IT, EARLY AND LATE, IN SEASON AND OUT OF SEASON, NOT LEAVING A STONE UNTURNED, AND NEVER DEFERRING FOR A SINGLE HOUR THAT WHICH CAN BE DONE JUST AS WELL AS NOW.

— P.T. BARNUM

The greatness of work is **inside** man.
— ANONYMOUS

If you want to build a ship, don't drum up the men to gather wood, divide the work and give orders. Instead, teach them to yearn for the vast and endless sea.

— ANTOINE DE SAINT-EXUPÉRY

The victory of **success** is half won when one gains the habit of **work**.
— SARAH KNOWLES BOLTON

Do not pray for easy lives. Pray to be stronger men. Do not pray for tasks equal to your powers. Pray for powers equal to your tasks. Then the doing of your work shall be no miracle, but **YOU** SHALL BE THE MIRACLE.

— PHILLIPS BROOKS

Diligence is the mother of good luck.
— BENJAMIN FRANKLIN

The heights by great men reached and kept
Were not attained by sudden flight,
But they, while their companions slept
Were toiling upward in the night.

— HENRY WADSWORTH LONGFELLOW

To make a man happy, fill his hands with work.

— FREDERICK E. CRANE

You can't *try* to do things;
you simply must *do* them.

— RAY BRADBURY

IT IS AMAZING HOW MUCH CAN BE ACCOMPLISHED IF NO ONE CARES WHO GETS THE CREDIT.

— JOHN WOODEN

FAR AND AWAY THE BEST PRIZE THAT
LIFE OFFERS IS THE CHANCE TO WORK
HARD AT WORK WORTH DOING.

— THEODORE ROOSEVELT

YOU cannot be really
first-rate at your work if
your WORK is all YOU ARE.

— ANNA QUINDLEN

WE EXIST TEMPORALLY THROUGH
WHAT WE TAKE, BUT WE LIVE FOREVER
THROUGH WHAT **WE GIVE**.
— DOUGLAS M. LAWSON

**The habit of giving only
enhances the desire to give.**
— WALT WHITMAN

*Gentle touches sweeten
sour days.*
— UNKNOWN

**The best place to find a
helping hand is at the
end of your own arm.**
— SWEDISH PROVERB

You give but little when you
give of your possessions. It
is when you give of yourself
that you truly give.
— KAHLIL GIBRAN

The hand that gives, gathers.
— JAMES HOWELL

*Anything that has real
and lasting value is
always a gift from
within.* — FRANZ KAFKA

The roots of happiness grow deepest in the soil of service.

— WILLIAM ARTHUR WARD

Not what we give, but what we share,
For the gift without the giver is bare.

— J.R. LOWELL

If we all tried to make other people's paths easy, our own feet would have a smooth, even place to walk on.

—MYRTLE REED

From what we get, we can make a living; what we give, however, makes a life.

— ARTHUR ASHE

Fragrance always stays in the hand that gives the rose.

— HADA BEJAR

Thee lift me and I'll lift thee and we'll both ascend together.

— JOHN GREENLEAF WHITTIER

Neither fire nor wind, birth nor death can erase our good deeds.

— BUDDHA

Service to others is the rent you pay for your room here on earth.

— MUHAMMAD ALI

Don't judge each day by the harvest you reap, but by the seeds you plant.

— ROBERT LOUIS STEVENSON

Kindness is the golden chain by which society is *bound* together.

— GOETHE

GOODNESS is the only investment that never fails.

— HENRY DAVID THOREAU

Help thy brother's boat across, and lo'! thine own has reached the shore.

— HINDU PROVERB

TREAT PEOPLE AS IF THEY WERE WHAT THEY **OUGHT TO BE**, AND YOU **HELP THEM** TO BECOME WHAT THEY ARE CAPABLE OF BEING.

— GOETHE

It is difficult to give away kindness.
It keeps coming back to you.

— CORT FLINT

A kind heart is a fountain of gladness, making everything in its vicinity freshen into smiles.

— WASHINGTON IRVING

Have you a **KINDNESS** shown?
PASS IT ON! 'Twas not given for thee alone,
PASS IT ON! Let it travel down the years,
Let it wipe another's tears,
Till in Heaven the deed appears —
PASS IT ON! — HENRY BURTON

Small kindnesses, small courtesies, small considerations, habitually practiced in our social intercourse, give a greater charm to the character than the display of great talent and accomplishments. — KELTY

The soul is awakened through service.

— ERICA JONG

Behold, I do not give lectures or a little charity, when I give I give myself.

— WALT WHITMAN

You cannot **LIFT ANOTHER SOUL** until you are standing on higher ground than he is... You cannot **LIGHT A FIRE IN ANOTHER** SOUL unless it is burning in your **OWN** SOUL.

— HAROLD B. LEE

Kindness is always fashionable.

— AMELIA E. BARR

JUST BECAUSE AN ANIMAL IS LARGE, IT DOESN'T MEAN HE DOESN'T WANT **KINDNESS**; HOWEVER BIG TIGGER SEEMS TO BE, REMEMBER THAT HE WANTS AS MUCH **KINDNESS** AS ROO.

— *POOH'S LITTLE INSTRUCTION BOOK*

If you can learn from hard knocks, you can also learn from soft touches.

— CAROLYN KENMORE

If... we should cast the gift of a loving thought into the heart of a friend, that would be giving as the angels give.

— GEORGE MACDONALD

What do we live for, if not to make life less difficult for each other?

— GEORGE ELIOT

If you haven't any
charity in your heart,
you have the worst
kind of heart trouble.

— LILLY PULITZER

When lives entwine, hearts
are bound together by little
gestures of kindness.

— UNKNOWN

A tiny bouquet of
flowers can fill a room
with sunshine, a
tiny act of kindness
can fill a heart
with joy.

— KATHERINE NELSON

Life is short and we have never too
much time for gladdening the hearts
of those who are traveling the dark
journey with us. Oh be swift to live,
make haste to be kind.

— HENRI FREDERICK AMIEL

In as much as ye have done it
unto one of the least of these...
ye have done it unto me.

— MATTHEW 23:40

If there is no joyous way to give
a festive gift, GIVE LOVE AWAY.

— ANONYMOUS

Quotes to Keep

Quotes to Keep

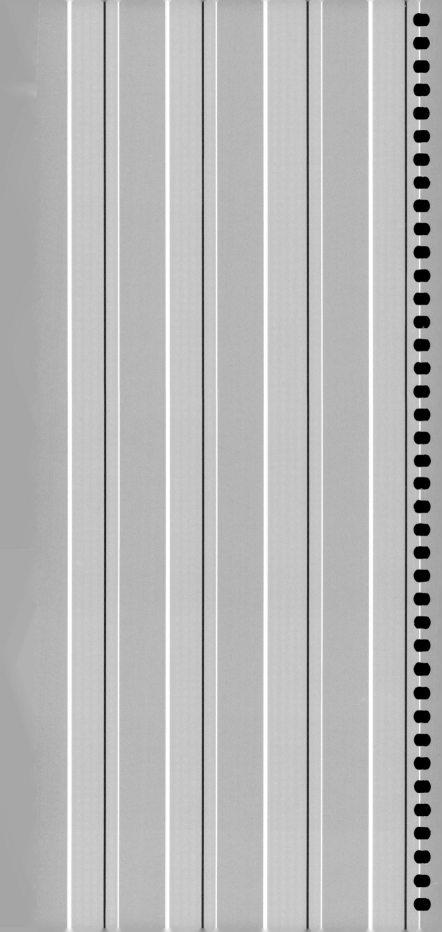

GUARD WELL your spare moments. They are like UNCUT DIAMONDS. Discard them and their value will never be known. IMPROVE THEM and they will become the BRIGHTEST GEMS in a USEFUL LIFE. — RALPH WALDO EMERSON

You may delay, but time will not.
— BENJAMIN FRANKLIN

As if you could kill time without injuring eternity.
— HENRY DAVID THOREAU

There is a time for work. And a time for love. That leaves no other time. — COCO CHANEL

Since Time is not a person we can overtake when he is gone, **let us honor him** with mirth and cheerfulness of heart while he is passing.
— GOETHE

Life is so daily. — INEZ TURLEY

The *inaudible* *and* **noiseless** foot of time. — SHAKESPEARE

SOMETIMES I WOULD ALMOST RATHER HAVE PEOPLE TAKE AWAY YEARS OF **MY LIFE** THAN TAKE AWAY **A MOMENT.**
— PEARL BAILEY

You have got to **own your days** *and live them, each one of them,* **every one of them,** *or else the years go right by and* **none of them** *belong to you.*
— HERB GARDNER

Time is a DRESSMAKER specializing in ALTERATIONS.
— FAITH BALDWIN

Let me tell thee, time is a very precious gift *of God;* so precious that it's only given to us moment by moment.
— AMELIA BARR

Take care of the MINUTES, for the HOURS will take care of themselves.

— LORD CHESTERFIELD

All my POSSESSIONS for one MOMENT of time.

— QUEEN ELIZABETH I

Dost thou love life? *Then do not squander time, for that's the stuff life is made of.*

— BENJAMIN FRANKLIN

TOMORROW I WILL LIVE,
THE FOOL DOES SAY;
TODAY ITSELF'S TOO LATE;
THE WISE LIVED YESTERDAY.

— MARTIAL

Time, you old gypsy man, Will you not stay, Put up your caravan Just for one day.

— R. HODGSON

The moments we forgo,
Eternity itself cannot retrieve.

— FRIEDRICH VON SCHILLER

The **reality** of **time**
exists
only within us.

— CHIN-NING CHU

*The bad news is time flies.
The good news is
you're the pilot.*

— MICHAEL ALTHSULER

TIME GOES, YOU SAY? AH NO!
ALAS, TIME STAYS, WE GO.

— HENRY AUSTIN DOBSON

How long a **M I N U T E**
is, depends on which side of
the bathroom door you're on.

— ZALL'S SECOND LAW

And what if you were told: One more hour?

— ELIAS CANETTI

O ACHING TIME!
O MOMENTS BIG AS YEARS!

— JOHN KEATS

THE ILLIMITABLE, SILENT, NEVER-RESTING
THING **CALLED TIME,** ROLLING, RUSHING
ON, SWIFT, SILENT, LIKE AN ALL EMBRACING
OCEAN-TIDE.... — THOMAS CARLYLE

Time does not change us.
It just
I U I N I F I O I L I D I S I *us.*
— MAX FRISCH

Time is a circus, always packing up and moving away.
— BEN HECHT

Little by little the time
goes by, Short if you sing it,
long if you sigh.
— ANONYMOUS

Nothing
is worth more
than this day.
— UNKNOWN

Since **TIME** is the one immaterial object
which we **CANNOT INFLUENCE—**
neither **SPEED** up nor **SLOW** down,
ADD to nor **DIMINISH—**
it is an imponderably **VALUABLE GIFT.**
— MAYA ANGELOU

The **butterfly counts** not months but **moments**, and has time enough.

— RABINDRANATH TAGORE

Time, like a snowflake,
disappears while
we're trying to decide
what to do with it. — UNKNOWN

TIME as he grows
old teaches all things.

— AESCHYLUS

DON'T SAY YOU DON'T HAVE ENOUGH TIME. YOU HAVE EXACTLY THE SAME NUMBER OF HOURS PER DAY THAT WERE GIVEN TO HELEN KELLER, PASTEUR, MICHELANGELO, MOTHER TERESA, LEONARDO DA VINCI, THOMAS JEFFERSON, AND ALBERT EINSTEIN.

— H. JACKSON BROWN, JR.

We need time to dream, time to remember, and time to reach the infinite. Time to be. — GLADYS TABER

The *time* which we have at our disposal

every day is *elastic*; the passions

that we feel *expand* it, those

that we inspire *contract* it; and

habit fills up what remains. — MARCEL PROUST

This time,
like all times, is a very good one, if we but know what to do with it.

— RALPH WALDO EMERSON

If you want to kill time, try working it to death.

— L.J. REARDON

These are the *magic years...*
and therefore *magic days...*
and therefore *magic moments.*

— ANONYMOUS

Treasure this day, and treasure yourself. Truly neither will ever happen again. — RAY BRADBURY

THE PAST
is never where you think you left it.

— KATHERINE ANNE PORTER

The **past** is a **guidepost,** not a **hitching post.**

— L. THOMAS HOLDCROFT

Men live by FORGETTING. Women live on MEMORIES.

— T.S. ELIOT

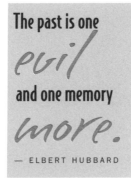

The past is one *evil* and one memory *more.*

— ELBERT HUBBARD

The **PAST** is not only that which happened but also that which could have happened but did not.

— TESS GALLAGHER

So we beat on, boats against the current, borne back ceaselessly into the past.

— F. SCOTT FITZGERALD

Ahh, **yes**
THE PAST CAN HURT,
BUT YOU CAN EITHER
RUN FROM IT **OR** LEARN FROM IT.

— *THE LION KING*

There is no such thing in anyone's life as an UNIMPORTANT DAY.

— ALEXANDER WOOLCOTT

> *The present is the outcome of the past; and it is the great hook upon which the future hangs.*
>
> — ORSON F. WHITNEY

LIFE CAN ONLY BE UNDERSTOOD BACKWARDS, BUT IT MUST BE LIVED FORWARDS.

— SÖREN KIERKEGAARD

Today, well lived, makes every yesterday a memory of happiness and every tomorrow a vision of hope. Look well, therefore, to this day.

— ANCIENT SANSKRIT PROVERB

Don't let **yesterday** use up too much of **today.**

— NATIVE AMERICAN PROVERB

All the flowers of all the tomorrows are in the seeds of today.

— INDIAN PROVERB

THE GREAT THING ABOUT GETTING OLDER IS THAT YOU DON'T LOSE ALL THE OTHER AGES YOU'VE BEEN!

— MADELINE L'ENGLE

The **present** is the necessary product of all the past, the necessary cause of all the **future**.

— ROBERT G. INGERSOLL

Happy the man, and happy he alone, He, who can **call today his own;** He who, secure within, can say; **"Tomorrow do thy worst,** for I have liv'd today."

— JOHN DRYDEN

The past is written! Close the book On pages sad and gray; Within the future do not look, But live today today.

— LYDIA AVERY COONLEY WARD

You can't bring back the past, and you're not promised the future, so enjoy life now.

— KIMO PAKI

This is the day that the Lord has made; let us rejoice and be glad in it. — PSALMS 118:24

To live is so startling it leaves little time for anything else.

— EMILY DICKINSON

THE PRESENT, like a note in *music,* is nothing but as it appertains to what is past and **WHAT IS TO COME.**

— WALTER SAVAGE LANDOR

People are always asking about the good old days. I say, why don't you say the good "now" days? Isn't "now" the only time you're living?

— ROBERT M. YOUNG

N O W is the only time we own; give, love, toil with a will. And place no faith in tomorrow, for the clock may then be still. — UNKNOWN

You are *younger today* than you ever will be again. Make use of it for the sake of tomorrow.
— ANONYMOUS

All of us tend to put off living. We are all dreaming of some MAGICAL ROSE GARDEN over the horizon instead of enjoying the ROSES THAT ARE BLOOMING outside our windows today. — DALE CARNEGIE

Live now,
believe me, wait not till tomorrow, gather the roses of life today.
— PIERRE DE RONSARD

Whether it's the BEST of times or the WORST of times, it's the ONLY TIME we've got.
— ART BUCHWALD

Today is that **tomorrow** you dreamt about.
Make it a **yesterday** worth remembering.

— MIKE PERRAS

You must live in the
|P|R|E|S|E|N|T|
launch yourself on every wave,
find your eternity in each moment.

— HENRY DAVID THOREAU

Remember, **today
is the tomorrow
you worried about
yesterday.** — DALE CARNEGIE

The living moment is
everything.

— D.H. LAWRENCE

Forever is composed of nows. — EMILY DICKINSON

IT IS ONLY POSSIBLE
TO LIVE
HAPPILY-EVER-AFTER
ON A
DAY-TO-DAY BASIS.

— MARGARET BONNANO

EVERYDAY HOLDS THE
POSSIBILITY OF A **MIRACLE.**

— ELIZABETH DAVID

The rainbow is more beautiful than the pot at the end of it, because the rainbow is now. And the pot never turns out to be quite what I expected.

— HUGH PRATHER

Learn to make the **MOST** of life,
Lose no **HAPPY** day,
Time can never bring thee back
Chances swept away. — UNKNOWN

Leave no tender word unsaid, Love while life shall last, The mill will never turn again With water that has past. — UNKNOWN

Yesterday is ashes; tomorrow wood.
Only today does the fire burn brightly.
— ESKIMO SAYING

Light **tomorrow** with **today!**
— ELIZABETH BARRETT BROWNING

Though no one can go back and make a brand new start, ANYONE CAN START from NOW and make A BRAND NEW ENDING
— CARL BARD

The FUTURE lies before you, like PATHS OF PURE WHITE snow. Be careful how you tread it, for every step will show.
— UNKNOWN

The best way to predict the future is to invent it. — ALAN KAY

The future belongs to those who see possibilities before they become obvious.
— JOHN SCULLY

THE BEST THING ABOUT THE FUTURE IS THAT IT ONLY COMES A DAY AT A TIME.
— ABRAHAM LINCOLN

I am not afraid of tomorrow, for I have seen yesterday and I love today. — WILLIAM ALLEN WHITE

123

When all else is lost, the **future** still remains.

— CHRISTIAN NESTELL BOVEE

Study the past if you would divine the future.

— CONFUCIUS

You can't turn back the clock. But you can wind it up again.

— BONNIE PRUDDEN

TOMORROW IS THE MOST IMPORTANT THING IN LIFE...IT PUTS ITSELF IN OUR HANDS AND HOPES WE'VE LEARNED SOMETHING FROM YESTERDAY.

— JOHN WAYNE

The **future** is purchased by the **present**.

— SAMUEL JOHNSON

TODAY WAS GOOD.
TODAY WAS FUN.
TOMORROW IS
ANOTHER ONE.

— DR. SEUSS

In the past we have had a light which flickered, in the present we have a light which flames, and IN THE FUTURE there will be a light which shines over all the land and sea. — SIR WINSTON CHURCHILL

I'M ALWAYS THINKING ABOUT

CREATING. MY FUTURE STARTS

WHEN I WAKE UP EVERY MORNING. . .

EVERY DAY I FIND SOMETHING

CREATIVE TO DO WITH MY LIFE.

— MILES DAVIS

The *future* is like the daytime moon, a diffident but faithful companion, *so elegant* as to be almost invisible, an inconspicuous marvel.

— ROBERT GRUDIN

Trust no future, howe'er pleasant!
Let the dead Past bury its dead!
Act, act in the living present!
Heart within, and God o'erhead!

— HENRY WADSWORTH LONGFELLOW

125

We are the | E | C | H | O | of the future.
— W. S. MERWIN

**THE FUTURE IS SOMETHING WHICH
EVERYONE REACHES AT THE RATE OF**

60 minutes an hour

WHATEVER HE DOES, WHOEVER HE IS.
— C.S. LEWIS

We steal if we touch tomorrow.

it is God's.
— HENRY WARD BEECHER

To know the road ahead, ask those coming back.
— CHINESE PROVERB

God made the world round so we would never be able to see too far down the road.
— ISAK DINESEN

Be not the slave of your own
past—plunge into the sublime
seas, **DIVE DEEP,** and **SWIM FAR,**
so you shall come back with
self-respect, with **new power,**
with an **advanced experience,**
that shall explain and overlook
the old. — RALPH WALDO EMERSON

FORTUNATELY FOR CHILDREN,
the uncertainties of the present always give
way to the enchanted possibilities of the future.
— GELSEY KIRKLAND

Weeping
may endure for a night, but
joy
cometh in the morning.

— PSALMS 30:5

**Let us then be up and doing,
with a heart for any fate.**

— HENRY WADSWORTH LONGFELLOW

The morning has gold in its mouth.
— GERMAN PROVERB

**Day's sweetest
moments are at dawn.**

— ELLA WHEELER WILCOX

I'd like mornings better if they started later.
— JIM DAVIS

**The sun is but a
morning star.**

— HENRY DAVID THOREAU

Every morning is a chance at a new day.
— MARJORIE PAY HINCKLEY

When I first open my eyes upon the morning meadows and look out upon the beautiful world, I thank God I am alive. — RALPH WALDO EMERSON

The morning pouring everywhere, its golden glory on the air.

— HENRY WADSWORTH LONGFELLOW

Do not say, "It is morning," and dismiss it with a name of yesterday. See it for the first time as a newborn child that has no name. — RABINDRANATH TAGORE

Do not shorten the morning by getting up late; look upon it as the quintessence of life, and to a certain extent sacred.
— ARTHUR SCHOPENHAUER

OFT WHEN THE WHITE, STILL DAWN **LIFTED THE SKIES** AND **PUSHED THE HILLS APART**, I HAVE FELT IT LIKE A **GLORY IN MY HEART**.

— EDWIN MARKHAM

Go to bed early, get up early — this is WISE.

— MARK TWAIN

Stars are the daisies that begem The blue fields of the sky. — D.M. MOIR

O bed! O bed! Delicious bed

That heaven on earth to the weary head!

— THOMAS HOOD

There they STAND, the innumerable stars, SHINING IN ORDER like a living hymn, WRITTEN IN LIGHT.

— N.P. WILLIS

A well-spent day brings |H|A|P|P|Y| |S|L|E|E|P|

— LEONARDO DA VINCI

The Sun's rim dips; the stars rush out; At one stride comes the dark.

— SAMUEL TAYLOR COLERIDGE

Sleep, Silence's child,
sweet father of soft rest,
Prince whose approach peace
to all mortals brings,
Indifferent host to shepherds
and kings, Sole comforter
to minds with grief oppressed.

— WILLIAM DRUMMOND

SLEEP...PEACE OF THE SOUL, WHO PUTTEST CARE TO FLIGHT.
— ANONYMOUS

SLEEP that knits up the ravelled sleeve of care
THE DEATH of each day's life, sore labour's bath
BALM OF HURT minds, great nature's second course,
CHIEF NOURISHER in life's feast.

— SHAKESPEARE

Oh, lightly, lightly tread! A holy thing is sleep.

— FELICIA DOROTHEA HEMANS

THE DAY IS DONE, AND THE DARKNESS FALLS FROM THE WINGS OF NIGHT, AS A FEATHER IS WAFTED DOWNWARD FROM AN EAGLE IN HIS FLIGHT.

— HENRY WADSWORTH LONGFELLOW

Thou driftest gently down the tides of sleep.

— HENRY WADSWORTH LONGFELLOW

SLEEP, BABY, SLEEP!

Thy father's watching
the sheep,
Thy mother's shaking
the dreamland tree,
And down drops a
little dream for thee.

SLEEP, BABY, SLEEP!

— ELIZABETH PRENTISS

THESE *blessed candles* OF THE NIGHT.

— SHAKESPEARE, REFERRING TO STARS

The night walked down the sky with the moon in her hand.

— FREDERICK L. KNOWLES

Twilight drops her curtain down, and pins it with a star.

— LUCY MAUD MONTGOMERY

Night time is really the **best time** to work. **All the ideas are there** to be yours **because everyone** else is **ASLEEP.**

— CATHERINE O'HARA

Day hath put on his jacket, and around His burning bosom buttoned it with stars.

— OLIVER WENDELL HOLMES

With finger on her solemn lip, Night hushed the shadowy earth. — MARGARET DELAND

Quotes to Keep

Quotes to Keep

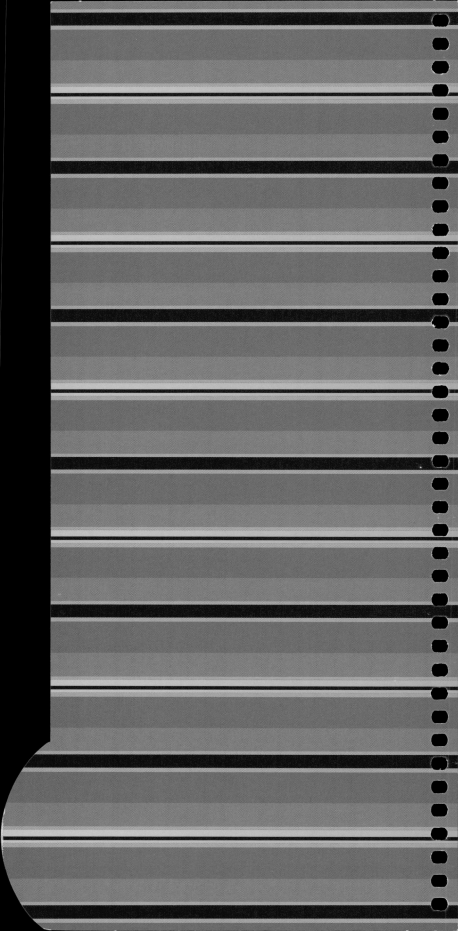

Adversity is the **diamond dust** that heaven polishes its jewels with. — LEIGHTON

If winter comes, can spring be far behind?

— PERCY BYSSHE SHELLEY

Sadness flies away on the wings of time.

— JEAN DA LA FONTAINE

THERE AIN'T NO CLOUD SO THICK **THAT THE SUN AIN'T SHININ' ON T'OTHER SIDE.**

— RATTLESNAKE, AN 1870'S MOUNTAIN MAN

Adversity causes some men to break, others to break records.

— WILLIAM A. WARD

Whenever **you FALL**, pick something **UP**.

— OSWALD AVERY

Life is a **grindstone**, and whether it grinds a man down or **polishes** him up depends on the stuff he's made of.

— JOSH BILLINGS

The world is round and the place which may seem like the END may also be only the BEGINNING.

— IVY BAKER PRIEST

SOME PEOPLE WALK IN THE RAIN... OTHERS JUST GET WET. — ROGER MILLER

To be TESTED is good. The CHALLENGED LIFE may be the BEST THERAPIST.

— GAIL SHEEHY

To *abolish* all valleys is to get rid of all mountains.

— ALAN W. WATTS

I will love the light, for it shows me the way, yet I will endure the darkness for it shows me the stars.

— OG MANDINO

Every exit is an entry somewhere.

— TOM STOPPARD

Sweet are the uses of adversity; Which, like the toad, ugly and venomous, **Wears yet a precious jewel in his head.** — SHAKESPEARE

However long the night, *the dawn will break.*

— AFRICAN PROVERB

A SMOOTH SEA NEVER MADE A SKILLFUL MARINER. — UNKNOWN

The cloud that darkens the present hour **may brighten** all our future days.

— UNKNOWN

WHAT THE **CATERPILLAR** CALLS THE **END OF THE WORLD**, THE MASTER CALLS A **BUTTERFLY**.

— RICHARD BACH

*Only if you have been
in the deepest valley
can you know how
magnificent it is to be on the
highest
mountain.*

— RICHARD M. NIXON

STRENGTH and **STRUGGLE** travel
together. — SPENCER W. KIMBALL

Into each life some rain must fall.

— HENRY WADSWORTH LONGFELLOW

THE BROOK WOULD LOSE ITS SONG
if we removed the rocks. — WALLACE STEGNER

As soon as we accept that life is difficult, it ceases to be so.

— SCOTT PECK

Earth has no sorrow that Heaven cannot heal.

— THOMAS MOORE

I have not failed. I've just found 10,000 ways that won't work.
— THOMAS EDISON

All the sugar is at the bottom of the cup. — UNKNOWN

Our greatest victory is not in never falling, but in rising every time we fall. — CONFUCIUS

Only the soul that KNOWS the mighty grief can know the MIGHTY RAPTURE.
— EDWIN MARKHAM

SORROWS ARE OUR BEST EDUCATORS.
A MAN CAN SEE FARTHER THROUGH A TEAR
THAN THROUGH A TELESCOPE.
— UNKNOWN

Should you shield the valleys from the windstorms, you would never see the beauty of their canyons. — ELISABETH KÜBLER-ROSS

If you run into a wall...figure out how to climb it, go through it, or work around it.
— MICHAEL JORDAN

139

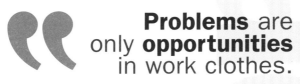

Problems are only **opportunities** in work clothes.

— FREDERICK R. KOPPEL

In **THREE WORDS** I can sum up everything I've learned about life: **IT GOES ON.**

— ROBERT FROST

Even I don't wake up looking like *Cindy Crawford.*

— CINDY CRAWFORD

The ultimate **measure of a man** is **not where he stands** in moments of comfort, but **where he stands** at times of challenge and controversy.

— MARTIN LUTHER KING, JR.

LET OTHER PENS DWELL ON GUILT AND MISERY. — JANE AUSTEN

A **bend** in the road is not the **end** of the road, unless you **fail to make the turn.**

— UNKNOWN

Sadness flies on the wings of the morning, and out of the heart of darkness comes the LIGHT.

— JEAN GIRAUDOUX

PERHAPS **SOMEDAY** IT WILL BE PLEASANT TO **REMEMBER** EVEN THIS.

— VIRGIL

Aerodynamically the bumblebee shouldn't be able to fly, but the bumblebee doesn't know that so it goes on flying anyway. — MARY KAY ASH

In times like these, it helps to recall that there have always been times like these. — PAUL HARVEY

Shadow owes its birth to light.

— GRAY

> DEATH IS THE OPENING OF A MORE SUBTLE LIFE. IN THE FLOWER, IT SETS FREE THE PERFUME; IN THE CHRYSALIS, THE BUTTERFLY; IN MAN, THE SOUL.
>
> — JULIETTE ADAM

> *It is foolish and wrong to mourn the men who died. Rather we should thank God that such men lived.*
>
> — GEORGE S. PATTON, JR.

DEATH — THE LAST SLEEP? NO, IT IS THE FINAL AWAKENING.

— WALTER SCOTT

> THE GENERATIONS OF LIVING THINGS PASS IN A SHORT TIME, AND LIKE RUNNERS, HAND ON THE TORCH OF LIFE.
>
> — LUCRETIUS

Death is a mere comma, not an exclamation point!

— NEAL A. MAXWELL

As a well spent day brings happy sleep, so life well used brings happy death.

— LEONARDO DA VINCI

IN THE NIGHT OF DEATH, HOPE SEES A STAR AND LISTENING, LOVE CAN HEAR THE RUSTLE OF A WING. — ROBERT INGERSOLL

Life is eternal, and love is immortal, and death is only a horizon; and a horizon is nothing save the limit of our sight.

— ROSSITER WORTHINGTON RAYMOND

For death is no more than a turning of us over from time to eternity.

— WILLIAM PENN

DEATH LIES ON HER, LIKE AN UNTIMELY FROST UPON THE SWEETEST FLOWER OF ALL THE FIELD. — SHAKESPEARE

Come, death, if you will: you cannot divide us; you can only unite us. — FRANZ GRILLPARGER

I CAN'T CHANGE THE DIRECTION OF THE WIND, *but I can* adjust *my* sails.

— JIMMY DEAN

GROWTH ITSELF CONTAINS THE GERM OF HAPPINESS. — PEARL S. BUCK

To change your life: start immediately; *do it flamboyantly; no exceptions.*

— WILLIAM JAMES

If you don't like something, change it.
If you can't change it, change your attitude.
Don't complain. — MAYA ANGELOU

If nothing ever changed, there would be no *butterflies.* — UNKNOWN

ALL THINGS CHANGE, NOTHING IS EXTINGUISHED... EVERYTHING FLOWS ONWARD.

— OVID

WE DID NOT CHANGE AS WE GREW OLDER; *we just became more clearly ourselves.*

— LYNN HALL

**BE YOURSELF.
WHO ELSE IS BETTER QUALIFIED?**

— FRANK J. GIBLIN, II

The noblest question in the world is,
"What good can I do in it?"

— BENJAMIN FRANKLIN

OUR GREATNESS LIES NOT SO MUCH IN
BEING ABLE TO REMAKE THE WORLD...AS
IN BEING ABLE TO REMAKE OURSELVES.

— GANDHI

The privilege of a lifetime is being who you are.

— JOSEPH CAMPBELL

People are like *stained-glass* **windows. They sparkle and shine when the sun is out, but when the darkness sets in, their true beauty is revealed only if their light is from within.**

— ELIZABETH KUBLER ROSS

Never be afraid to sit awhile and think.

— LORRAINE HANSBERRY

**MEDITATE.
LIVE PURELY. BE QUIET.
DO YOUR WORK WITH
MASTERY.
LIKE THE MOON, COME OUT
FROM BEHIND THE CLOUDS!
SHINE.**

— BUDDHA

Better keep yourself clean and bright; you are the window through which you must see the world.

—GEORGE BERNARD SHAW

JUST TRUST YOURSELF, then you will know how to live.

—GOETHE

ALWAYS BE A **FIRST-RATE VERSION OF YOURSELF**, INSTEAD OF A SECOND-RATE VERSION OF SOMEBODY ELSE.

—JUDY GARLAND

Compete against yourself, not others, for that is who is truly your best competition.

—PEGGY FLEMING

Whatever you are, be a **good one.**

—ABRAHAM LINCOLN

THE MAN WHO FOLLOWS THE CROWD WILL USUALLY GET NO FURTHER THAN THE CROWD. THE MAN WHO WALKS ALONE IS LIKELY TO FIND HIMSELF IN PLACES NO ONE HAS EVER BEEN.

—ALAN ASHLEY-PITTS

The molecules of your body are the same molecules that make up the nebulae, that burn inside the stars themselves. We are star stuff.

—VICTOR TENBAUM

*Yes'm, old friends is always best,
'less you can catch a new one that's
fit to make an old one out of.*
— SARAH ORNE JEWETT

Those friends thou hast,
and their adoption tried,
grapple them to thy soul
with hoops of steel.
— SHAKESPEARE

Silences make the real conversations between friends.
— MARGARET LEE RUNBECK

...the most valuable antiques are old friends.
— H. JACKSON BROWN, JR.

Each friend represents a world in us, a world possibly not born until
they arrive, and it is only by this meeting that a new world is born.
— ANAIS NIN

A friend is, as it were, a second self.
— MARCUS T. CICERO

Our friends see the **best**
in us, and by that very fact
call forth the **best from us.**
— JOHN BLACK

*Only your **real friends** will tell you
when your face is dirty.*
— SICILIAN PROVERB

147

Piglet sidled up to Pooh from behind.
"Pooh!" he whispered. "Yes, Piglet?" "Nothing,' said
Piglet, taking Pooh's paw. "I just wanted to be sure of you."

— A.A. MILNE

Constant use will not wear ragged the fabric of friendship.

— DOROTHY PARKER

Friends are kisses blown to us by angels.

— UNKNOWN

Let us be grateful to people who make us happy; they are the charming gardeners who make our souls blossom.

— MARCEL PROUST

Strangers are just friends waiting to happen.

— UNKNOWN

I HAVE FRIENDS IN OVERALLS WHOSE
FRIENDSHIP I WOULD NOT SWAP FOR THE
FAVOR OF THE KINGS OF THE WORLD.

— THOMAS A. EDISON

Friends give full color to our lives.

— UNKNOWN

The warmth of a friend's presence brings joy to our hearts, sunlight to our souls, and pleasure to all of life.

— UNKNOWN

We cannot tell the precise moment when **friendship is formed**. As in filling a vessel drop by drop, there is at last a drop which makes it run over; so in a series of kindnesses there is at last one which makes the heart run over.

— JAMES BOSWELL

FRIENDS are those rare people who ask how we are and then wait to hear the answer.

— ED CUNNINGHAM

A good friend is a connection to life, a tie to the past, a road to the future, the key to sanity in a totally insane world.

— LOIS WYSE

FRIEND.
GOOD.

— *FRANKENSTEIN*

My lifetime listens to yours.

— MARGARET PETERS

FRIENDS ARE ANGELS WHO LIFT US TO OUR FEET WHEN OUR WINGS HAVE TROUBLE REMEMBERING HOW TO FLY.

— UNKNOWN

149

Having a **family** is like having a bowling alley installed in your brain.

— MARTIN MULL

My home is not a place, it is people.

— LOIS MCMASTER BUJOLD

You can never go home again, but the truth is you can never leave home, so it's all right.

— MAYA ANGELOU

HOME IS A PLACE NOT ONLY OF STRONG AFFECTIONS, BUT OF ENTIRE UNRESERVE; IT IS LIFE'S UNDRESS REHEARSAL, ITS BACKROOM, ITS DRESSING ROOM.

— HARRIET BEECHER STOWE

Home had nothing to do with the boards and nails that made our residence. Home was here, in my husband's arms. Here was my refuge. Here was my love.

— JANENE WOLSEY BAADSGAARD

Home, the spot of earth supremely blest, a dearer, sweeter spot than all the rest.

— ROBERT MONTGOMERY

I do not understand how anyone can live without one small place of enchantment to turn to.

— MARJORIE KINNAN RAWLINGS

Ah! There is nothing
like staying at HOME,
for real comfort.
— JANE AUSTEN

Home is an invention on which
no one has yet improved.
— ANN DOUGLAS

It's not the HOME I love,
but the **life** that is
LIVED there.
— ELSIE DE WOLFE

SWEET IS THE SMILE OF HOME; THE MUTUAL
LOOK WHEN HEARTS ARE OF EACH OTHER SURE.
— JOHN KEBLE

*A child on a farm sees a plane fly
overhead and dreams of a faraway place.
A traveler on the plane sees the
farmhouse — and dreams of home.*
— CARL BURNS

His house was perfect, whether you liked
food, or sleep, or work, or story-telling,
or singing, or just sitting and thinking,
best, or a pleasant mixture of them all.
— J.R.R. TOLKIEN

Parents are people who bear children,
bore teenagers and board newlyweds.
— ANONYMOUS

She walks in beauty, like the night
Of cloudless climes and starry skies;
And all that's best of dark and bright
Meet in her aspect and her eyes.

— LORD BYRON

Oh, thou art fairer than the evening air
Clad in the beauty of a thousand stars.

— CHRISTOPHER MARLOWE

An ounce of mother is worth a pound of clergy.

— SPANISH PROVERB

If evolution really works, how come mothers only have two hands?

— MILTON BERLE

mother —
that was the bank where we
deposited all our hurts and worries.

— T. DEWITT TALMAGE

Motherhood is not for the faint-hearted. Frogs, skinned knees, and the insults of teenage girls are **not meant for the wimpy.**

— DANIELLE STEEL

To a child's ear, "mother" is magic in any language.

— ARLENE BENEDICT

Her grandmother, as she gets older, is not fading but rather becoming more concentrated.

— ANONYMOUS

Men are what their mothers made them.

— RALPH WALDO EMERSON

Who ran to help me when I fell,
And would some pretty story tell,
Or kiss the place to make it well?
MY MOTHER. — JANE TAYLOR

Real sisterhood is a bunch of dames in bathrobes throwing back M&M's and making each other laugh.

— MAXINE WILKE

Sometimes the strength of motherhood is greater than natural laws.

— BARBARA KINGSOLVER

By the time a man realizes that maybe his father was right, he usually has a son who thinks he's wrong.

— CHARLES WADSWORTH

I FELT SOMETHING IMPOSSIBLE FOR ME TO EXPLAIN IN WORDS. THEN WHEN THEY TOOK HER AWAY, **IT HIT ME.** I GOT SCARED ALL OVER AGAIN AND BEGAN TO FEEL GIDDY. THEN IT CAME TO ME — I WAS A FATHER.

— NAT KING COLE

A truly rich man is one whose children run into his arms when his hands are empty.

— ANONYMOUS

A father carries **pictures** where his **money** used to be.

— ANONYMOUS

IT IS ADMIRABLE FOR A MAN TO TAKE HIS SON FISHING, BUT THERE IS A SPECIAL PLACE IN HEAVEN FOR THE FATHER WHO TAKES HIS DAUGHTER SHOPPING.

— JOHN SINOR

The most important thing that a father can do for his children is to love their mother.

— THEODORE M. HESBURGH

There's no pillow quite so soft as a father's strong shoulder.

— RICHARD L. EVANS

You can learn many things from children. How much patience you have, for instance.
— FRANKLIN P. JONES

What is a home without children?
QUIET. — HENNY YOUNGMAN

There are only two things a child will share willingly — communicable diseases and his mother's age.
— BENJAMIN SPOCK

I actually remember feeling delight, at two o'clock in the morning, when the baby woke for his feed, because I so longed to have another look at him.
— MARGARET DRABBLE

The greatest poem ever known
Is one all poets have outgrown:
The poetry, innate, untold,
Of being only four years old.
— CHRISTOPHER MORLEY

THERE IS A GARDEN IN **EVERY CHILDHOOD**, AN ENCHANTED PLACE WHERE COLORS ARE BRIGHTER, THE AIR SOFTER, AND THE MORNING MORE FRAGRANT THAN EVER AGAIN.
— ELIZABETH LAWRENCE

When I grow up
I want to be
a little boy.

— JOSEPH HELLER

IF CHILDREN GREW UP ACCORDING TO
EARLY INDICATIONS, WE SHOULD HAVE
NOTHING BUT GENIUSES. — GOETHE

Children's games are hardly games.
Children are never more serious
than when they *play*.

— MONTAIGNE

So, like a forgotten
fire, a *childhood*
can always flare up
again within us.

— GASTON BACHELARD

Ah, the sweetness of YOUTH
GROW OLD, yes
But age with LOVE
And YOUTH is yours forever

— MARK BALDOCK

The first child is
made of glass, the
second porcelain,
the rest of rubber,
steel and granite.

— RICHARD J. NEEDHAM

I'm youth, I'm joy, I'm a little bird that has broken out of the egg.

— SIR JAMES MATTHEW BARRIE

Our youth we can have but today,
We may always find time to grow old.
— BISHOP GEORGE BERKELEY

WE CANNOT ALWAYS **BUILD THE FUTURE** FOR OUR YOUTH, BUT WE CAN **BUILD OUR YOUTH** FOR THE FUTURE.
— FRANKLIN D. ROOSEVELT

Like a kite cut from the string, Lightly the **soul of my youth** has taken flight. — ISHIKAWA TAKUBOKU

KISS your children **goodnight,** even if they are already **asleep.**
— H. JACKSON BROWN

A child is a beam of sunlight from the Infinite and Eternal.
— LYMAN ABBOTT

How soft and fresh he breathes!
Look! He is dreaming! Visions sure of joy
Are gladdening his rest; and, ah! who knows
But waiting angels do converse in sleep
With babies like this!

— BISHOP COXE

Children *are the anchors that* hold *a mother to* life. — SOPHOCLES

You rock a sobbing child without wondering if today's world is passing you by, because you know YOU HOLD TOMORROW tightly in your arms.

— NEAL A. MAXWELL

Youth! Stay close to the young, and a little rubs off. — ALAN JAY LERNER

To bring up a **child** in the way he should go, travel that way **yourself** once in a while.

— JOSH BILLINGS

Quotes to Keep

Quotes to Keep

STUDENT STUDY GUIDE FOR

HOLE'S
ANATOMY&
PHYSIOLOGY

FIFTEENTH EDITION

PREPARED BY:
DELON WASHO-KRUPPS

McGraw Hill Education

STUDENT STUDY GUIDE FOR HOLE'S ANATOMY & PHYSIOLOGY, FIFTEENTH EDITION

Published by McGraw-Hill Education, 2 Penn Plaza, New York, NY 10121. Copyright © 2019 by McGraw-Hill Education. All rights reserved. Printed in the United States of America. Previous editions © 2016, 2013, and 2010. No part of this publication may be reproduced or distributed in any form or by any means, or stored in a database or retrieval system, without the prior written consent of McGraw-Hill Education, including, but not limited to, in any network or other electronic storage or transmission, or broadcast for distance learning.

Some ancillaries, including electronic and print components, may not be available to customers outside the United States.

This book is printed on acid-free paper.

3 4 5 6 7 8   QVS   23 22 21 20 19

ISBN 978-1-260-16544-9
MHID 1-260-16544-2

Portfolio Manager: *Matthew Garcia*
Product Developer: *Michelle Gaseor*
Marketing Manager: *Kristine Rellihan*
Content Project Manager: *Mary Jane Lampe*
Buyer: *Sandy Ludovissy*
Design: *Tara McDermott*
Content Licensing Specialist: *Lori Hancock*
Compositor: *SPi Global*

The Internet addresses listed in the text were accurate at the time of publication. The inclusion of a website does not indicate an endorsement by the authors or McGraw-Hill Education, and McGraw-Hill Education does not guarantee the accuracy of the information presented at these sites.

mheducation.com/highered

Table of Contents

CHAPTER 1

INTRODUCTION TO HUMAN ANATOMY AND PHYSIOLOGY

OVERVIEW

This chapter begins your exploration of anatomy and physiology by describing the origins of this field of study and outlining the rationale for understanding the human body (Learning Outcome 1). The chapter continues by defining anatomy and physiology and by describing their relationship to each other (Learning Outcome 2). The levels of organization of the human body, and common themes are discussed (Learning Outcomes 3–5). Next, the characteristics of life, and the mechanisms that maintain life are outlined and explained (Learning Outcomes 6–10). The discussion moves on to the description of major body cavities and the organs they contain, the locations of membranes associated with these cavities, and descriptions of the major organ systems and their functions (Learning Outcomes 11–15). This foundation then leads to your ability to identify the impact of life-span changes on these anatomical components (Learning Outcome 16). Your exploration ends with an introduction to the appropriate terminology used to describe relative positions of body parts, body sections, and body regions to one another (Learning Outcome 17).

This chapter defines the characteristics and needs common to all human beings and the manner in which the human body is organized to accomplish life processes. Some of the language specific to anatomy and physiology is also introduced.

LEARNING OUTCOMES

After you have studied this chapter, you should be able to do the following:

1.1   Origins of Medical Science
1.   Identify some of the early discoveries that led to our current understanding of the human body.
1.2   Anatomy and Physiology
2.   Explain how anatomy and physiology are related.
1.3   Levels of Organization
3.   List the levels of organization in the human body and the characteristics of each.
1.4   Common Themes in Anatomy and Physiology
4.   List and describe the key concepts in anatomy and physiology.
5.   List and describe the underlying mechanisms in anatomy and physiology.
1.5   Life and the Maintenance of Life
6.   List and describe the major characteristics of life.
7.   Give examples of metabolism.
8.   List and describe the major requirements of organisms.
9.   Explain the importance of homeostasis to survival.
10.   Describe the parts of a homeostatic mechanism and explain how they function together.
1.6   Organization of the Human Body
11.   Identify the locations of the major body cavities.
12.   List the organs located in each major body cavity.
13.   Name and identify the locations of the membranes associated with the thoracic and abdominopelvic cavities.
14.   Name the major organ systems, and list the organs associated with each.
15.   Describe the general function of each organ system.
1.7   Life-Span Changes
16.   Identify changes related to aging, from the microscopic to the whole-body level.
1.8   Anatomical Terminology
17.   Properly use the terms that describe relative positions, body sections, and body regions.

FOCUS QUESTION

How is the human body organized to accomplish those tasks that are essential to maintain life?

MASTERY TEST

Now take the mastery test. Do not guess. Some questions may have more than one correct answer. As soon as you complete the test, check your answers and correct any errors. Note your successes and failures so that you can reread the chapter to meet your learning needs.

1. What events and circumstances are thought to have stimulated ancient peoples' curiosity about how their bodies worked?

2. List the lifestyle changes in the ancient world that altered the spectrum of human illnesses, and identify the illnesses associated with these changes.

3. As knowledge about the structure and function of the body increased, it was necessary to develop a new specialized language.
   a. True
   b. False

4. What two languages form the basis for the language of anatomy and physiology?

5. The branch of science that studies the structures (morphology) of the body is known as what?

6. The branch of science that studies what these structures do and how they do it is known as what?

7. The function of a part is (always/sometimes/never) related to its structure.

Questions 8–12. Match the structures listed in the first column with the functions listed in the second column.

Structure	Function
8. atoms, molecules, macromolecules	a. groups of cells that have a common function
9. cells	b. chemical structures required for life
10. tissues	c. allow life to continue despite changing environments and reproduce to continue the species
11. organisms	d. simplest living units
12. subatomic particles	e. parts of an atom

13. List the five levels of organization of the body in order of increasing complexity, beginning with the cell.

14. List the characteristics of life.

15. What are the physiological changes that obtain, release, and use energy called?

16. What is the force necessary to maintain life?

17. What is the most abundant chemical substance in the human body?

18. Food is used as an _____ source, to build new _____ _____, and to participate in chemical reactions.

19. What is the purpose of oxygen?

20. Generally, an increase in temperature (increases/decreases) the rate of chemical reactions.

21. Atmospheric pressure plays a part in what bodily process?

22. Homeostasis means
   a. maintenance of a stable internal environment.
   b. integrating the functions of the various organ systems.
   c. preventing any change in the organism.
   d. never deviating from a value.

23. In most circumstances, how is homeostasis maintained in the broad sense?

24. List the components of a homeostatic mechanism.

25. Body temperature is maintained around a set point of 37°C.
   a. True
   b. False

26. The set point for the body's temperature is controlled by which of the following structures?

   a. skin

   b. circulatory system

   c. lungs

   d. hypothalamus

27. Blood glucose levels (are/are not) maintained by a negative feedback mechanism.

28. Positive feedback mechanisms usually lead to (restored health/illness).

29. The portion of the body that contains the head, neck, and trunk is called the _____ portion.

30. The arms and legs are called the _____ portion.

31. What is the inferior boundary of the thoracic cavity called?

32. The heart, esophagus, trachea, and thymus gland are located in the _____ of the thoracic cavity.

33. The pelvic cavity is best defined as

   a. the lower one-third of the abdominopelvic cavity.

   b. the portion of the abdomen that contains the reproductive organs.

   c. the portion of the abdomen surrounded by the pelvic girdle.

   d. separated from the abdominal cavity by the urogenital diaphragm.

34. The visceral and parietal pleural membranes secrete a serous fluid into a potential space that is known as what?

35. The heart is covered by the _____ membranes.

36. The peritoneal membranes are located in the _____ cavity.

37. Match the systems listed in the first column with the functions listed in the second column.

   1. nervous system

   2. muscular system

   3. cardiovascular system

   4. respiratory system

   5. skeletal system

   6. digestive system

   7. lymphatic system

   8. endocrine system

   9. urinary system

   10. reproductive system

   11. integumentary system

   a. reproduction

   b. transporting

   c. integration and coordination

   d. support and movement

   e. body covering

   f. absorption and excretion

38. On average, when do you begin to be aware of your own aging?

   a. 2nd decade

   b. 3rd decade

   c. 4th decade

   d. 5th decade

39. The recommendation that people over sixty five years of age receive influenza and pneumonia vaccines is based on age-related changes in which of the following structures or processes?

   a. skin

   b. lungs

   c. immune response

   d. mucosa of the upper respiratory system

40. A slower metabolism due to aging can lead to:

   a. weight gain

   b. increased body temperature

   c. cold intolerance

   d. fatigue

41. Which of the following positions of body parts is/are in correct *anatomical position*?

   a. palms of hands turned toward sides of body

   b. standing erect

   c. arms at side

   d. face toward left shoulder

42. Terms of relative position are used to describe
   a. the relationship of siblings within a family.
   b. the importance of the various functions of organ systems in maintaining life.
   c. the location of one body part with respect to another.
   d. the differences between the practitioner and the patient.

43. A sagittal section divides the body into
   a. superior and inferior portions.
   b. right and left portions.
   c. anterior and posterior portions.
   d. proximal and distal portions.

44. Locate the epigastric, hypochondriac, and iliac regions of the body and list some structures or organs within these.

STUDY ACTIVITIES

Definition of Word Parts

Define the following word parts used in this chapter.

append-

cardi-

cerebr-

cran-

dors-

homeo-

-logy

meta-

nas-

orb-

pariet-

pelv-

peri-

pleur-

-stasis

super-

-tomy

4

1.1 Origins of Medical Science

A. Why did the study of the human body begin with attempts to understand illness and injury rather than attempts to understand the human body?

B. List the changes in the disease spectrum that came with the change in lifestyle from hunting and gathering to agriculturally based functions.

C. Describe the ways in which the study of science paralleled human pre-history and history.

D. Dissection of the human body became an important activity in the study of the human body during the _____ century.

1.2 Anatomy and Physiology

A. 1. Anatomy is the study of what?

    2. Physiology is the study of what?

B. Explain how the structure of the following parts is related to the function given.

fingers: grasping

heart: pumping

blood vessels: moving blood in the proper direction

mouth: receiving food

leg bones: support

urinary bladder: receiving and holding urine

C. 1. A newly discovered part of the brain identified by imaging techniques is the planum temporale. What is its function?

    2. What are the functions of taste receptors found in the tongue and the small intestine?

    3. Proteins released by a damaged spinal cord are the same as those released by damage to the skin. How was this discovery made?

1.3 Levels of Organization

Arrange the following structures in increasing levels of complexity: subatomic particles, atoms, organ systems, organelles, organism, organs, macromolecules, cells, tissue, and molecules. Then give an example of something found in the level, for example, subatomic particles are electrons, protons, and neutrons.

1.4 Common Themes in Anatomy and Physiology

Describe the following underlying mechanisms/processes. Then give an example of each.

1. gradients

2. permeability

5

3.   cellular differentiation

4.   cell-to-cell communication

5.   balance

6.   energy

1.5   Life and the Maintenance of Life

A.   Describe the following ten characteristics of life. Then give an example of the process in the body and how it is important for life, for example, movement would be blood delivered to cells. Life depends on this movement to provide oxygen and nutrients to cells.

1.   movement

2.   responsiveness

3.   growth

4.   reproduction

5.   respiration

6.   digestion

7.   absorption

8.   circulation

9.   assimilation

10. excretion

B.   What is *metabolism*?

C.   Match the terms in the first column with the statements in the second column that define their role in the maintenance of life.
   1.   water   a.   essential for metabolic processes
   2.   food   b.   governs the rate of chemical reactions

3. oxygen
4. heat
5. pressure

c. force that moves most molecules
d. necessary for release of energy
e. provides chemicals for building new living matter

D. Answer the following regarding homeostasis.

1. How would you define homeostasis?

2. List the components of a homeostatic mechanism.

3. How is body temperature maintained at 37°C (98.6°F) in spite of the environmental fluctuations from below zero to 110°C?

4. Describe negative and positive feedback mechanisms. Give examples of each.

1.6 Organization of the Human Body

A. 1. List the parts of the axial portion of the human body.

2. List the parts of the appendicular portion of the human body.

3. What body cavities are found in the axial portion of the body?

4. The organs found within the thoracic and abdominopelvic cavities are known by what collective term?

5. List the several organs or structures found within the various body cavities.

6. Describe the regions within the thoracic and abdominopelvic cavities.

7. List the small cavities found within the head.

B. 1. What lines the walls of the thoracic and abdominopelvic cavities?

2. What is the name of the membrane that lines the right and left thoracic compartments?

3. What is the name of the membrane that covers the lungs?

4. Why is the pleural cavity called a "potential space"?

C. Name and describe the membranes covering the heart.

D. 1. What is the membrane that lines the wall of the abdominopelvic cavity called?

2. What is the name of the membrane which covers the organs within the cavity called?

7

E. Fill in the following chart concerning the structure and function of organ systems.

Function	Organ System	Organs in System
Body covering		
Support and movement		
Integration and coordination		
Transportation		
Absorption and excretion		
Reproduction: female		
Reproduction: male		

1.7 Life-Span Changes

A. What is *aging*?

B. When do we begin to be aware of aging?

C. Signs of aging are due to changes at what levels of organization?

D. List some examples of the impact of the aging process on the human body.

E. What is believed to be the reason for centenarians?

1.8 Anatomical Terminology

A. Use the illustration on this page to specify the terms that describe the relationship of one point on the body to another.

1. Point (a) in relation to point (d)

2. Point (f) in relation to point (h)

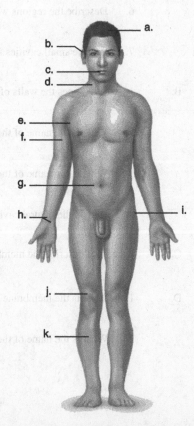

3.   Point (g) in relation to point (i)

4.   Point (i) in relation to point (j)

5.   Point (i) in relation to point (g)

B.   On the previous illustration do the following to reinforce understanding.

1.   Draw a line through the drawing to indicate a midsagittal section. How is this different from a frontal section?

2.   Draw a line through the drawing to indicate a transverse section.

3.   Define a frontal (coronal) section.

4.   Locate and label the following body regions: epigastric; umbilical; hypogastric; the right & left: hypochondriac, lateral (lumbar), and inguinal (iliac). Then locate these regions on yourself or on a partner.

Clinical Focus Questions

Now can you apply all this information? Identify the organ(s) likely to be involved in each of the following assessments. You may find it helpful to consult reference plates 1–7.

A resonant sound when the intercostal spaces of the posterior chest are tapped. _____

Pain with deep palpation of the upper right quadrant. _____

Dullness to tapping (percussion) of the left lower thorax in the axillary to mid axillary line. _____

Palpation of a smooth-bordered, globelike structure over the pelvis. _____

Gurgling sounds via a stethoscope placed on the abdomen. _____

Discomfort on palpation of the left lower quadrant of the abdomen. _____

Sharp pain on percussion of the posterior flank. _____

When you have completed the study activities to your satisfaction, retake the mastery test and compare your performance with your initial attempt. If there are still areas you do not understand, repeat the appropriate study activities.

CHAPTER 2
CHEMICAL BASIS OF LIFE

OVERVIEW

This chapter introduces you to some basic concepts of chemistry, a science that studies the composition of substances and the changes that occur as elements combine. The chapter begins with examples of important chemicals involved in the maintenance of health and life (Learning Outcome 1). It explains what atoms are and how they combine or react to make up molecules and compounds (Learning Outcomes 2, 3, and 5). You will learn how the composition of compounds is expressed in formulas (Learning Outcome 4); what the definition of *acids, bases,* and *buffers* are and how they interact to maintain pH (Learning Outcomes 6, 7, and 8). Lastly, the major groups of inorganic and organic substances and their functions are described (Learning Outcomes 9 and 10).

Knowledge of basic chemical concepts is essential to your understanding of the functions of cells and of the human body.

LEARNING OUTCOMES

After you have studied this chapter you should be able to
2.1 The Importance of Chemistry in Anatomy and Physiology
1. Give examples of how the study of living materials requires an understanding of chemistry.
2.2 Structure of Matter
2. Describe the relationships among matter, atoms, and compounds.
3. Describe how atomic structure determines how atoms interact.
4. Explain how molecular and structural formulas symbolize the composition of compounds.
5. Describe the three types of chemical reactions.
6. Describe the differences among acids, bases, and salts.
7. Explain the pH scale.
8. Explain the function of buffers.
2.3 Chemical Constituents of Cells
9. List the major inorganic chemicals common in cells and explain the function(s) of each.
10. Describe the general functions of the main classes of organic molecules in cells.

FOCUS QUESTION

How does chemistry influence the structure and function of living things?

MASTERY TEST

Now take the mastery test. Do not guess. Some questions may have more than one correct answer. As soon as you complete the test, check your answers and correct your errors. Note your successes and failures so that you can reread the chapter to meet your learning goals.

1. The discipline that deals with the chemistry of living things is called what?

2. What is matter and in what forms can it be found?

3. What are the basic units of matter?

4. When two elements are found in combination, the substance is called a _____.

5. Elements required by the body in large amounts are known as _____ elements.

6. Give examples of these elements.

7. Many trace elements are important parts of what bodily processes?

8. An atom is made up of
   a. a nucleus.
   b. protons.
   c. electrons.
   d. neutrons.

9. Match the following:
   1. neutron
   2. proton
   3. electron
   a. positive electrical charge
   b. negative electrical charge
   c. no electrical charge

10. The atomic number of an element is determined by the number of what?

11. The atomic weight of an element is determined by adding the number of _____ and the number of _____.

12. An isotope has the same atomic _____ but a different atomic _____.

13. The atoms of the same element have the same number of _____ and _____.

14. When an isotope decomposes and gives off energy, it is
   a. unstable.
   b. radioactive.
   c. explosive.
   d. destroyed.

15. The interaction of atoms is determined primarily by the number of _____ they possess.

16. Atomic radiation that travels the most rapidly and is the most penetrating is
   a. alpha.
   b. beta.
   c. gamma.
   d. delta.

17. The time it takes for one-half of the amount of an isotope to decay to a nonradioactive form is known as its what?

18. Radioactive isotopes of iodine can be used both to diagnose and to treat thyroid problems because
   a. iodine is only concentrated in the thyroid gland.
   b. iodine is intrinsically destructive to the thyroid gland.
   c. both a and b.
   d. neither a nor b.

19. An element is chemically inactive if
   a. it has a high atomic weight.
   b. its outer electron shell is filled.
   c. it has an odd number of protons.
   d. the atomic number is greater than 20.

20. An ion is
   a. an atom that is electrically charged.
   b. an atom that has gained an electron.
   c. an atom that has lost an electron.
   d. all of the above.

21. Positively charged ions are known as _____; negatively charged ions are known as _____.

22. Regarding a covalent bond, electrons are
   a. shared by two atoms.
   b. given up by the atom.
   c. taken up by the atom.
   d. none of the above.

23. The ionizing radiation to which people in the United States are exposed is generated by
   a. radioactive substances that occur naturally in the earth's surface.
   b. medical and dental X-rays.
   c. the use of radioactive materials for power generation.
   d. the inclusion of radioactive substances in consumer products.

24. A compound is always a molecule but a molecule is not always a compound. Do you agree with this statement? Why or why not?

25. $C_6H_{12}O_6$ is an example of what kind of formula?

11

26. The following is an example of what kind of formula?

27. Chemical reactions in which molecules are formed are called _____. Chemical reactions in which molecules are broken apart are called _____.

28. A + B ⟷ AB is known as a _____ _____.

29. The speed of a chemical reaction is affected by the presence of a _____.

30. Match the following.
   1. accepts hydrogen ions in water   a.   acid
   2. product of an acid and a base reacting together   b.   base
   3. releases hydrogen ions in water ·   c.   salt

31. What is the pH of a neutral solution? _____ An acid solution? _____ A basic solution? _____

32. A blood pH of 7.8 indicates a condition known as what?

33. Inorganic substances usually dissolve in _____.

34. A molecule is (more/less) likely than an ion to take part in a chemical reaction when dissolved in water.

35. Organic substances are most likely to dissolve in _____ or _____.

36. Which of the following substances does not play a role in the polarization of the cell membrane?
   a. sodium ions   c. bicarbonate ions
   b. potassium ions   d. sulfate ions

37. Identify the following cell constituents with an *O* if they are organic and an *I* if they are inorganic:

   a. water ( ), b. carbohydrate ( ), c. glucose ( ), d. oxygen ( ), e. protein ( ), f. carbon dioxide ( ), g. fats ( ).

38. What are the three most common atoms in carbohydrates?

39. What are the "building blocks" of fat molecules?

40. What are the "building blocks" of protein molecules?

41. The function of nucleic acids is to
   a. store information and control life processes.   c. neutralize bases within the cell.
   b. act as receptors for hydrogen ions.   d. provide energy to the cell.

42. The three-dimensional shapes of proteins are called _____.

43. Molecules that have polar regions are (hydrophilic/lipophilic).

STUDY ACTIVITIES

Definition of Word Parts

Define the following word parts used in this chapter.

bio-

di-

glyc-

iso-

lip-

-lyt

mono-

poly-

sacchar-

syn-

2.1 The Importance of Chemistry in Anatomy and Physiology

1. What is the subject matter that chemists study?

2. What subdivision of chemistry is of particular interest to physiologists? Why?

2.2 Structure of Matter

A. Complete the sentences and answer the following questions concerning elements and atoms.

1. Anything that has weight and takes up space is known as _____.

2. Fundamental substances are called _____.

3. What is a bulk element? Give examples.

4. What is a trace element? For what processes are they used?

5. What is an ultratrace element?

13

B.   Fill in the following chart.

Element	Symbol	Element	Symbol
Oxygen		Sodium	
Carbon		Magnesium	
	H	Cobalt	
Nitrogen			Cu
	Ca		F
	P	Iodine	
	K		Fe
Sulfur			Mn
	Cl	Zinc	

C.   Answer the questions that pertain to the diagram on
      this page.

      1.   What is the atomic number of this atom?

      2.   What is its atomic weight?

      3.   How many total electrons are needed to fill its
            outer shell?

      4.   Identify this element.

      5.   Label the parts of the atom.

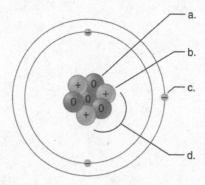

D.   Answer the following questions about isotopes.

      1.   How does the isotope of any element differ from the element?

      2.   How does this difference affect the way an isotope interacts with other elements? Explain your answer.

      3.   What is a radioactive isotope?

      4.   List the three types of radiation.

      5.   Describe what is meant by the term "half-life of an isotope."

      6.   Describe at least two clinical uses of radioactive isotopes.

E.   Explain the difference between an ionic bond and a covalent bond.

14

F.   Answer the following questions about ionizing radiation.

    1.   Define *ionizing radiation*.

    2.   Describe the effects of ionizing radiation on the health of living things.

    3.   List the sources of ionizing radiation. Which of these sources can be controlled by humans?

G.   Answer the following questions concerning molecules and compounds.

    1.   Two or more atoms combine to form a _____.

    2.   A formula that is a shorthand notation of the kinds and numbers of atoms in a molecule is a _____ formula.

    3.   If atoms of different elements combine, they form a _____.

    4.   In order to combine with another atom, the number of electrons in the outer orbital must be
       a.   more than two in the inner shell.   c   less than eight in the third shell.
       b.   more than eight in the second shell.   d.   less than two in the inner shell.

    5.   Ionically bound compounds exist as
       a.   molecules.   c.   crystals.
       b.   salts.   d.   compounds.

    6.   When atoms bond by sharing a pair of electrons, a _____ bond is formed.

H.   Answer the following questions about chemical reactions.

    1.   Identify the type of chemical reaction in these equations.
       a. $AB \rightarrow A + B$ c. $AB + CD \rightarrow AD + CD$
       b. $A + B \rightarrow AB$

    2.   What is the role of a catalyst in a chemical reaction?

I.   Identify these substances as being *acid, base*, or *salt*.
       a.   HCl   d. $Mg(OH)_2$
       b.   NaOH   e. $NaHCO_3$
       c. H_2SO_4 f.   NaCl

J.   Answer the following concerning acid and base concentrations.

    1.   What is meant by *pH*?

    2.   Identify these substances as being an acid or base according to the pH.
       a.   carrot: pH 5.0   d.   tomato: pH 4.2
       b.   milk of magnesia: pH 10.5   e.   lemon: pH 2.3
       c.   human blood: pH 7.4   f.   distilled water: pH 7.0

    3.   What is *alkalosis* and what are its clinical signs and symptoms?

    4.   What is *acidosis* and what are its clinical signs and symptoms?

2.3 Chemical Constituents of Cells

A.   1.   What is the role of the following inorganic substances in the cell? Be specific.
       a.   water

       b.   oxygen

     c.   carbon dioxide

     d.   inorganic salts or electrolytes (Na, K, Ca, HCO_3, PO_4)

B.   How do NO (nitric oxide) and CO (carbon monoxide) affect body function?

C.   Answer the following questions concerning carbohydrates.

     1.   What is the role of carbohydrates in maintaining the cell?

     2.   What are the major elements found in carbohydrates?

     3.   Describe simple and complex carbohydrates.

D.   Answer the following questions that pertain to the accompanying diagram.

     1.   What is the molecular formula of this substance?

     2.   What is this compound?

E.   Answer the following questions concerning lipids.

     1.   What elements are found in lipids?

     2.   What is the role of lipids in maintaining the cell?

     3.   What are the "building blocks" of fats?

     4.   Fats with single-bonded carbon atoms are known as what?

     5.   Fats containing double-bonded carbon atoms are known as what?

     6.   Describe the composition and characteristics of a phospholipid molecule.

     7.   List commonly occurring steroids in body cells.

F. Answer the following questions concerning proteins.

1. What is the role of protein in maintaining the cell?

2. What elements are found in protein?

3. What are the "building blocks" of proteins?

4. A protein molecule that has become disorganized and lost its shape is said to have become _____.

5. What is the primary structure of a protein?

6. What are the two forms of secondary protein structure?

7. How does the tertiary structure form in a protein?

G. Answer the following regarding nucleic acids.

1. Describe the roles of deoxyribonucleic acid, DNA, and ribonucleic acid, RNA.

2. Describe the structures of DNA and RNA.

H. Describe positron-emission tomography (PET) imaging. What makes it especially useful?

I. Describe computerized tomography (CT) scanning. What makes it a particularly useful technique?

17

Clinical Focus Questions

Vomiting and diarrhea lead to loss of both fluid and electrolytes. How might these losses be most effectively treated? Why is prompt treatment important?

When you have finished the study activities to your satisfaction, retake the mastery test and compare your results with your initial attempt. If you are not satisfied with your performance, repeat the appropriate study activities.

OVERVIEW

You begin your examination of the human body in this chapter by studying the structural and functional unit of life: the cell. The chapter begins by comparing and contrasting the different types of cells in the human body. You will reinforce the relationship of structure and function by examining how the range in cell sizes and characteristics determines the functional aspects of the individual cells (Learning Outcomes 1 and 2). The chapter will then describe specific components of the cell in detail, the structure of the cell membrane, the various types of organelles and their functions, the role of the cytoskeleton and the structure and function of the cell nucleus (Learning Outcomes 3–6). Since cells perform a number of biochemical reactions necessary for life, you will be introduced to the mechanisms used to allow molecules and ions in and out of cells (Learning Outcome 7). Our cells are vital for life but they are not immortal so you will study the orderly processes of cell reproduction (Learning Outcomes 8 and 9). This process is carefully controlled to ensure replacement of a normal cell without creating an abnormal cell (Learning Outcome 10). You will then be introduced to what stem cells and progenitor cells are and what role they have in cell growth, repair, and differentiation (Learning Outcomes 11 and 12). Lastly, you will read about cell death and the process of apoptosis, which along with mitosis will allow you to maintain a stable number of normal functioning cells necessary for a healthy life (Learning Outcomes 13–15).

An understanding of cell structure is basic to understanding how cells support life.

LEARNING OUTCOMES

After you have studied this chapter, you should be able to

3.1 Cells Are the Basic Units of the Body
1. Explain how cells differ from one another.
3.2 A Composite Cell
2. Describe the general characteristics of a composite cell.
3. Explain how the components of a cell's membrane provide its function.
4. Describe each kind of cytoplasmic organelle and explain its function.
5. Describe cellular structures that are parts of the cytoskeleton and explain their functions.
6. Describe the cell nucleus and its parts.
3.3 Movements into and out of the Cell
7. Explain how substances move into and out of cells.
3.4 The Cell Cycle
8. Describe the cell cycle.
9. Explain how a cell divides.
3.5 Control of Cell Division
10. Describe several controls of cell division.
3.6 Stem and Progenitor Cells
11. Explain how stem cells and progenitor cells make possible growth and repair of tissues.
12. Explain how two differentiated cell types can have the same genetic information but different appearances and functions.
3.7 Cell Death
13. List the steps of apoptosis.
14. Distinguish between apoptosis and necrosis.
15. Describe the relationship between apoptosis and mitosis.

FOCUS QUESTION

Cells are the units of life so explain how they manifest all the characteristics of life discussed in Chapter 1. More specifically explain how cells acquire energy, reproduce, carry out chemical reactions, for example, synthesis and hydrolysis. Then after days or years of doing these functions, how do cells die?

MASTERY TEST

Now take the mastery test. Do not guess. Some questions may have more than one correct answer. As soon as you complete the test, check your answers and correct any errors. Note your successes and failures so that you can reread the chapter to meet your learning needs.

1. What is a cell?

2. How many cells are found in the human body? How much do cells vary in size? What cell can be seen without the aid of a microscope?

3. Cells develop the ability to perform different functions in a process known as what?

4. Match the structures in the first column with the proper functions in the second column.

   1. cells

   2. cell membrane

   3. nucleus

   4. various cytoplasmic organelles

   a. performance of various cellular activities such as protein synthesis, metabolism, and cell respiration

   b. control of all cellular activities; contains the genetic material of the cell

   c. controls movement of substances into and out of the cell; allows the cell to respond to certain stimuli

   d. the smallest living units

5. Which of the following statements about the hypothetical composite cell is/are true?

   a. It is necessary to construct a composite cell because cells vary so much based on their function.

   b. It contains structures that occur in many kinds of cells.

   c. It contains only structures that occur in all cells, although the characteristics of the structure may vary.

   d. It is an actual cell type chosen because it occurs most commonly in the body.

6. What are the three major portions of a cell?

7. The organelles are located in the

   a. nucleolus.

   b. cytoplasm.

   c. cell matrix.

   d. cell membrane.

8. Which of the following statements about the cell membrane is false?

   a. An intact cell membrane is essential to the life of the cell.

   b. The cell membrane is composed of phospholipids and protein.

   c. The cell membrane does not participate in chemical reactions.

   d. The cell membrane is selectively permeable.

9. The cell membrane is essential to the ability to receive and respond to chemical messages.

   a. True

   b. False

10. What characteristic of the cell membrane makes it impermeable to such substances as water, amino acids, and sugars?

    a. an intercellular matrix that makes it difficult for water-soluble substances to get close to the cell membrane

    b. the phosphate groups that form the outermost and innermost layers of the cell membrane

    c. the fatty acid portions of phospholipids that make up the inner layer of the cell membrane

    d. the fibrous proteins that span the width of the cell membrane

11. Which of the following substances on the cell membrane surface help/helps cells to recognize and bind to each other as well as recognizing "nonself" substances such as bacteria?

    a. proteins

    b. cholesterol

    c. glycerol

    d. glycoproteins

12. Water-soluble substances such as ions cross the cell membrane via

    a. active transport mechanisms.

    b. protein channels.

    c. carrier mechanisms.

    d. phagocytosis.

20

13. Receptors on the cell membrane are composed of
    a. carbohydrates.
    b. proteins.
    c. fats.
    d. triglycerides.

14. Faulty ion channels can cause disease and sudden death.
    a. True
    b. False

15. A class of drugs that are used to treat hypertension and angina affects which of the following transmembrane channels?
    a. calcium channels
    b. sodium channels
    c. chloride channels
    d. potassium channels

16. Cell adhesion molecules are proteins that
    a. provide the "glue" for cells to adhere to each other permanently.
    b. attract cells to an area in which they are needed.
    c. are part of a mechanism that allows cells to interact in a totally different manner than usual.
    d. act like enzymes to catalyze chemical reactions.

17. Which organelle functions as a communication system for the cytoplasm?

18. The chemical activity in the endoplasmic reticulum results in
    a. synthesis of protein.
    b. dissemination of amino acids.
    c. oxidation of glucose.
    d. synthesis of lipid molecules.

19. Which of the following statements about ribosomes is false?
    a. Ribosomes are part of rough endoplasmic reticulum.
    b. Ribosomes are made up of protein and RNA.
    c. Ribosomes secrete proteins used as enzymes.
    d. Ribosomes are found primarily in the nucleus of the cell.

20. What is the function of the Golgi apparatus?

21. The mitochondria are also known as the _____ of cells.

22. Cells with very high energy requirements are likely to have (more/less/the same number of) mitochondria than cells with low energy requirements.

23. Which of the following organelles is/are most likely to be of interest to evolutionary biologists?
    a. nucleolus
    b. cell membrane
    c. lysosome
    d. mitochondria

24. The enzymes of the lysosome function to
    a. control cell reproduction.
    b. digest bacteria and damaged cell parts.
    c. release energy from its storage place within the cell.
    d. control the Krebs cycle.

25. Peroxisomes are found most commonly in the cells of the
    a. liver.
    b. heart muscle.
    c. kidney.
    d. central nervous system.

26. Which of the following statements about the centrosome is/are false?
    a. It is located near the nucleus.
    b. The centrioles of the centrosome function in cellular reproduction.
    c. The centrosome is concerned with the distribution of genetic material.
    d. It helps provide energy for the cell.

27. What are the mobile, hairlike projections that extend outward from the surface of the cell called?

28. A membranous sac formed when the cell membrane folds inward and pinches off is a
    a. microtubule.
    b. cytoplasmic inclusion.
    c. vesicle.
    d. lysosome.

29. Thin, threadlike structures found within the cytoplasm of the cell are called _____ and _____.

30. The structures that float in the nucleoplasm of the nucleus are the _____ and the _____.

31. Which of the following structures is made of nucleic acids and proteins?
    a. nucleus
    b. nucleolus
    c. cell membrane
    d. chromatin

32. The process that allows the movement of gases and ions from areas of higher concentration to areas of lower concentration until equilibrium has been achieved is known as what?

33. The process by which substances are moved through the cell membrane by a carrier molecule is called what?

34. The process by which water moves across a semipermeable membrane from areas of high concentration of solute to areas of lower concentration of solute is called what?

35. A hypertonic solution is one that
    a. contains a greater concentration of solute than the cell.
    b. contains the same concentration of solute as the cell.
    c. contains a lesser concentration of solute than the cell.

36. The process by which molecules are forced through a membrane by hydrostatic pressure that is greater on one side than on the other is known as what?

37. The process that uses energy to move molecules or ions across a concentration gradient from an area of lower concentration to an area of higher concentration is known as _____ _____.

38. The process by which cells engulf liquid molecules by creating a vesicle is known as _____.

39. A process that allows cells to take in molecules of solids by surrounding them to create a vesicle is known as _____.

40. Which of the following statements best describes what happens when solid material is taken into a vacuole?
    a. A ribosome enters the vacuole and uses the amino acids in the "invader" to form new protein.
    b. A lysosome combines with a vacuole and decomposes the enclosed solid material.
    c. The vacuole remains separated from the cytoplasm and the solid material persists unchanged.
    d. Oxygen enters the vacuole and oxidizes the enclosed solid material.

41. The selective and rapid transport of a substance from one end of a cell to the other is known as
    a. endocytosis.
    b. transcytosis.
    c. pinocytosis.
    d. exocytosis.

42. When does the duplication of DNA molecules in cells preparing to reproduce occur?

43. Match these events of cell reproduction with the correct description.
    1. Microtubules shorten and pull chromosomes toward centrioles.
    2. Chromatin forms chromosomes; nuclear membrane and nucleolus disappear.
    3. Chromosomes elongate, and nuclear membranes form around each chromosome set.
    4. Chromosomes become arranged midway between centrioles; duplicate parts of chromosomes become separated.

    a. prophase
    b. metaphase
    c. anaphase
    d. telophase

44. The period of cell growth and duplication of cell parts is known as _____.

45. Different cells in the human body reproduce themselves according to limits that seem inherent to the cell type.
    a. True
    b. False

46. Identify the following cells using *A* if they reproduce continually throughout life, *B* if they reproduce when an injury occurs, and *C* if they are no longer able to reproduce.

    a. skin cells   d. nerve cells

    b. liver cells   e. cells of intestinal lining

    c. blood-forming cells

47. Which of the following characteristics is typical of a benign tumor?

    a. a lump that may be discernible by palpation   c. causes pressure on surrounding tissue that may cause pain

    b. travels to distant sites via the circulation   d. can interfere with normal function

48. Name two gene families that are known to be involved in cancer formation.

49. The daughter cells of stem cells can follow several developmental pathways but not all pathways and are known as what?

50. The process that sculpts organs from tissues that naturally overgrow is _____.

STUDY ACTIVITIES

Definition of Word Parts

Define the following word parts used in this chapter.

apo-

cyt-

endo-

hyper-

hypo-

inter-

iso-

lys-

mit-

phag-

pino-

pro-

-som

vesic-

3.1 Cells Are the Basic Units of the Body

A.   Cell sizes are measured in units called _____.

B.   What human cell is visible to the unaided eye?

C.   How do cells differ from one another?

3.2 A Composite Cell

A.   Answer the following concerning a composite cell.

1.   List the three major parts of a cell.

2.   Structures within the cytoplasm that serve specific functions necessary for cell survival are called _____.

3.   The _____ directs the overall activities of the cell.

4.   Cells of the human body are eukaryotic. What does this mean? Are bacteria also eukaryotic?

B.   Answer the following concerning the cell membrane.

1.   Describe the general characteristics and functions of the cell membrane.

2.   Why is a membrane semipermeable?

3.   Label the "heads" and "tails" of the phospholipid molecules in the following diagram of a cell membrane. Then explain why this chemical relationship occurs.

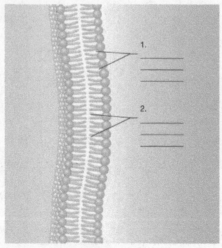

1. _____
   _____
   _____

2. _____
   _____
   _____

Cell membrane

C.   Answer the following questions about the structure of the membrane proteins.

1.   What are the functions of integral proteins and peripheral proteins?

2.   What are the functions of glycoproteins?

3.   Explain what the role of cell adhesion molecules (CAM) is in injury.

D.   Answer the following questions about the cytoplasm of a cell and what is found there.

1.   Describe the appearance of cellular cytoplasm.

2.   Fill in the following chart concerning the structure and function of these cellular organelles.

Organelle	Structure	Function
Endoplasmic reticulum		
Ribosome		
Golgi apparatus		
Mitochondria		
Lysosomes		
Peroxisomes		

3.   How do abnormalities of organelles affect health?

a.   What does the acronym MELAS stand for?

b.   Describe Krabbe disease and how it is treated.

c.   What is adrenoleukodystrophy and how can it be treated?

E.   Answer the following questions regarding other cellular structures

1.   What is the function of the centrosome and where do you find it in the cell?

2.   What do the cilia and flagella have in common? Name cells which contain these structures.

3.   How are microfilaments, intermediate filaments and microtubules distinguished from each other?

4.   Describe and give examples of microfilaments in a cell.

5.   Describe and give examples of the microtubules in a cell.

F.   Answer the following questions regarding the cell nucleus.

1.   What do you find in the cell nucleus? Name all the parts.

2.   Why is the nucleus important necessary for cellular function?

3.3 Movements into and out of the Cell

A. Answer the following questions regarding how substances enter and leave the cell through the cell membrane.

1. List the physical processes used in the movement of substances across the cell membrane.

2. List the physiological processes used to move substances across the cell membrane.

B. Answer the following concerning movement by diffusion and facilitated diffusion.

1. What factors are important for diffusion?

2. When does diffusion stop?

3. What substances in the human body are transported by diffusion?

4. What transport mechanism is illustrated in the following pictures?

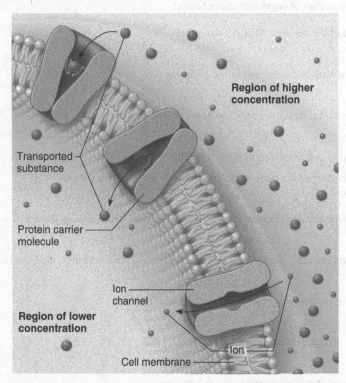

5. Describe the mechanism and the types of molecules moved this way.

C. Following are three micrographs of a red blood cell in solutions of varying tonicity. Label the solution that the cell is surrounded by in each drawing and then explain what is happening and why.

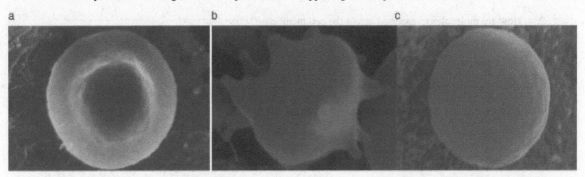

a   b   c

© David M. Phillips/Visuals Unlimited

D. Answer these questions concerning the illustration at right.

1. What process is illustrated here?

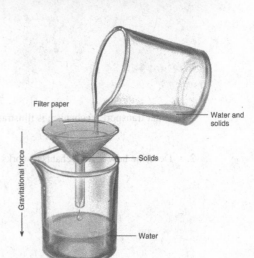

2. What provides the force needed to pull the liquid through the solids?

3. Where within the body does this process occur?

E. Answer the questions that follow the accompanying diagram.

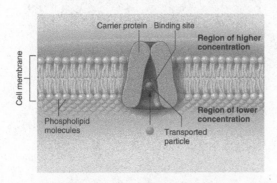

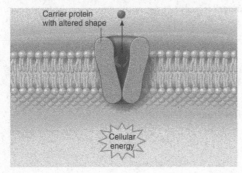

1.   What transport mechanism is illustrated here?

2.   How are molecules transported across the cell membrane?

3.   What substances are transported by this mechanism?

F.   Answer the questions concerning the process of endocytosis.

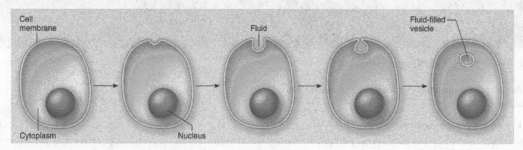

1.   What transport mechanism is illustrated in this drawing?

2.   Describe how this mechanism works and what substances are transported this way?

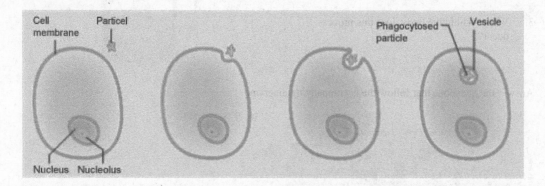

3.   What mechanism is illustrated in this drawing?

4.   What organelles are involved?

5.   What kinds of substances are transported in this manner?

6.   How is receptor-mediated endocytosis different from these other two forms of endocytosis?

G.   What is the importance of exocytosis and how does it differ from endocytosis?

H.   Transcytosis combines both of these processes, describe how this is utilized by HIV in the process of infection.

3.4 The Cell Cycle

A.   The series of changes that a cell undergoes from its formation until its reproduction is called its _____ _____.

B.   What events occur during interphase?

C.   Describe each of the following events in mitosis.

prophase

metaphase

anaphase

telophase

D.   Describe the events of cytoplasmic division and when they occur in the cell cycle.

3.5 Control of Cell Division

A.   Describe the internal mechanisms that are thought to control reproduction of cells.

B.   Describe the external mechanisms that are thought to control reproduction of cells.

C.   List the characteristics that make cancer cells different from normal cells.

3.6 Stem and Progenitor Cells

A.   What is differentiation? Why does it occur?

B.   What is a stem cell?

C.   What are progenitor cells?

D.   What is the difference between totipotent and pluripotent stem cells?

E.   How can all the cells in the body have the same genetic code but have completely different structures and functions?

3.7 Cell Death

A.   What is apostosis?

B.   What is its role in normal development?

C.   What happens in a cell undergoing apoptosis?

Clinical Focus Questions

A.   How is knowledge of the mechanism of cellular reproduction applied to the treatment of disease and development of drugs especially in regards to cancer?

B.   Select a disease with which you are familiar. How does your understanding of cell function help you understand the symptoms of that disease and approaches to its treatment?

When you have completed the study activities to your satisfaction, retake the mastery test and compare your performance with your initial attempt. If there are still areas you do not understand, repeat the appropriate study activities.

OVERVIEW

This chapter deals with the cell's ability to convert and utilize energy to carry out the functions described in the previous chapter. You will examine the processes of synthesis and decomposition that occur in cells (Learning Outcomes 1), how these vital processes are regulated (Learning Outcomes 2 and 3), and what the role of ATP is in these processes (Learning Outcome 4). You will learn about the process of cellular respiration, which synthesizes ATP, and how carbohydrates are used for this (Learning Outcomes 5 and 6). You will also explore the storage of genetic information by the cell and how this information can be transmitted and used to synthesize proteins (Learning Outcomes 7–9). You will compare and contrast the nucleic acids and examine their roles in the process of protein synthesis (Learning Outcomes 10 and 11). The chapter then discusses the impact of changes in genetic information, how these changes originate, the types of changes that occur, and the diseases that can result from these changes (Learning Outcomes 12 and 13).

LEARNING OUTCOMES

After you have studied this chapter, you should be able to

4.1   Metabolic Processes
   1.   Compare and contrast anabolism and catabolism.
4.2   Control of Metabolic Reactions
   2.   Describe the role of enzymes in metabolic reactions.
   3.   Explain how metabolic pathways are regulated.
4.3   Energy for Metabolic Reactions
   4.   Explain how ATP stores chemical energy and makes it available to a cell.
4.4   Cellular Respiration
   5.   Explain how the reactions of cellular respiration release chemical energy.
   6.   Describe the general metabolic pathways of carbohydrate metabolism.
4.5   Nucleic Acids and Protein Synthesis
   7.   Describe how DNA molecules store genetic information.
   8.   Describe how DNA molecules are replicated.
   9.   Explain how protein synthesis relies on genetic information.
   10.   Compare and contrast DNA and RNA.
   11.   Describe the steps of protein synthesis.
4.6   Changes in Genetic Information
   12.   Describe how genetic information can be altered.
   13.   Explain how a mutation may or may not affect an organism.

FOCUS QUESTION

How does the food we eat become converted to energy that drives all body processes and supplies the building material for new cells?

MASTERY TEST

Now take the mastery test. Do not guess. Some questions may have more than one correct answer. As soon as you complete the test, check your answers and correct your mistakes. Note your successes and failures so that you can reread the chapter to meet your learning needs.

1. The sum total of chemical reactions within the cell is known as what?

2. The speed of intracellular chemical reactions that are essential to life is controlled by
   a. mitochondria.
   c. RNA.
   b. enzymes.
   d. the permeability of the cell membrane.

3. The metabolic process that synthesizes materials for cellular growth and requires energy is called _____.

4. The metabolic process that breaks down complex molecules into simpler ones and releases energy is called _____.

5. The process by which two molecules are joined together to form a more complex molecule and water is called
   a. dehydration synthesis.
   c. atomization.
   b. chemical bonding.

6. Glycerol and fatty acids become joined to form water and
   a. cholesterol.
   c. fat molecules.
   b. phospholipids.
   d. wax.

7. Amino acids are joined by a peptide bond to form water and _____.

8. The process by which water is added to a complex molecule to break it down as represented by the equation $C_{12}H_{22}O_{11} + H_2O \rightarrow C_6H_{12}O_6 + C_6H_{12}O_6$ is called _____.

9. Anabolism must be (greater than/balanced with/less than) catabolism to maintain the life of the cell.

10. Catabolic reactions typically _____ energy, while anabolic reactions _____ energy.

11. Enzymes are a type of
    a. lipid.
    c. protein.
    b. carbohydrate.
    d. inorganic salt.

12. Enzymes work by (increasing/decreasing) the amount of energy needed to begin a reaction in the cell.

13. An enzyme acts only on a particular substance that is called its
    a. binding site.
    c. complement.
    b. substrate.
    d. product.

14. An enzyme's ability to recognize the substance upon which it will act seems to be based on
    a. atomic weight.
    c. structural formula.
    b. molecular shape or conformation.
    d. number of carbons.

15. A substance needed to convert an inactive form of an enzyme to an active form is called a _____ or a _____.

16. Cofactors are frequently _____; coenzymes are often _____.

17. A chemical that interferes with cellular metabolism by denaturing its enzymes is called a(n)
    a. antienzyme.
    c. caustic metal.
    b. metabolic poison.
    d. reversible inhibitor.

18. The form of energy utilized by most cellular processes is
    a. chemical.
    c. thermal.
    b. electrical.
    d. mechanical.

19. The process by which the energy in a molecule of glucose is released within the cell is called _____.

20. The three main components of a molecule of ATP are _____, _____, and _____.

21. Re-synthesis of ATP from ADP is accomplished by the process of _____.

22. The initial phase of respiration that occurs in the cytoplasm which does not require oxygen and produces two pyruvic acid molecules plus energy is called _____ respiration or _____.

23. The energy needed to prime glucose is provided by
   a. oxygen.
   b. ATP.
   c. ADP.
   d. heat.

24. NADH is a coenzyme that carries energy in
   a. a nitrogen bond.
   b. adenosine molecules.
   c. high-energy electrons.
   d. a large nucleus.

25. The second phase of respiration that occurs in the mitochondria, requires oxygen, and produces carbon dioxide, water, and energy is called _____ respiration.

26. What molecule is needed for this second phase, but not for the first? _____

27. Which of the two phases of cellular respiration can yield or release more energy? _____

28. Coupling of energy and ATP synthesis is accomplished by a series of enzyme complexes located within the
   a. mitochondria.
   b. DNA.
   c. Golgi apparatus.
   d. muscle cells.

29. Muscle fatigue and cramps following strenuous exercise are due to the production of what compound? _____

30. The function of electron carriers such as nicotinamide adenine dinucleotide (NAD⁺) is to
   a. act as an oxygen storage molecule.
   b. preserve the structure of glucose molecules.
   c. temporarily store the energy released from chemical bonds of glucose molecules.
   d. act as catalysts for oxidation reactions.

31. What is the fate of carbohydrate that is in excess of the amount that can be stored as glycogen?
   a. It is excreted in the urine.
   b. The cells are forced to increase their metabolic rate to burn it.
   c. It is converted to fat molecules and deposited into fat tissue.
   d. It remains in the blood.

32. The main storage reservoirs for glycogen are _____ cells and the _____.

33. What is the fate of amino acids that are in excess of the amount that can be used for protein synthesis when there is plenty of energy?
   a. They are stored as glycogen.
   b. They are excreted by the kidneys.
   c. They are converted to fat.
   d. They are made into proteins.

34. We inherit traits from our parents because
   a. DNA contains genes that are the carriers of inheritance.
   b. genes tell the cells to construct protein in a unique way for each individual.
   c. sexual reproduction is required for a new individual.
   d. our cells undergo mitosis after conception.

35. All of the DNA in the cell constitutes the _____.

36. A molecule consisting of a double helix with sugar and phosphates forming the outer strands and organic bases joining the two strands is known as what?

37. List the four nitrogenous bases of the DNA molecule.

38. DNA base pairs A and G are _____; T and C are _____.

39. Which of the following complementary base pairs is correct?
   a. A, T
   b. C, G
   c. C, T
   d. G, A

40. DNA molecules are located in the _____. Protein synthesis takes place in the _____.

41. What are the three types of RNA used for protein synthesis?

42. The function of ribozymes is
   a. the formation of lipids, such as cholesterol.
   b. to guide the breakdown of polysaccharides.
   c. to control the bonding of amino acids.
   d. to transfer amino acids to the ribosome.

43. Each amino acid can be specified by only one codon.
   a. True
   b. False

44. mRNA molecules and ribosomes act together to synthesize
   a. protein.
   b. carbohydrate.
   c. fats.
   d. genes.

45. The amino acids in a molecule of protein are arranged in the correct sequence by
   a. ribosomes.
   b. transfer RNA.
   c. messenger RNA.
   d. DNA.

46. The energy for the synthesis of protein molecules is supplied by _____ molecules.

47. Which of the following factors is capable of causing mutation?
   a. radiation
   b. poor diet
   c. sunlight
   d. chemicals

48. The two general types of mutations are _____ mutations and _____ mutations.

49. "Common genetic variants with no discernible effects" are known as what?

50. What protects against mutation in the cell?

STUDY ACTIVITIES

Definition of Word Parts

Define the following word parts used in this chapter.

aer-

an-

ana-

cata-

co-

de-

mut-

-strat

sub-

-zym

4.1 Metabolic Processes

A. Answer the following concerning anabolic metabolism.

1. Define *anabolism*.

2. This formula is an example of anabolism. What specific molecules are being joined here and what is the name of this process?

3. Glycerol and fatty acid molecules joined by dehydration synthesis form what compound?

4. Amino acids joined by dehydration synthesis form what compound?

B. Answer these questions concerning catabolic metabolism.

1. Define *catabolism*.

2. Why are these processes in the body called hydrolysis?

3. Why are anabolism and catabolism balanced in healthy individuals?

4.2 Control of Metabolic Reactions

A. Answer the following regarding enzymes and enzyme actions.

1. Describe the structure and function of most enzymes.

2. Explain why enzymes are needed only in very small quantities.

3. Enzymes promote chemical reactions in cells by (increasing/decreasing) the amount of energy needed to initiate a reaction.

4. What is the relationship between an enzyme and a substrate? Explain how this works.

5. List the factors that can alter the shapes of enzymes and therefore their activities.

B. Answer the following regarding metabolic pathways.

1. A sequence of enzyme-controlled reactions that lead to the synthesis or breakdown of biochemicals is called what?

2. What is a rate-limiting enzyme and how does this inhibit a metabolic pathway?

C. Answer the following regarding cofactors and coenzymes.

  1. What is a coenzyme? What substances are coenzymes?

  2. What is a cofactor? What substances are cofactors?

4.3 Energy for Metabolic Reactions

A. Answer the following regarding energy and its fate.

  1. What is energy? What are some common forms of energy?

  2. What happens to energy in a reaction?

  3. What is cellular respiration?

  4. What role do enzymes have in this process and where do you find them?

B. Answer the following regarding ATP molecules.

  1. What is the importance or function of ATP?

  2. Describe an ATP molecule.

  3. Energy is released by what set of chemical reactions is donated to ADP? The energy released from ATP is then used to do what set of chemical reactions?

C. What is oxidation and how is it different from burning of a chemical substance?

4.4 Cellular Respiration

A. Answer the following regarding the overview of cellular respiration.

  1. What are the three main reactions that occur in cellular respiration?

  2. What are the requirements and the products of these reactions?

  3. What happens to the energy released by these reactions?

  4. Reactions that require oxygen are _____; those that do not require oxygen are _____.

  5. Which of the above reactions produces the greatest number of ATP molecules?

B.   Answer the following regarding glycolysis.

      1.   Which phase of cellular respiration is this and why?

      2.   Describe the three main events of glycolysis.

      3.   What is the coenzyme necessary for transporting energy?

      4.   What is the net number of ATP molecules produced and where is the rest of the energy?

C.   Answer the following regarding anaerobic respiration.

      1.   What is oxygen's role in cellular respiration?

      2.   When oxygen is not available, how does NADH unload its electrons?

      3.   What is produced by this and why is this not a good solution to your energy needs?

D.   Answer the following regarding the aerobic reactions.

      1.   What happens to pyruvic acid produced by glycolysis to get it ready for citric acid cycle?

      2.   Describe the citric acid (Krebs) cycle, include what molecule this set of reactions begins with, how many ATP are formed, what coenzymes are needed and how many of each.

      3.   What is released by this process and what molecules does it need to continue?

      4.   Describe what happens in the electron transport chain, explain what happens to the coenzymes and how much ATP is produced.

      5.   What is the role for oxygen in this and what is produced in the process?

E.   When, how, and where is excess glucose stored?

4.5 Nucleic Acids and Protein Synthesis

A.   Answer these questions concerning genetic information.

      1.   What is the genetic code and how is it passed between organisms?

      2.   What is a gene?

      3.   What is a genome? What is the exome?

4. Name and describe the building blocks of nucleic acids.

5. Describe the structure of DNA.

6. Which of the bases are purines and which ones are pyrimidines?

7. What is complementary base pairing?

B. Answer the following regarding DNA replication.

1. Describe the process of DNA replication.

2. When does DNA replicate?

3. If you had the following sequence on one strand of DNA: ATTTACCGCGATTGGCAATCCGAT, what would the sequence on the new strand of DNA that formed from this be?

C. Answer the following regarding the genetic code.

1. What is meant by the "genetic code"?

2. Why is the genetic code said to be universal?

3. What molecule will transfer the information from the nucleus to the cytoplasm?

D. Answer the following regarding RNA molecules.

1. Fill in the following table comparing DNA and RNA molecules.

	DNA	RNA
Main location		
5-carbon sugar		
Basic molecular structure		
Nitrogenous bases included		
Major functions		

2. What is the process of copying DNA into RNA called?

3. Describe how messenger RNA is formed.

4. What are codons?

5. Where must messenger RNA go and what must it bind to for translation to occur?

E. Answer the following regarding protein synthesis.
1. Describe a transfer RNA molecule.

2. What is the role of transfer RNA in protein synthesis?

3. What are ribosomes and what is their role in this process?

4. What are the overall requirements for protein synthesis?

5. Describe the process of translation.

6. Why is it stated that protein synthesis is economical?

4.6 Changes in Genetic Information

A. Answer the following regarding the nature of mutations.

1. What is a mutation?

2. Differentiate between spontaneous and induced mutations.

3. When or under what circumstances do mutations become harmful?

4. How does a mutation get transmitted to the next generation?

B.   Answer the following regarding the protection against mutation.

1.   What are some molecular mechanisms that protect against mutations?

2.   How does having several different codons for the same amino acid prevent a mutation from changing the protein's function?

3.   How does having two copies of each chromosome help to maintain function?

4.   Explain how the timing of a mutation affects the seriousness of its effect on health.

Clinical Focus Questions

Why could you make the following statement? "Knowledge of DNA is a necessary component for treating and curing every pathology we encounter."

When you have completed the study activities to your satisfaction, retake the mastery test and compare your performance with your initial attempt. If there are still areas you do not understand, repeat the appropriate study activities.

OVERVIEW

After learning about cells and cellular processes important for life, in this chapter you will study how cells cooperate structurally and functionally to form the four basic types of tissue in the human body (Learning Outcomes 1–3). The chapter considers epithelial and connective tissues in more detail, describing their general characteristics and functions and giving specific examples of organs that contain each of these types of tissue (Learning Outcomes 4, 5, 7, 8 and 9). The classification of glands and the different types of membranes are also addressed (Learning Outcomes 6 and 10). The chapter concludes with an overview of the three types of muscle (Learning Outcome 11) and a general description of nervous tissue (Learning Outcome 12) because both of these tissues will be explored in depth in later chapters.

The characteristics of tissues remain the same regardless of where they occur in the body. Knowledge of these characteristics is essential to understanding how a specific tissue contributes to the function of an organ.

LEARNING OUTCOMES

After you have studied this chapter, you should be able to

5.1   Cells Are Organized into Tissues
1.   Describe how cells are organized into tissues.
2.   Identify the intercellular junctions in tissues.
3.   List the four major tissue types in the body, then indicate locations and functions of each type.
5.2   Epithelial Tissues
4.   Describe the general characteristics and functions of epithelial tissue.
5.   Name the types of epithelium, and identify an organ in which each is found.
6.   Explain how glands are classified.
5.3   Connective Tissues
7.   Describe the general characteristics of connective tissue.
8.   Compare and contrast the ground substance, cells, and fibers in different types of connective tissue.
9.   Describe the major functions of each type of connective tissue, and identify where each type of connective tissue is found.
5.4   Types of Membranes
10.   Describe and locate each of the four types of membranes.
5.5   Muscle Tissues
11.   Distinguish among the three types of muscle tissue.
5.6   Nervous Tissues
12.   Describe the general characteristics and functions of nervous tissue.

FOCUS QUESTION

Tissue is the "fabric" of life. With only four broad classifications, how can we accomplish the assembly and operations of all the body's components?

MASTERY TEST

Now take the mastery test. Do not guess. Some questions may have more than one correct answer. As soon as you complete the test, check your answers and correct any errors. Note your successes and failures so that you can reread the chapter to meet your learning needs.

1.   In complex organisms, cells of similar structure and function are organized into groups known as what?

2.   What is the term for the structures that connect the cell membranes?

3.   Which of the following is a junction that is found in the lining of blood vessels and the digestive tract?

    a.   desmosome

    b.   gap junction

    c.   tight junction

    d.   extracellular matrix

4. Which of the following allows ions and small nutrients to move between cells?
   a. desmosome
   b. gap junction
   c. tight junctions
   d. extracellular matrix

5. List the four major tissue types found in the human body.

6. The function of epithelial tissue is to
   a. support body parts.
   b. cover body surfaces.
   c. bind body parts together.
   d. form the framework of organs.

7. Which of the following statements about epithelial tissue is/are true?
   a. Epithelial tissue has no blood vessels.
   b. Epithelial cells reproduce slowly.
   c. Epithelial cells are nourished by substances diffusing from connective tissue.
   d. Injuries to epithelial tissue do not heal.

8. The blood-brain barrier shields brain cells from toxins by
   a. stimulation of brain cells to secrete a special lipid to coat the cell membranes.
   b. modifications of the walls of capillaries in the brain.
   c. increasing the protein in the cell membranes of capillaries and brain cells.
   d. creating a fatty matrix in which brain cells are embedded.

9. Epithelial cells are classified according to _____ and number of _____.

10. Match the following types of epithelial cells with their correct location.
    1. simple squamous epithelium
    2. simple cuboidal epithelium
    3. simple columnar epithelium
    4. pseudostratified columnar epithelium
    5. stratified squamous epithelium
    6. stratified cuboidal epithelium
    7. stratified columnar epithelium
    8. transitional epithelium
    9. glandular epithelium

    a. within columnar or cuboidal epithelium
    b. lining of the ducts of salivary glands
    c. lining of respiratory passages
    d. epidermis of skin
    e. air sacs of lungs, walls of capillaries
    f. lining of digestive tract
    g. lining of urinary tract
    h. lining of developing ovarian follicle
    i. conjunctiva of the eye

11. Glands that secrete their products into ducts are called _____ glands.

12. Glands that lose small portions of their glandular cell bodies during secretion are
    a. merocrine glands.
    b. apocrine glands.
    c. alveolar glands.
    d. holocrine glands.

13. Most exocrine secretory cells in a gland are
    a. merocrine.
    b. holocrine.
    c. apocrine.
    d. endocrine.

14. The function(s) of connective tissue is/are
    a. support.
    b. protection.
    c. covering.
    d. fat storage.

15. The most common kind of cell in connective tissue is the _____.

16. A connective tissue cell that can become detached and move about is the _____.

17. Mast cells secrete _____ and _____.

18. An important characteristic of collagenous fibers is their
    a. elasticity.
    b. rigidity.
    c. tensile strength.
    d. inability to reproduce rapidly.

19. Elastic fibers have (more/less) strength than collagenous fibers, but are easily _____.

20. Which of the following statements is/are true about adipose tissue?
    a. It is a specialized form of loose connective tissue.
    b. It occurs around the kidneys, behind the eyeballs, and around various joints.
    c. It serves as a conserver of body heat.
    d. It serves as a storehouse of energy for the body.

21. Which of the following statements is/are true of connective tissue?
    a. Dense connective tissue has many collagen fibers.
    b. Areolar connective tissue contains both elastic and collagenous fibers.
    c. Elastin is prominent in reticular connective tissue.
    d. All types have a rich blood supply.

22. Sprains heal slowly because dense regular connective tissue has a relatively poor blood supply.
    a. True
    b. False

23. The chondromucoprotein is part of the intercellular substance of
    a. muscle.
    b. bone.
    c. cartilage.
    d. nerves.

24. Where are the blood vessels that supply blood to cartilage cells?

25. What are the three types of cartilage?

26. Which of these is the most common cartilage?
    a. hyaline
    b. fibrous
    c. elastic
    d. serous

27. The mechanism used to supply nutrients to cartilage cells is _____.

28. The model for the developing bones of a fetus is
    a. hyaline cartilage.
    b. elastic cartilage.
    c. fibrocartilage.
    d. areolar connective tissue.

29. The most rigid connective tissue is _____.

30. The extracellular matrix in vascular tissue is known as what?

31. The membrane that lines body cavities that open to the outside of the body is a
    a. serous membrane.
    b. mucous membrane.
    c. cutaneous membrane.
    d. synovial membrane.

32. The three types of muscle tissue are _____, _____, and _____.

33. Which type of muscle is involuntary and striated in appearance?
    a. skeletal
    b. dense regular
    c. smooth
    d. cardiac

34. The coordination and regulation of body functions are the functions of _____ tissue.

35. The cells that bind nerve cells and support nervous tissue are _____ cells.

STUDY ACTIVITIES

Definition of Word Parts

Define the following word parts used in this chapter.

adip-

chondr-

-cyt

epi-

-glia

hist-

hyal-

inter-

macr-

neur-

os-

phag-

pseud-

squam-

strat-

stria-

5.1 Cells Are Organized into Tissues

A.   List the four major tissue types found in the body.

B.   Describe and locate the following intercellular junctions: tight junctions, desmosomes, and gap junctions.

C.   Describe the blood-brain barrier.

5.2 Epithelial Tissues

A.   1.   Describe the general characteristics of epithelial tissue.

         2.   Where in the body is epithelial tissue present?

         3.   Epithelial tissue is anchored to connective tissue by the _____ _____.

         4.   How does epithelial tissue receive nutrients?

         5.   How are epithelial cells classified?

B.   Answer the following concerning simple squamous epithelium.

         1.   Describe the structure of simple squamous epithelium.

         2.   Simple squamous epithelium is found where _____ and _____ take place.

C.   Answer the following concerning simple cuboidal epithelium.
1.   Describe the structure of simple cuboidal epithelium.

2.   Where is this type of tissue found?

3.   The functions of simple cuboidal epithelium are _____ and _____.

D.   Answer the following concerning simple columnar epithelium.
1.   Describe the structure of simple columnar epithelium.

2.   Where do you find this tissue in the body?

3.   What is its function?

4.   What cellular features are often found on these cells?

E.   Answer the following concerning pseudostratified columnar epithelium.
1.   Microscopic, hairlike projections called _____ are a characteristic of pseudostratified columnar epithelium.

2.   Where is this tissue found?

3.   What is its function?

F.   Answer the following concerning stratified squamous epithelium.
1.   Describe the structure and function of stratified squamous epithelium.

2.   Where is this tissue found?

G.   Answer these questions concerning stratified cuboidal epithelium.
1.   Where is this tissue located?

2.   What are its functions?

H.   Answer these questions concerning stratified columnar epithelium.
1.   What is the structure of this tissue?

2.   Where is this tissue located?

I.   Answer these questions concerning transitional epithelium.
1.   Where is this tissue located?

2.   What are its functions?

J.   Answer these questions concerning glandular epithelium.
        1. Epithelial cells specialized to secrete substances into ducts are called _____.

        2. In what type of tissue are such cells usually located?

        3. Fill in the following chart regarding the types of exocrine glands.

Type	Characteristics	Example
Unicellular glands		
Multicellular glands		
Simple glands		
a. Simple tubular gland		
b. Simple coiled tubular gland		
c. Simple branched tubular gland		
d. Simple branched alveolar gland		
Compound glands		
a. Compound tubular gland		
b. Compound alveolar gland		

        4. Answer the following questions about glandular secretions.
            a. Compare the how merocrine, apocrine, and holocrine glands secrete their products.

            b. Differentiate between serous cells and mucous cells.

5.3 Connective Tissues

A.   1. What are the functions of connective tissue?

        2. What are the characteristics of connective tissue?

B.   1. What are the major cell types in connective tissue?

        2. What are the functions of these cells?

C.   Describe the major fibers found in connective tissue.

D.   How does a disturbance in the ability to synthesize collagen affect the body? Give examples.

E.   Fill in the following table regarding connective tissue proper.

Type	Description	Function	Location
Areolar connective tissue			
Adiose connective tissue			
Reticular connective tissue			
Dense regular connective tissue			
Dense irregular connective tissue			
Elastic connective tissue			

F.   Fill in the following table regarding specialized connective tissue and answer the questions below.

Type	Description	Function	Location
Hyaline cartilage			
Elastic cartilage			
Fibrocartilage			
Bone			
Blood			

1.   How do the cartilage cells receive nutrients?

2.   What cells do you find in osseous tissue?

3.   Bone injuries heal relatively rapidly. Why is this true?

4.   List the types of cells in blood and identify what is unique about this matrix.

5.4 Types of Membranes

A.   Fill in the following chart concerning membranes.

Type	Tissues Contained	Location	Function
Serous			
Mucous			
Cutaneous			
Synovial			

5.5 Muscle Tissues

A.   What are the characteristics of muscle tissue?

B.   Fill in the following chart regarding the different types of muscle tissue.

Type	Structure	Control	Location
Skeletal			
Smooth			
Cardiac			

5.6 Nervous Tissues

A.   1.   Name and describe the basic cell of nervous tissue.

2.   What are the functions of neuroglial cells in nervous tissue?

3.   What is the function of nervous tissue?

Clinical Focus Questions

Describe the impact of the loss of several feet of small intestine on an individual's nutritional status. How does the structure of the simple columnar epithelium intensify the impact of such a loss?

When you have completed the study activities to your satisfaction, retake the mastery test and compare your performance with your initial attempt. If there are still areas you do not understand, repeat the appropriate study activities.

OVERVIEW

In this chapter, you will begin combining the tissues to form organs and examine how these cooperate to form systems. The first system you study is the integument. The chapter describes the functions and structures of skin as well as the factors that determine skin coloration (Learning Outcomes 1 and 2). You will then read about the accessory structures and how they contribute to the function of integument (Learning Outcomes 3 and 4). The integument's role in maintaining body temperature is presented (Learning Outcome 5) followed by an introduction to the mechanisms of repair, which occur when skin has been damaged (Learning Outcomes 6 and 7). Last, you will read of the changes that occur in the integument as we age (Learning Outcome 8).

Study of the integumentary system is essential to understanding how the body controls interaction between the internal and external environments.

LEARNING OUTCOMES

After you have studied this chapter, you should be able to:
6.1   Skin and Its Tissues
    1.   Describe the structure of the layers of the skin.
    2.   Summarize the factors that determine skin color.
6.2   Accessory Structures of the Skin
    3.   Describe the accessory structures associated with the skin.
    4.   Explain the functions of each accessory structure of the skin.
6.3   Skin Functions
    5.   List various skin functions, and explain how the skin helps regulate body temperature.
6.4   Healing of Wounds and Burns
    6.   Describe wound healing.
    7.   Distinguish among the types of burns, and include a description of healing with each type.
6.5   Life-Span Changes
    8.   Summarize life-span changes in the integumentary system.

FOCUS QUESTION

You have spent the day on the beach in 90°F heat. You return to your air-conditioned home and notice that you have a deep partial thickness burn. How does the skin help you to adjust to the changes in temperature? How will the integument heal in over the next week and what will prevent an infection from occurring?

MASTERY TEST

Now take the mastery test. Do not guess. Some questions may have more than one correct answer. As soon as you complete the test, check your answers and correct any mistakes. Note your successes and failures so that you can reread the chapter to meet your learning needs.

1.   Define an *organ*.

2.   The largest organ in the body by weight is the _____.

3.   List the functions of the skin.

4.   The outer layer of skin is called the _____.

5.   The inner layer of skin is called the _____.

6. The mass of connective tissue beneath the inner layer of skin is called the _____ _____.

7. The cells of the skin that reproduce are in the
   a. keratin.
   b. stratum corneum.
   c. stratum basale (germinativum).
   d. collagen.

8. Blood vessels supplying blood to the skin are located in the
   a. dermis.
   b. epidermis.
   c. subcutaneous layer.
   d. muscle.

9. When a person does not change his or her position for a long time, a _____ _____ may develop.

10. The symptoms of psoriasis are due to
    a. increased cell division in the epidermis.
    b. increased keratinization of epidermal cells.
    c. impaired circulation to the epidermis.
    d. separation of the dermal and epidermal layers.

11. The pigment that gives color to the skin is
    a. melanin.
    b. trichosiderin.
    c. biliverdin.
    d. bilirubin.

12. Skin cancer is associated with high exposure to _____.

13. Which protein accumulates in the epidermal cells and provides a protective barrier to water loss and damage?
    a. collagen
    b. keratin
    c. melanin
    d. hemoglobin

14. The dermis of the skin (contains/does not contain) smooth muscle cells.

15. The accessory organs of the skin are _____, _____, _____, and _____ _____.

16. The dermis is composed of two layers of connective tissue. Name the layers and the specific type of connective tissue associated with them.

17. Hair color is determined by the amount and type of _____ the hair contains.

18. The glands usually associated with hair follicles are _____ glands.
    a. apocrine
    b. endocrine
    c. sebaceous
    d. exocrine

19. The active, growing part of the nail is the _____.

20. The sweat glands associated with the regulation of body temperature are the _____ glands.
    a. endocrine
    b. eccrine
    c. exocrine
    d. apocrine

21. Mammary glands are modified _____ glands.

22. The most common skin problem in adolescence is
    a. acne.
    b. blisters.
    c. contact dermatitis.
    d. cancers.

23. Which of the following organs and tissues produce the most heat?
    a. kidneys
    b. bones
    c. muscles
    d. lungs

24. The primary process(es) by which the body loses heat is/are
    a. radiation.
    b. conduction.
    c. evaporation.
    d. convection.

25. Those at highest risk for hypothermia are
    a. infants.
    b. school-age children.
    c. young adults.
    d. the elderly.

26. The normal response to injury or stress in the body is known as
   a. inflammation.
   b. anemia.
   c. hypoxia.
   d. metabolism.

27. When a cut extends into the dermis, the cells that form the new tissue to hold the edges of the wound together are
   a. reticulocytes.
   b. fibroblasts.
   c. phagocytes.
   d. neutrophils.

28. In large, open wounds, the healing process may be accompanied by the formation of _____.

29. In a partial-thickness burn, when large areas of the epidermis are destroyed, the cells are replaced by
   a. stem cells of accessory organs of the skin, such as hair follicles or glands.
   b. the dermis.
   c. the stratum basale.
   d. an autograft.

30. A full-thickness burn many times requires skin grafting in order to supply skin cells usually produced in the dermis.
   a. True
   b. False

31. Skin changes and behaviors in the elderly affect the structure of bones adversely.
   a. True
   b. False

STUDY ACTIVITIES

Definition of Word Parts

Define the following word parts used in this chapter.

alb-

cut-

derm-

epi-

follic-

hol-

kerat-

melan-

por-

seb-

sudor-

6.1 Skin and Its Tissues

A.   Answer the following questions regarding the skin.

1.   The layers of the skin are the _____ and _____.

2.   What kinds of tissue are found in each of these layers?

3.   Describe the structure and function of the subcutaneous layer.

4.   Describe the ways in which drugs can be delivered through the skin.

B.   Answer the following questions regarding the epidermis.

1.   Fill in the following chart concerning the layers of the epidermis.

Layer	Location	Characteristics
Stratum basale		
Stratum spinosum		
Stratum granulosum		
Stratum lucidum		
Stratum corneum		

2.   Why is water not absorbed through the skin?

3.   How is the production of epidermal cells related to the development of calluses and corns?

4.   List the functions of the epidermis.

5.   What is the purpose of melanin and how do epithelial cells acquire this pigment?

6.   What other factors affect skin color?

C.   Answer the following questions about pressure sores (decubitus ulcers).

1.   How does a pressure sore develop?

2. How can the development of pressure sores be prevented?

3. Would you expect a very thin person to be at increased risk for a pressure sore? Why or why not?

D. Answer the following questions regarding cancer.
   1. Cancer of the skin can arise from the deep layers of the _____ or from pigmented _____.
   2. How can you reduce your risk for skin cancer?

E. Answer the following questions regarding the dermis.
   1. How do the patterns of fingerprints form?

   2. Describe the structure and function of the dermis.

   3. What types of muscle cells are found in the dermis?

   4. What is the function of nervous tissue in the skin?

6.2 Accessory Structures of the Skin

A. Label the structures in the drawing below.

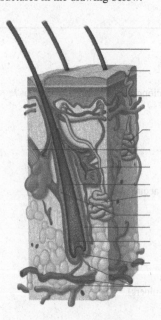
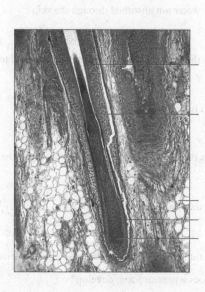

B.   Answer the following questions about hair follicles.

     1.   What is hair and how does it develop?

     2.   Explain how various hair colors are produced.

     3.   Describe how hair responds to cold temperature or strong emotion.

C.   How is baldness treated? How effective are the various treatments for baldness?

D.   Answer the following questions regarding the skin glands.

     1.   Where are sebaceous glands located, and what is the function of the substance they secrete?

     2.   Compare apocrine and merocrine sweat glands in relation to location, association with other skin structures, and activating stimuli.

E.   Describe the mechanisms that lead to acne. How is it treated?

6.3 Skin Functions

A.   List the basic functions of the skin

B.   Answer the following questions regarding regulation of body temperature

     1.   Match the terms in the first column, which are processes of heat loss, with their definitions in the second column.

a.	radiation	1.	Heat is lost by continuous circulation of air over the body.
b.	conduction	2.	Sweat changes to vapor and carries heat away from the body.
c.	convection	3.	Heat moves from the warm body to cooler air via infrared heat waves.
d.	evaporation	4.	Heat moves away from the body by contact with a cool object.

     2.   Describe the roles of the nervous, muscular, circulatory, and respiratory systems in heat regulation.

C.   Answer the following questions regarding problems in temperature regulation.

     1.   Explain the events that can produce an increase in body temperature.

2. What are the symptoms of hypothermia?

3. What groups are at increased risk of hypothermia?

4. How can hypothermia be prevented?

6.4 Healing of Wounds and Burns

A. Answer the following questions regarding cuts.

1. What cells are involved in a shallow break in the skin?

2. What happens when there is an injury that extends into the dermis or subcutaneous layer?

3. What are granulations and when do they typically form?

B. Answer the following questions regarding burns.

1. What is the difference between a superficial and a deep partial-thickness burn?

2. What factors determine or drive the healing process in deep partial-thickness burns?

3. What is a typical treatment with full-thickness burns?

4. What does the "rules of nines" pertain to?

6.5 Life-Span Changes

Describe the changes that occur as skin ages. Which of these changes are simply cosmetic and which can compromise the individual's health?

Clinical Focus Questions

As summer and the hot weather approach, your family is concerned about your grandmother. Your grandmother is a healthy, 83-year-old woman who lives alone and is proud of her independence. She does not have an air conditioner, despite your family's offer to purchase and install one for her. She says she is too old to get used to "newfangled things now." What suggestions could you offer to help your grandmother maintain her health during the hot weather? Explain your rationale.

When you have completed the study activities to your satisfaction, retake the mastery test and compare your performance with your initial attempt. If there are still areas you do not understand, repeat the appropriate study activities.

OVERVIEW

This chapter deals with the skeletal system—the tissues that form the framework for the body, facilitate movement, regulate calcium, and even produce blood cells. The chapter begins with a description of these tissues, outlining the general functions of bone, and an explanation of how bones are classified for your understanding (Learning Outcome 1). You will then explore the unique microscopic and macroscopic features that provide these specific functions (Learning Outcome 2). You will study the way that bone develops and grows as well as the intrinsic and extrinsic factors that affect these processes (Learning Outcomes 3 and 4). Functions of bone and the organization of the skeleton will follow this (Learning Outcomes 5 and 6). Once you have examined the basic organization and the specific functions, you will locate and name most of the bones in the skeleton (Learning Outcomes 7–13). This chapter will end by discussing how the skeletal system changes throughout life (Learning Outcome 14).

Movement is a characteristic necessary for life. A study of the skeletal system will help you understand how a complex organism, the human being, is organized to accomplish movement.

LEARNING OUTCOMES

After you have studied this chapter you should be able to

7.1   Bone Shape and Structure
   1.   Classify bones according to their shapes, and name an example from each group.
   2.   Describe the macroscopic and microscopic structure of a long bone, and list the functions of these parts.
7.2   Bone Development and Growth
   3.   Distinguish between intramembranous and endochondral bones, and explain how such bones develop and grow.
   4.   Describe the effects of sunlight, nutrition, hormonal secretions, and exercise on bone development and growth.
7.3   Bone Function
   5.   Discuss the major functions of bones.
7.4   Skeletal Organization
   6.   Distinguish between the axial and appendicular skeletons, and name the major parts of each.
7.5   Skull
   7.   Locate the bones that compose the skull and identify their major features.
7.6   Vertebral Column
   8.   Locate the bones that compose the vertebral column and identify their major features.
7.7   Thoracic Cage
   9.   Locate the bones that compose the thoracic cage and identify their major features.
7.8   Pectoral Girdle
   10.   Locate the bones that compose the pectoral girdle and identify their major features.
7.9   Upper Limb
   11.   Locate the bones that compose the upper limb and identify their major features.
7.10   Pelvic Girdle
   12.   Locate the bones that compose the pelvic girdle and identify their major features.
7.11   Lower Limb
   13.   Locate the bones that compose the lower limb and identify their major features.
7.12   Life-Span Changes
   14.   Describe life-span changes in the skeletal system.

FOCUS QUESTION

You are playing basketball. Despite your effort to avoid it, the ball strikes you in the head. How has the skeletal system contributed to your ability to move around the court and how has it protected you from injury?

MASTERY TEST

Now take the mastery test. Do not guess. Some questions have more than one correct answer. As soon as you complete the test, check your answers and correct any mistakes. Note your successes and failures so that you can reread the chapter to meet your learning needs.

1. Which of the following tissues is/are found in bones?
   - a. cartilage
   - b. nervous tissue
   - c. fibrous connective tissue
   - d. blood

2. A bone with a long longitudinal axis and expanded ends is classified as what type of bone?

3. Ribs are examples of which classification of bones?
   - a. long
   - b. short
   - c. flat
   - d. sesamoid

4. The "shaft" of a long bone is known as the what?
   - a. epiphysis
   - b. diaphysis
   - c. lacunae
   - d. central canal

5. Which of the following statements regarding the periosteum is/are correct?
   - a. The periosteum contains nerve tissue and is responsible for feeling in the bone.
   - b. The fibers of the periosteum are continuous with ligaments and tendons.
   - c. The metabolic activity of the bone occurs in the periosteum.
   - d. The periosteum has an important role in bone formation and repair.

6. The function of a bony process is to provide a
   - a. passage for blood vessels.
   - b. place of attachment for tendons and ligaments.
   - c. smooth surface for articulation with another bone.
   - d. location for exchange of electrolytes.

7. Bone that consists of tightly packed osseous tissue is what type of bone?

8. Bone that consists of numerous bony plates that are separated by irregular spaces is what type of bone?

9. The medullary cavity is filled with
   - a. spongy bone.
   - b. fatty connective tissue.
   - c. marrow.
   - d. collagen.

10. The extracellular material of bone is _____ and _____ _____.

11. Severe bone pain caused by abnormally shaped red blood cells that obstruct circulation is a symptom of what disease?

12. Bones that develop from layers of membranous connective tissue are called _____ _____.

13. Bones that develop from layers of hyaline cartilage are called _____ _____.

14. The band of cartilage between the primary and secondary ossification centers in long bones is called the
   - a. osteoblastic band.
   - b. calcium disk.
   - c. periosteal plate.
   - d. epiphyseal plate.

15. The primary ossification center in a long bone is found at the
   - a. epiphysis.
   - b. center of the diaphysis.
   - c. epiphyseal plate.
   - d. articular surface of the joint.

16. Cells undergoing mitosis in the cartilaginous cells of the epiphyseal disk are found in
   - a. zone one, closest to the epiphyseal end.
   - b. zone two.
   - c. zone three.
   - d. zone four near the diaphyseal end.

17. Which of the following statements about osteoclasts is/are true?
   - a. Osteoclasts are large cells that originate by the fusion of monocytes.
   - b. Osteoclasts are cells that give rise to new bone tissue.
   - c. Osteoclasts become inactive with aging, giving rise to osteoporosis.
   - d. Osteoclasts get rid of the inorganic component of the oldest cartilaginous cells and allow osteoblasts to invade the region.

18. List the factors that affect bone development, growth, and repair.

19. In a developing bone, compact bone is deposited
    a. on the outside of bone just under the periosteum.
    b. in the center of the bone within the marrow.
    c. on the inner surface of compact bone close to the marrow.
    d. in a random fashion within compact bone.

20. Osteoclasts and osteoblasts remodel bone throughout life. Osteoclasts cause resorption of bone tissue, and osteoblasts replace bone tissue.
    a. True
    b. False

21. Vitamin D affects bone development and repair by
    a. influencing the rate at which calcium is deposited in bone.
    b. exchanging phosphorus for calcium in bone tissue.
    c. allowing absorption of calcium in the small intestine.
    d. maintaining the degree of ionization of calcium salts.

22. The mass of fibrocartilage that fills the gap between two ends of a broken bone in the early stages of healing is called
    a. a hematoma.
    b. cartilaginous callus.
    c. hyaline cartilage.
    d. granulation tissue.

23. The speed with which a fractured bone heals is dependent, in part, on how closely the fractured parts lie in relation to one another.
    a. True
    b. False

24. Which of the following are functions of bone?
    a. provide shape and support of the body
    b. protect body structures
    c. produce blood cells
    d. store inorganic salts

25. The two types of bone marrow are _____ marrow and _____ marrow.

26. In an adult, the marrow in which blood cell formation takes place is found primarily in the
    a. skull.
    b. long bones of the legs.
    c. vertebrae.
    d. metacarpals.

27. List some of the metabolic processes that require calcium.

28. Which of the following hormone(s) stimulate/stimulates osteoclasts to break down bone tissue?
    a. calcitonin
    b. thyroxine
    c. parathyroid hormone
    d. adrenal hormones

29. What is the term for the process of blood cell formation?

30. What is/are the effect(s) of calcitonin?
    a. to increase osteoclast activity
    b. to increase osteoblast activity
    c. to activate vitamin D
    d. to increase calcium reabsorption

31. How many bones are normally present in adult skeletons?

32. Small bones that develop in tendons where they reduce friction in places where tendons pass over bony prominences are called
    a. sesamoid bones.
    b. irregular bones.
    c. wormian bones.
    d. flat bones.

33. List the five parts of the axial skeleton.

34. List the four major parts of the appendicular skeleton.

35. The only movable bone of the skull is the
    a. nasal.
    b. mandible.
    c. maxillae.
    d. vomer.

36. Air-filled cavities in the cranial bones (sinuses) function to
   a. reduce the weight of the skull.
   b. act as a reservoir for mucus.
   c. control the temperature of structures within the skull.
   d. increase the intensity of the voice by acting as sound chambers.

37. The bone that forms the back of the skull and joins the skull along the lambdoidal suture is the _____ bone.

38. The cranial bone containing the sella turcica, which protects the pituitary gland, is the _____ bone.

39. The bones that enclose the brain are collectively known as the _____.

40. A cleft palate is due to incomplete fusion of the _____ _____ of the maxilla.

41. The membranous areas (soft spots) of an infant's skull are called _____.

42. Which bone(s) form(s) the "bridge" of the nose?
   a. lacrimal
   b. ethmoid
   c. nasal
   d. palatine

43. The adult vertebral column has how many parts?
   a. 33
   b. 23
   c. 26
   d. 30

44. The intervertebral disks are attached to what part of the vertebrae?
   a. lamina
   b. vertebral body
   c. spinous process
   d. pedicle

45. What condition is the result of the laminae of the vertebrae failing to unite during development?

46. Which of the vertebrae contain the densest osseous tissue?
   a. cervical
   b. thoracic
   c. lumbar
   d. sacral

47. The posterior wall of the pelvic girdle is formed by the _____.

48. An exaggeration of the thoracic curve is called
   a. lordosis.
   b. scoliosis.
   c. kyphosis.
   d. halitosis.

49. The function(s) of the thoracic cage include(s)
   a. production of blood cells.
   b. contribution to breathing.
   c. protection of heart and lungs.
   d. support of the shoulder girdle.

50. True ribs attach to the _____ directly by costal cartilage.

51. The middle section of the sternum is known as the
   a. manubrium.
   b. tubercle.
   c. xiphoid process.
   d. body.

52. The union of the manubrium and body of the sternum is an important clinical landmark of the chest and is called the _____ _____.

53. The pectoral girdle is made up of two _____ and two _____.

54. What is commonly referred to as the "elbow bone" is actually
   a. the surgical neck of the humerus.
   b. the olecranon process of the ulna.
   c. the radial tuberosity.
   d. the styloid process.

55. The wrist consists of
   a. 8 carpal bones.
   b. 5 metacarpal bones.
   c. 14 phalanges.
   d. distal segments of the radius and the ulna.

56. The bones found in the palm of the hand are the _____ bones.

57. When the hands are placed on the hips, they are placed over
   a. the iliac crest.
   b. the acetabulum.
   c. the ischial tuberosity.
   d. the ischial spines.

58. The longest bone in the body is the
   a. tibia.
   c. femur.
   b. fibula.
   d. patella.

59. The lower end of the fibula can be felt as an "ankle bone". The correct name for this feature is the
   a. head of the fibula.
   c. tibial tuberosity.
   b. lateral malleolus.
   d. lesser trochanter.

60. The largest of the tarsal bones is the _____.

61. Loss of bone mass normally begins around age
   a. 35.
   c. 55.
   b. 45.
   d. 65.

62. Loss of trabecular bone in the aging process results in an increase risk in fractures of the _____ and _____.

STUDY ACTIVITIES

Definition of Word Parts

Define the following word parts used in this chapter.

acetabul-

ax-

-blast

canal-

carp-

-clast

clav-

condyl-

corac-

cribr-

crist-

fov-

glen-

inter-

intra-

lamell-

meat-

odont-

poie-

7.1 Bone Shape and Structure

A.   Describe the characteristics of each of the following types of bone and give examples within the body: long bones, short bones, flat bones, irregular bones, and sesamoid bones.

B.   Answer the following questions about the parts of a long bone.
    1.   The expanded articular part of a long bone is called the _____.
    2.   The articulating surface is coated with a layer of _____ _____.
    3.   The shaft of a long bone is known as its _____.
    4.   Describe the periosteum and its functions.

    5.   Describe compact and spongy bone. Where are they found and how are they typically arranged in bones?

    6.   Label the following parts in this figure of a long bone: proximal epiphysis, diaphysis, distal epiphysis, articular cartilage, spongy bone, space containing red marrow, compact bone, medullary cavity, yellow marrow, periosterum, epiphyseal plates, endosteum.

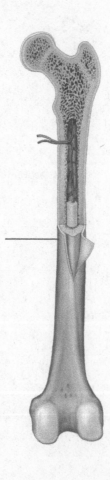

C.   Answer the following concerning the microscopic structure of bone.

    1.   Bone cells (osteocytes) are located in _____, which are arranged in concentric circles around _____ _____.

    2.   What are the extracellular materials of bone? What are the functions of these materials?

    3.   What are the structural differences in compact bone and spongy bone?

    4.   Why do patients who suffer from sickle-cell disease have bone pain?

7.2 Bone Development and Growth

A.   What bones are intramembranous bones? How do these develop?

B.   What bones are endochondral bones? How do these develop? Be sure to include descriptions and the locations of the primary ossification center, the secondary ossification center, and the epiphyseal plate.

C.   Answer these questions about growth at the epiphyseal plate.

    1.   Describe the four zones in the epiphyseal plate between the diaphysis and epiphysis.

    2.   In what zone of the epiphyseal plate is the process of mitosis occurring?

    3.   How does the bone lengthen?

    4.   What is the role of osteoclasts in bone growth and development?

D.   Describe the process of bone remodeling that occurs throughout life.

E.   Answer the following questions regarding bone development, growth, and repair.

    1.   What are the roles of vitamins A, D, and C in bone development and growth?

    2.   What hormones are involved in the development of bone?

    3.   What hormones are responsible for ossification of the epiphyseal plates?

    4.   How does exercise influence bone growth and development?

7.3 Bone Function

A. Answer the following questions regarding the general functions of bones.

    1. What bones function primarily to provide support?

    2. What bones function primarily to protect viscera?

    3. Are all bones capable of movement?

B. Answer the following questions concerning blood cell formation.

    1. Where are blood cells formed in the embryo? In the infant? In the adult?

    2. What is the difference between red and yellow marrow?

    3. What is the process of blood cell formation called?

C. Answer these questions concerning inorganic salt storage in bone.

    1. What are the major inorganic salts stored in bone?

    2. How is calcium released from bone so that it is available for physiological processes?

    3. What metabolic processes depend on calcium ions in the blood?

D. Answer the following regarding fragility fractures

    1. What are these and what are the risk factors associated with them?

    2. What recommendations would you give a person to help prevent these?

7.4 Skeletal Organization

A. The adult skeleton usually contains _____ bones. What causes this number to vary?

B. 1. What are the two major divisions of the skeleton?

    2. List the major parts and the bones found in each of these major divisions.

7.5 Skull

A. Answer these questions concerning the bones in the skull.

    1. How many bones are found in the human skull?

2. Which, if any, of these bones is mobile?

3. What are the two divisions of the skull?

B.   Answer the following questions concerning the cranial bones.
1. Using your own head or that of a partner, locate the following cranial bones and identify the suture lines that form their boundaries: occipital bone, temporal bones, frontal bone, and parietal bones.

2. What are the remaining two bones of the cranium? Where are they located?

3. Fill in the following table of the cranial bones

Name of Bone	Description	Special Features
Frontal		
Parietal		
Occipital		
Temporal		
Sphenoid		
Ethmoid		

4. Which of these bones contains sinus or air cells? What is the purpose of these features?

C.   Answer the following questions concerning the facial bones.
1. Using yourself or a partner, locate the following facial bones: maxilla, palatine, zygomatic, lacrimal bones, nasal bones, vomer bone, inferior nasal conchae, and mandible.

2. Which of these bones contains a sinus?

3. Which of these bones makes up the orbits of the eyes?

4. Which of these bones makes up the nasal cavity?

5. Which of these bones forms the hard palate?

6. How does a cleft palate develop?

D.   Describe the differences between the infant skull and the adult skull.

7.6 Vertebral Column

A. Answer the following questions about the vertebral column.

    1. What is the function of the vertebral column?

    2. What are the divisions and how many bones are in each?

    3. What is the difference between the vertebral column of an infant and that of an adult? How does this occur?

B. Label the features of a typical vertebra.

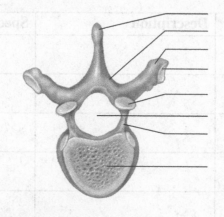

C. Answer the following questions regarding the cervical vertebrae.

    1. What are the special features found in this region?

    2. What is the first vertebra called? What are its unique features?

    3. What is the second vertebra called? What are its unique features?

D. Answer the following questions regarding the thoracic vertebrae.

    1. In what ways is the structure of the thoracic vertebrae unique?

    2. Abnormal curvature of this area is known as what?

E. In what ways is the structure of the lumbar vertebrae unique?

F. Describe the sacrum and name the unique features found in this bone.

7.7 Thoracic Cage

A.   Name the bones and the function of the thoracic cage.

B.   Describe the differences among true, false, and floating ribs. Include their articulations.

C.   Describe the sternum including manubrium, body, sternal angle, and xiphoid process. Locate these structures on yourself or a partner.

D.   Label the features of the thoracic cage.

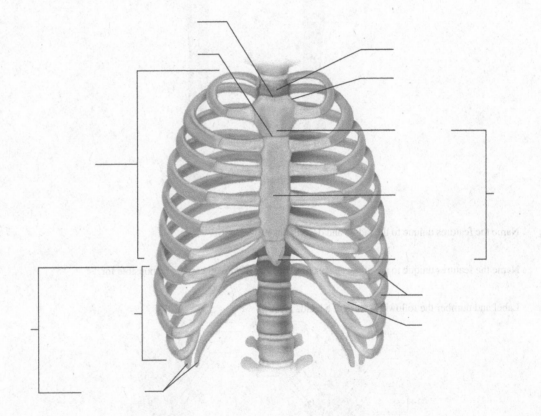

7.8 Pectoral Girdle

A.   Use yourself or a partner to locate and list the bones of the pectoral girdle. What is the function of the pectoral girdle?

B.   Describe the clavicles.

C.   Name the unique feature of the scapulae and state their purpose.

7.9 Upper Limb

A.   Use yourself or a partner to locate and list the bones of the upper limb.

B.   Label the following features of the humerus.

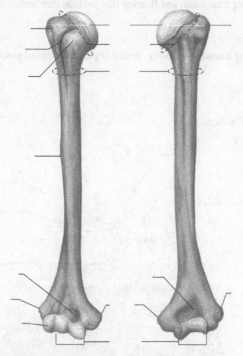

C.   Name the features unique to the radius and describe its movement.

D.   Name the features unique to the ulna and describe the type of movement it is responsible for.

E.   Label and number the following bones of a hand.

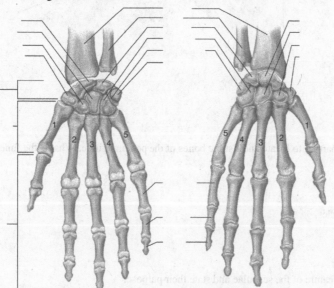

68

Fill in the following table to summarize anatomy of the pectoral girdle and upper limbs.

Name of Bone	Location	Special Feature
Clavicle		
Scapulae		
Humerus		
Radius		
Ulna		
Carpal		
Metacarpal		
Phalanx		

7.10 Pelvic Girdle

A.   List the bones and the function of the pelvic girdle.

B.   Identify the bone in which each of the structures in the following table is located, and explain the function of each of these structures.

Structure	Bone	Function
Acetabulum		
Anterior superior iliac spine		
Symphysis pubis		
Obturator foramen		
Ischial tuberosity		
Ischial spine		

C.   Describe the differences between the male and female skeletons.

Part or Feature	Male	Female
Skull		
Mastoid process		
Supraorbital ridge		
Chin		
Jaw angle		
Forehead		

Orbit		
Palate		
Pelvis		
Obturator foramen		
Acetabulum		
Pubic arch		
Sacrum		
Coccyx		
Cavity		

7.11 Lower Limb

A.   List the bones of the lower limb.

B.   Label the features on this figure of the femur.

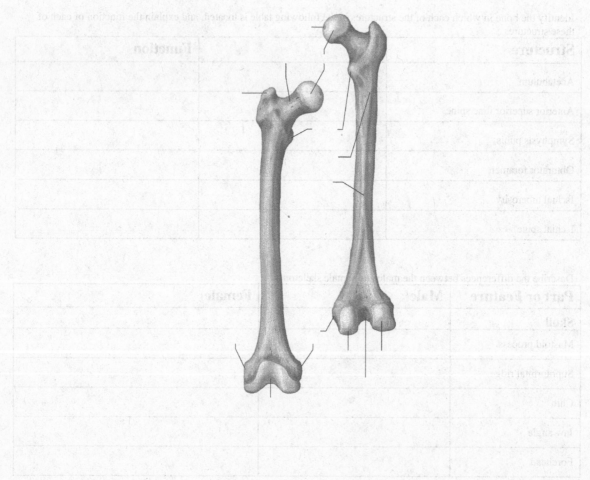

C.   Name the features unique to the tibia and note their functions.

D.   Label bones in the foot.

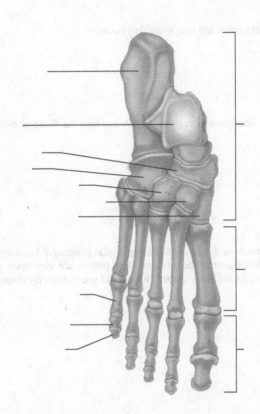

E.   Fill in the following table to summarize your knowledge of the pelvic girdle and lower limb.

Name of the Bone	Location	Special Feature
Hip bone		
Femur		
Patella		
Tibia		
Fibula		
Tarsal		
Metatarsal		
Phalanx		

F.	Note the similarities between the upper and lower limbs and then detail why there are differences.

7.12 Life-Span Changes

A.	List the changes in the skeletal system and note when they occur.

B.	What are the reasons that the elderly are more prone to falls and how can these be avoided?

Clinical Focus Questions

Your neighbors' two-week-old infant has been diagnosed as having a mild congenital hip displacement, and the doctor has told the parents that the use of a thick diaper should correct the problem. Both parents are very upset and state that they do not understand what is wrong with the baby or the reason for the heavy diaper. How would you explain the diagnosis and treatment to them?

When you have completed the study activities to your satisfaction, retake the mastery test and compare your performance with your initial attempt. If there are still areas you do not understand, repeat the appropriate study activities.

OVERVIEW

This chapter will help you appreciate how the skeletal system and muscular system can cooperate to produce various movements necessary for life. An understanding of how joints work is basic to understanding how the body moves. You will study the functions of joints and how joints are classified according to the type of tissue that binds the bones together (Learning Outcome 1). You will look at the organization and structure of specific fibrous joints (Learning Outcome 2) and specific cartilaginous joints (Learning Outcome 3). You will be able to describe the structure of a synovial joint and distinguish among six types of these joints as well as be able to name or give an example of each type (Learning Outcomes 4 and 5). You will be able to explain how skeletal muscles produce movements at joints, and identify types of joint movements (Learning Outcomes 6 and 7) You will then examine some specific joints in the body and be able to describe the joint and how its articulating parts are held together (Learning Outcomes 8 and 9). Finally, you will be able to describe life-span changes in joints (Learning Outcome 10).

An understanding of how joints work is basic to understanding how the body moves.

LEARNING OUTCOMES

After you have studied this chapter you should be able to:
8.1   Types of Joints
1.   Explain how joints may be classified according to the type of tissue that binds the bones together and the degree of movement possible at the joint.
2.   Describe how bones of fibrous joints are held together, and name an example of each type of fibrous joint.
3.   Describe how bones of cartilaginous joints are held together, and name an example of each type of cartilaginous joint.
4.   Describe the general structure of a synovial joint.
5.   Distinguish among the six types of synovial joints, and name an example of each type.
8.2   Types of Joint Movements
6.   Explain how skeletal muscles produce movements at joints.
7.   Identify several types of joint movements.
8.3   Examples of Synovial Joints
8.   Describe the shoulder joint, and explain how its articulating parts are held together.
9.   Describe the elbow, hip, and knee joints, and explain how their articulating parts are held together.
8.4   Life-Span Changes
10.   Describe life-span changes in joints.

FOCUS QUESTION

You finish transcribing your class notes, rise from your chair, and stretch. Which joints are involved what type of movement are you performing, and how are the joints enabling you to perform these movements?

MASTERY TEST

Now take the mastery test. Do not guess. Some questions may have more than one correct answer. As soon as you complete the test, check your answers and correct any mistakes. Note your successes and failures so that you can reread the chapter to meet your learning needs.

1.   The function(s) of joints is/are to
a.   bind parts of the skeletal system together.
b.   allow movement in response to skeletal muscle contraction.
c.   permit bone growth.
d.   protect underlying structures.

2   Name three classifications of joints according to range of movement and the type of tissue that binds them together.

3. Which of the following are characteristics of fibrous joints?
    a. The bones of the joint have a space between them.
    b. The bones of the joint are held firmly together by fibrous connective tissue.
    c. This type of joint is found in the skull.
    d. The structure of these joints is fixed early in life.

4. Syndesmosis, suture, and gomphosis are types of _____ joints.

5. The epiphyseal plate is an example of a _____ or a _____ joint.

6. Movement in a vertebral column and the symphysis pubis (is/is not) due to compressing a pad of cartilage.

7. The function of articular cartilage is to
    a. provide flexibility in the joint.
    b. provide insulation.
    c. minimize friction.
    d. secrete synovial fluid.

8. Extra cushioning and distribution of weight in a synovial joint is provided by which feature?

9. Which of these structures is a fluid-filled sac found in synovial joints to reduce friction between skin and bone?
    a. meniscus
    b. bursa
    c. symphysis
    d. ligament

10. If aspirated synovial fluid is cloudy, red-tinged, and contains pus, the most likely cause is
    a. a fracture.
    b. osteoarthritis.
    c. a bacterial infection.
    d. a collagen disease, rheumatoid arthritis.

11. The joint structures that limit movement in a joint in order to prevent injury are the
    a. articulating surfaces of the bones.
    b. ligaments.
    c. tendons.
    d. synovial membranes.

12. The inner layer of the joint capsule is the _____ _____.

13. Which of the following are functions of synovial fluid?
    a. lubrication of the joint surfaces
    b. prevention of infection within the joint
    c. nutrition of the cartilage within the joint
    d. absorption of shock within the joint

14. Which type of synovial joint allows rotation and is found between the atlas and the axis?
    a. a saddle joint
    b. a plane joint
    c. a hinge joint
    d. a pivot joint

15. How are bursae named?

16. Where is articular cartilage found?

17. The type of joint that permits the widest range of motion is a
    a. pivot joint.
    b. hinge joint.
    c. gliding joint.
    d. ball-and-socket joint.

18. Match the joint in the first column with the type of joint it represents.
    1. shoulder
    2. elbow
    3. ankle
    4. thumb
    a. saddle
    b. gliding
    c. ball-and-socket
    d. pivot
    e. hinge

19. Bending parts of a joint so that the angle between parts of the joint is decreased is
    a. flexion.
    b. extension.
    c. inversion.
    d. elevation.

20. Movement that brings the foot farther from the shin is
    a. adduction.
    b. abduction.
    c. plantar flexion.
    d. dorsiflexion.

21. The two bones that form the shoulder joint are the _____ and the _____.

22. The shoulder (is/is not) an extremely stable joint.

23. The kind of injury to which the shoulder joint is prone is _____.

24. The _____ and the _____ make up the hinge joint of the elbow.

25. What movements are made possible by the rotation of the head of the radius?

26. An instrument used to visualize the interior of a joint is the _____.

27. The head of the femur fits into the _____ of the _____ bone.

28. List the six possible movements of the hip joint.

29. The largest and most complex of the synovial joints is the _____ joint.

30. Rotation at the knee joint is possible when the knee is
   a. flexed.
   b. extended.
   c. abducted.
   d. adducted.

31. A joint injury that involves stretching and tearing of ligaments and tendons is a _____.

32. Elderly persons should restrict regular exercise to limit wear and tear on increasingly fragile joints.
   a. True
   b. False

STUDY ACTIVITIES

Definition of Word Parts

Define the following word parts used in this chapter.

anul-

arth-

burs-

glen-

labr-

ov-

sutur-

syn-

syndesm-

8.1 Types of Joints

A. Address the following concerning the general types of joints.
   1. List and explain the three structural classifications of joints.

   2. List and explain the three functional classifications of joints.

B. Answer the following questions about fibrous joints (synarthroses).
   1. List the characteristics of fibrous joints.

2. Describe and give an example of each of the following fibrous joints.
   a. syndesmosis

   b. suture

   c. gomphosis

3. Label this drawing of a gomphosis.

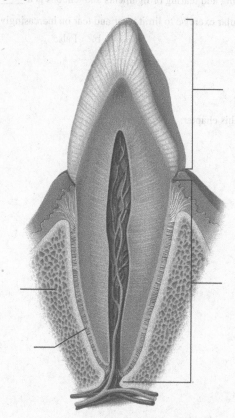

4. Areas in the infant skull that permit the shape of the skull to change during childbirth are called _____.

C. Answer the following questions concerning cartilaginous joints (amphiarthroses).
1. List and describe the two types of cartilaginous joints.

2. Label the parts of cartilaginous joints.

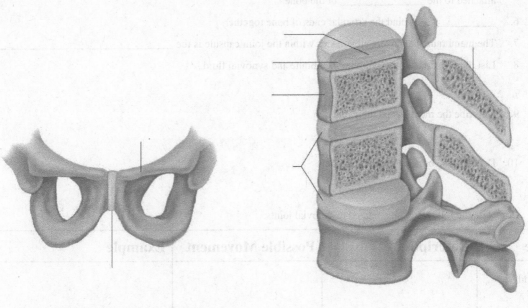

3. Describe the function of an intervertebral disk.

4. A symphysis important in childbirth is the _____ _____.

D. Answer the following questions about synovial joints.
1. Label the parts of a generic synovial joint.

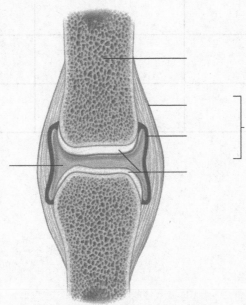

2. List the conditions that can be diagnosed by examining synovial fluid. Include the clinical findings or conclusions for each condition.

3. The parts of bones that come together in a joint are covered by a layer of _____ _____.

4. The bones of a synovial joint are held together by a _____ _____.

5. The outer layer of the structure in the previous question is composed of _____ connective tissue and is attached to the _____ of the bone.

6. _____ bind the articular ends of bone together.

7. The membrane that covers all surfaces within the joint capsule is the _____ _____.

8. List the functions of the synovial membrane and synovial fluid.

9. Describe the menisci and their function.

10. Describe the bursae and their function.

E. Complete the following table related to synovial joints.

Type	Description	Possible Movement	Example
Ball-and-Socket			
Condylar			
Plane			
Hinge			
Pivot			
Saddle			

8.2 Types of Joint Movements

Describe the following joint movements. You may also wish to perform these movements as you describe them. Note that identifying the movements which are paired may help you to learn these.

flexion

extension

hyperextension

dorsiflexion

plantar flexion

abduction

adduction

rotation

circumduction

supination

pronation

eversion

inversion

protraction

retraction

elevation

depression

8.3 Examples of Synovial Joints

A. Answer the following questions and attempt the assessments regarding the shoulder joint.

1. Label the parts on the drawing of a shoulder joint.

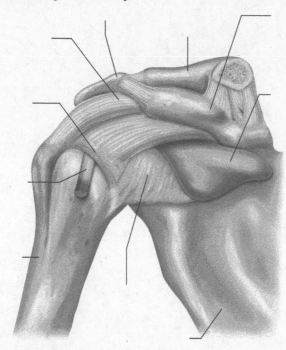

2. Explain the relationship between the wide range of movement at the shoulder joint and the relative ease with which the shoulder can be dislocated.

3. List the ligaments that help prevent shoulder dislocation.

B. Answer the following questions and attempt the assessments regarding the elbow joint.

1. Describe the structure of the elbow joint and list the movements possible at this joint.

2. The procedure used to diagnose and treat injuries to the elbow, shoulder, and knee via a thin fiber-optic instrument is called _____.

C. Answer the following questions and attempt the assessments concerning the hip joint.

1. The hip joint is a _____ and _____ joint.

2. Describe the structure of the hip joint.

3. The hip joint is (more/less) movable than the shoulder joint. Give the rationale for your answer.

4. List the major ligaments of the hip and identify the function of each.

D. Attempt the following assessments and answer the questions about the knee joint.

1. Label the parts of the knee joint.

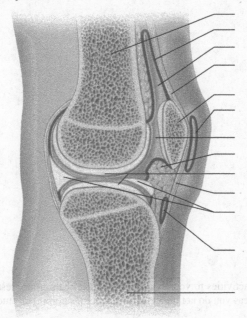

2. List the five major ligaments of the knee joint.

3. What is the function of the cruciate ligaments?

4. List the movements possible in the knee joint.

5. What additional structures are found in the knee joint to cushion and help reduce friction?

8.4 Life-Span Changes

Describe the joint changes that occur over the life span.

Clinical Focus Questions

After fracturing your humerus just distal to the surgical neck, your arm was immobilized in a sling that bound your upper arm to your trunk for six weeks. The sling has just been removed and your physician has prescribed physical therapy for you. Why was your arm immobilized in this fashion? What kinds of exercises can you anticipate the physical therapist will prescribe for you?

When you have completed the study activities to your satisfaction, retake the mastery test and compare your performance with your initial attempt. If there are still areas you do not understand, repeat the appropriate study activities.

OVERVIEW

This chapter presents the muscular system. The muscular system is responsible for all the different types of movement required for life. Most of the chapter focuses on skeletal muscle named for the necessary association of this type of muscle with the skeleton to achieve the movements with which we are most familiar. You will begin by reading of the relationship of skeletal muscle structure and organization to its unique functions (Learning Outcomes 1 and 2). The chapter will then discuss how the nervous system is responsible for controlling and regulating the process of muscle contraction (Learning Outcomes 3 and 4), You will also examine what the physiological processes are that provide energy and adequate oxygen to prevent fatigue and loss of function (Learning Outcomes 5–7). You will be able to distinguish between a twitch and a sustained contraction (Learning Outcome 8), describe how muscles produce movement and sustain posture (Learning Outcome 9), and distinguish between fast- and slow-twitch muscles (Learning Outcome 10). You will then compare and contrast the mechanisms of contraction in smooth muscle, cardiac muscle, and skeletal muscle, (Learning Outcomes 11–13). You will be able to explain how the attachments, locations, and interactions of skeletal muscles produce movement (Learning Outcome 14), and you will be able to identify and locate the skeletal muscles of each body region and describe their actions (Learning Outcome 15). Finally, you will be able to describe age-related changes in the muscular system and discuss how exercise can help maintain a healthy muscular system (Learning Outcomes 16 and 17).

The skeletal system can be thought of as the passive partner in producing movement; the muscular system can be thought of as the active partner. This chapter explains how muscles interact with bones to maintain posture and produce movement. In addition, the chapter compares the characteristics and functions of skeletal, smooth, and cardiac muscles. This understanding is fundamental for the study of other organ systems, such as the digestive system, the respiratory system, and the cardiovascular system.

LEARNING OUTCOMES

After you have studied this chapter you should be able to:

9.1   Structure of a Skeletal Muscle
1.   Describe the structure of a skeletal muscle.
2.   Name the major parts of a skeletal muscle fiber and describe the functions of each.
9.2   Skeletal Muscle Contraction
3.   Describe the neural control of skeletal muscle contraction.
4.   Identify the major events of skeletal muscle fiber contraction.
5.   List the energy sources for skeletal muscle fiber contraction.
6.   Describe oxygen debt.
7.   Describe how a muscle may become fatigued.
9.3   Muscular Responses
8.   Distinguish between a twitch and a sustained contraction.
9.   Explain how various types of muscular contractions produce body movements and help maintain posture.
10.   Distinguish between fast and slow twitch muscle fibers.
9.4   Smooth Muscle
11.   Distinguish between the structures and functions of multiunit smooth muscle and visceral smooth muscle.
12.   Compare the contraction mechanisms of skeletal and smooth muscle cells.
9.5   Cardiac Muscle
13.   Compare the contraction mechanisms of skeletal and cardiac muscle cells.
9.6   Skeletal Muscle Actions
14.   Explain how the attachments, locations, and interactions of skeletal muscles make possible certain movements.
9.7   Major Skeletal Muscles
15.   Identify and locate the skeletal muscles of each body region and describe the action(s) of each muscle.
9.8   Life-Span Changes
16.   Describe aging-related changes in the muscular system.
17.   Discuss how exercise can help maintain a healthy muscular system as the body ages.

FOCUS QUESTION

How do muscle cells utilize energy and interact with bones to accomplish such diverse movements as "texting" a message to a friend and playing a basketball game?

MASTERY TEST

Now take the mastery test. Do not guess. Some questions may have more than one correct answer. As soon as you complete the test, check your answers and correct any mistakes. Note your successes and failures so that you can reread the chapter to meet your learning needs.

1. The kind of muscle under conscious control is _____ muscle.

2. A skeletal muscle is separated from adjacent muscles and kept in place by layers of connective tissue called

   a. fascia.   c. perimysium.
   b. aponeuroses.   d. sarcolemma.

3. Connective tissues that attach muscle to the periosteum are called

   a. ligaments.   c. aponeuroses.
   b. tendons.   d. elastin.

4. Bundles of muscle fibers are known as what?

5. The layer of connective tissue that closely surrounds a skeletal muscle is the _____.

6. The connective tissue that penetrates and divides the individual muscles into fascicles is the

   a. deep fascia.   c. epimysium.
   b. subcutaneous fascia.   d. perimysium.

7. A surgical procedure to relieve pressure within a muscle compartment is a _____.

8. The characteristic striated appearance of skeletal muscle is due to the arrangement of alternating protein filaments composed of _____ and _____.

9. The units that form the repeating pattern along each muscle fiber are called

   a. transverse tubules.   c. sarcoplasmic reticulum.
   b. sarcomeres.   d. myosin filaments.

10. The main muscle protein found in I bands is (actin/myosin).

11. Membranous channels formed by invaginations of the sarcolemma into the sarcoplasm are known as _____ _____.

12. In addition to actin and myosin, two other proteins associated with actin filaments are _____ and _____.

13. When muscle fibers are overstretched, the injury sustained is a _____ _____.

14. The union between a nerve fiber and a muscle fiber is the

   a. motor neuron.   c. neuromuscular junction.
   b. motor end plate.   d. neurotransmitter.

15. The axon of a motor nerve (does/does not) physically contact the muscle fiber it stimulates.

16. Contraction of skeletal muscle is initiated by _____ released into the synaptic cleft.

17. The substance used by motor neurons to transmit stimuli to skeletal muscle is

   a. norepinephrine.   c. acetylcholine.
   b. dopamine.   d. serotonin.

18. When the filaments of actin and myosin form cross-bridges within the myofibril, the result is

   a. contraction of the muscle fiber.   c. release of acetylcholine.
   b. membrane polarization.   d. relaxation of the muscle fiber.

19. What ion is necessary in relatively high concentrations to allow the formation of cross-bridges between actin and myosin?

20. When a muscle fiber is at rest, the protein complex _____ prevents the formation of cross-bridges between actin and myosin.

21. Contraction of skeletal muscle after death is known as what?

22. The energy used in muscle contraction is supplied by the breakdown of _____ _____.

23. The substance that halts stimulation of muscle tissue is
    a. acetylcholine.
    b. calcium.
    c. acetylcholinesterase.
    d. sodium.

24. A disease caused by a decreased amount of acetylcholine receptors is _____ _____.

25. The primary source of energy to regenerate ATP from ADP and phosphate is a substance called _____ _____.

26. What is the substance stored in large quantities in muscle that can store oxygen called?

27. A person feels out of breath after vigorous exercise because of oxygen debt. Which of the following statements help(s) explain this phenomenon?
    a. Anaerobic respiration increases during strenuous activity.
    b. Lactic acid is metabolized more efficiently when the body is at rest.
    c. Conversion of lactic acid to glycogen occurs in the liver and requires energy.
    d. Priority in energy use is given to ATP synthesis.

28. After prolonged muscle use, muscle fatigue occurs due to an accumulation of what substance?

29. Muscle tissue is a major source of
    a. fat.
    b. glucose.
    c. water.
    d. heat.

30. The minimal strength stimulus needed to elicit contraction of a single muscle fiber is called the _____ _____.

31. A muscle's contractile response to a stimulation is called a _____.

32. The period of time following a muscle response to a stimulus when it will not respond to a second stimulus is called the
    a. latent period.
    b. contraction.
    c. refractory period.
    d. relaxation.

33. Muscle tone refers to
    a. a state of sustained, partial contraction of muscles that is necessary to maintain posture.
    b. a feeling of well-being following exercise.
    c. the ability of a muscle to maintain contraction against an outside force.
    d. the condition athletes attain after intensive training.

34. The force generated by muscle contraction in response to different levels of stimulation is determined by the
    a. level of stimulation delivered to individual muscle fibers.
    b. number of fibers that respond in each motor unit.
    c. number of motor units stimulated.
    d. diameter of the muscle fibers.

35. A contraction during which muscle shortens is known as what?

36. A contraction in which tension is generated without a change in muscle length is known as what?

37. When exercise activates primarily the slow-twitch or red fibers, the result is
    a. increased muscle strength.
    b. increased use of glucose.
    c. increased resistance to fatigue.
    d. increased anaerobic tolerance.

38. The muscles that move the eye are (fast/slow)-twitch fibers.

39. The precision of movement produced by a muscle is due to
    a. the size of the muscle fiber, small fibers being more precise.
    b. the small muscle fiber–to–neuron ratio within a motor unit.
    c. many muscle fibers being present for each neuron in a motor unit.
    d. the number of branches in the neuron, many branches being associated with precise stimulation.

40. Smooth muscle contracts (more slowly/more rapidly) than skeletal muscle following stimulation.

41. Two types of smooth muscle are _____ muscle and _____ muscle.

42. The protein that binds to calcium in smooth muscle is _____.

43. Peristalsis is due to which of the following characteristics of smooth muscle?

   a. the capacity of smooth muscle fibers to excite each other
   c. rhythmicity
   b. lack of fatigue
   d. sympathetic innervation

44. The neurotransmitter(s) in smooth muscle is/are

   a. norepinephrine.
   c. acetylcholine.
   b. dopamine.
   d. serotonin.

45. In the following statements, does statement a explain statement b? _____

   a. Cardiac muscle remains refractory until a contraction is completed.
   b. Sustained tetanic contraction is not possible in heart muscle.

46. Drugs that stop irregular contractions in cardiac muscle by interfering with the movement of calcium ions across the cardiac muscle cell membranes are called _____ _____ _____.

47. In producing movement of body parts, muscles and bones interact similar to mechanical devices known as _____.

48. The attachment of a muscle to a relatively fixed part is called the _____; the attachment to a relatively mobile part is called the _____.

49. Smooth body movements depend on _____ giving way to prime movers.

50. The muscle that compresses the cheeks inward when it contracts is the

   a. orbicularis oris.
   c. platysma.
   b. epicranius.
   d. buccinator.

51. Excessive use of jaw muscles to clench the jaw may lead to _____ _____ syndrome.

52. The muscle that moves the head so that the face turns to the opposite side when one side contracts is the

   a. sternocleidomastoid.
   c. semispinalis capitis.
   b. splenius capitis.
   d. longissimus capitis.

53. The large triangular muscle that extends horizontally from the base of the skull and the cervical and thoracic vertebrae to the shoulder is named the _____.

54. The muscle that abducts the upper arm and can both flex and extend the humerus is the

   a. biceps brachii.
   c. infraspinatus.
   b. deltoid.
   d. triceps brachii.

55. The muscle that extends the arm at the elbow is the

   a. biceps brachii.
   c. supinator.
   b. brachialis.
   d. triceps brachii.

56. The band of tough connective tissue that extends from the xiphoid process to the symphysis pubis and serves as an attachment for muscles of the abdominal wall is the _____ _____.

57. The heaviest muscle in the body, which serves to straighten the leg at the hip during walking, is the

   a. psoas major.
   c. adductor longus.
   b. gluteus maximus.
   d. gracilis.

58. The tendon that connects the gastrocnemius muscle with the calcaneus is the _____ tendon, or the _____ tendon.

STUDY ACTIVITIES

Definition of Word Parts

Define the following word parts used in this chapter.

calat-

erg-

fasc-

-gram

hyper-

inter-

iso-

laten-

myo-

reticul-

sarco-

syn-

tetan-

-tonic

-troph

voluntar-

9.1 Structure of a Skeletal Muscle

A.   How would you describe or define skeletal muscle?

B.   Provide answers to the following questions and assessments regarding the connective tissue coverings.

1.   A skeletal muscle is held in position by layers of fibrous connective tissue called _____.

2.   This tissue extends beyond the end of a skeletal muscle to form a cordlike _____.

3.   When this tissue extends beyond the muscle to form a sheet-like structure, it is called a(n) _____.

4. Label these parts in the following figure.

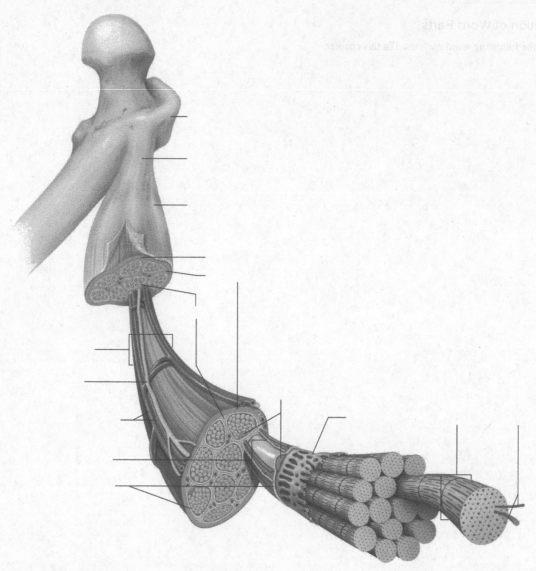

5. Where are deep, subcutaneous, and subserous fascia located?

6. What is compartment syndrome?

C. Provide answers to the following questions and assessments concerning skeletal muscle fibers.

1. List components of a muscle fiber and describe its appearance.

2. Threadlike parallel structures abundantly present in sarcoplasm are called what?

3. The protein filaments found in the threadlike structures are _____ and _____. Describe the structure of these myofilaments.

4. Describe or draw a sarcomere. *Be sure to include I bands, A bands, Z lines, H zones, and M lines.*

5. List the proteins found in a sarcomere.

6. The network of membranous channels in the cytoplasm of muscle fibers is known as the what?

7. What structure in other cells does this resemble?

8. What is a triad?

9.2 Skeletal Muscle Contraction

A. Provide answers to the following questions and assessments regarding the neuromuscular junction.
   1. Label these structures in the accompanying illustration of a neuromuscular junction.

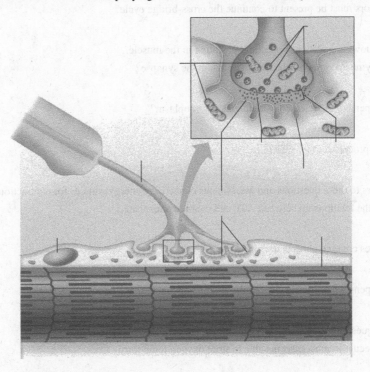

   2. Describe what the function or role of the structures are at the junction.

B. Provide answers to the following questions and assessments concerning stimulus for contraction.
   1. How is a muscle stimulated to contract?

   2. What happens after the neurotransmitter binds its receptor?

   3. Describe the changes in membrane permeability to ions that occur during the spread of the impulse.

4. Describe the roles of actin, myosin, tropomyosin, and troponin in muscle contraction.

C. What is myasthenia gravis and how is it treated?

D. What is the role of the sarcoplasmic reticulum in contraction and relaxation?

E. What is the sliding filament model and what happens to the bands and zones in the sarcomere as muscle contracts?

F. Answer the following questions regarding cross bridge cycling.
   1. What is a cross-bridge and when does it form in a contraction?

   2. What is the role of ATPase?

   3. What factors must be present to continue the cross-bridge cycle?

G. Answer the following questions regarding relaxation in the muscle.
   1. What enzyme decomposes the acetylcholine in the synapse?

   2. What happens to the released calcium in the sarcoplasm?

   3. Does this process require ATP?

H. Provide answers to these questions and assessments concerning energy sources for contraction.
   1. Describe the relationship between ATP and creatine phosphate.

   2. Where does creatine phosphate come from?

   3. What happens when muscle uses all the creatine phosphate?

I. Answer these questions concerning oxygen supply and cellular respiration.
   1. What molecule in muscle seems able to store oxygen temporarily?

   2. Why is it important for muscle to be able to store oxygen?

   3. How is oxygen usually transported to muscle cells?

   4. Why is oxygen necessary for muscle contraction?

J. Answer the following questions regarding oxygen debt
   1. How does muscle continue to contract in the absence of oxygen?

2. What is meant by *oxygen debt*? How is it paid off?

K. Answer the following questions concerning muscle fatigue.

1. What is meant by *muscle fatigue*? What causes it?

2. What are muscle cramps? What cause them?

L. Heat production is an important function of muscle. What happens to the heat that is generated by all the energy transfers?

9.3 Muscular Responses

A. Define *threshold stimulus*.

B. Provide answers to the following questions and assessments regarding the recording of muscle contraction.

1. The accompanying illustration shows a myogram of a type of muscle contraction known as a twitch. Explain what is happening on the molecular level in the muscle fiber during the latent period, the period of contraction and the period of relaxation.

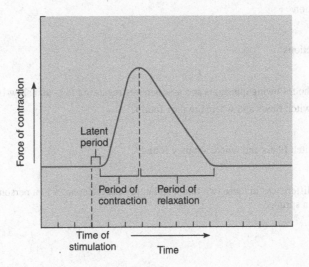

2. What is meant by the *all-or-none* response?

3. What happens if a muscle fiber is stretched beyond its normal resting length? What if it is compressed?

C.   Answer the following questions regarding summation.
1.   How does this increase the force of contraction?

2.   What is it called when there is no period of relaxation?

D.   Answer the following questions regarding recruitment of motor units.
1.   What is a motor unit?

2.   How does recruitment increase the force of contraction?

E.   Answer the following questions regarding sustained contractions.
1.   What happens during sustained contractions?

2.   What is muscle tone important for?

F.   Describe the following types of contractions.
1.   isometric contraction

2.   isotonic contraction

3.   eccentric contractions

G.   Provide answers for the following questions and assessments regarding fast- and slow-twitch muscle fibers.
1.   What are slow-twitch fibers and where are they found?

2.   What are fast-twitch fibers and where are they found?

3.   Summarize the differences in these two fibers and apply the differences to a person who runs marathons versus someone who is a sprinter.

9.4 Smooth Muscle

A.   Provide answers to the following questions and assessments concerning smooth muscle fibers.
1.   The contractile mechanisms of smooth muscle are (the same/different) compared to skeletal muscle.

2.   List the structural differences between smooth muscle cells and skeletal muscle cells.

3.   What are the two types of smooth muscle and where is each found?

4. What is the process of peristalsis?

5. What does rhythmicity entail?

B. Describe smooth muscle contraction and compare it to skeletal muscle contraction.

9.5 Cardiac Muscle

Fill in the following chart, which compares skeletal and cardiac muscle.

	Skeletal	Cardiac
Major location		
Major function		
Cellular characteristics		
striations		
nucleus		
special features		
Mode of control		
Contraction characteristics		

9.6 Skeletal Muscle Actions

A. Provide answers to the following questions and assessments concerning body movement.

1. What are the parts of a lever?

2. Describe the difference between first-, second-, and third-class levers.

3. Give examples of these types of levers in the human body.

B. A skeletal muscle has at least two places of attachment to bone. For instance, the gluteus maximus, which extends the leg at the hip, is attached to the posterior surface of the ilium, the sacrum, and the coccyx at one end and to the posterior surface of the femur and the iliotibial tract at the other. One place of attachment is the origin and the other is the insertion. Explain the difference between the two.

C.   Match the terms in the first column with the statements in the second column that best describe the role of muscle groups in producing smooth muscle movement.

1.   prime mover

a.   muscle that returns a part to its original position

2.   synergist

b.   muscle that makes the action of the prime mover more effective

3.   antagonist

c.   muscle that has the major responsibility for producing a movement

9.7 Major Skeletal Muscles

A.   How are muscles named?

B.   Fill in the following table regarding muscles for facial expression to help you learn them.

Muscle	Origin	Insertion	Action
Epicranius			
Orbicularis oculi			
Orbicularis oris			
Buccinator			
Zygomaticus major			
Zygomaticus minor			
Platysma			

C.   Address the following about the muscles of mastication.
1.   List and locate the muscles of mastication.

2.   Describe TMJ syndrome.

D.   Locate the muscles that move the head and vertebral column then group them by their actions.
1.   Which of the muscles are flexors?

2.   Which of the muscles are extensors?

3.   Which muscles are rotators?

4.   Do you notice a pattern regarding the location of these grouped muscles?

E.   Locate the muscles that move the pectoral girdle and group them by their actions.
1.   Where do you find the extensors?

2.   Where do you find the flexors?

F.   Locate the muscles that move the upper arm and group them by their actions.
1.   Which of the muscles are abductors?

2.   Which of the muscles are rotators?

3.   Which of the muscles are extensors?

4.   Which of the muscles are flexors?

G.   Locate the muscles that move the forearm and group them by their actions.
1.   Which of the muscles are the flexors and where are they located?

2.   Which of the muscles are the extensors and where are they located?

3.   What muscles do rotation and what do you call this movement specifically?

H.   Name the muscles of the abdominal wall. What actions are they responsible for?

I.   What actions are performed by the muscle of the pelvic outlet?

J.   Locate the muscles that move the thigh and group them by their actions.
       1.   What muscles are found anterior and what action(s) are they responsible for?

       2.   What muscles are found posterior and what action(s) are they responsible for?

       3.   Where do you find the adductors?

K.   Locate the muscles that move the leg and group them by their actions.
       1.   Where are the flexors found here? What is the collective name of this group of muscles?

       2.   Where are the extensors found? What is the collective name for this group of muscles?

L.   Locate the muscles that move the ankle, foot, and toes and describe the unique actions or movements of the foot.

9.8 Life-Span Changes

A.   Describe the effects of aging on the muscular system.

B.   Why is exercise recommended to everyone?

Clinical Focus Questions

Your sister, age 28, is very excited about the opening of a gym in her neighborhood. Many of her friends have joined and she is planning to get in shape. She had her second child three months ago and has been experiencing difficulty losing weight. Your sister is known in the family as a couch potato. What advice will you give her about her plans? Explain your rationale.

When you have completed the study activities to your satisfaction, retake the mastery test and compare your performance with your initial attempt. If there are still areas you do not understand, repeat the appropriate study activities.

97

NERVOUS SYSTEM I: BASIC STRUCTURE AND FUNCTION

OVERVIEW

Two systems coordinate and integrate the functions of the other body systems so that your internal environment remains stable in spite of changes in the environment. These systems are the nervous system and the endocrine system. Chapter 10 begins with a discussion of the general functions of the nervous system, the types of cells that comprise nervous tissue, and the two major groups of nervous system organs (Learning Outcomes 1–3). The chapter continues with discussion of sensory receptors and how they respond to stimuli (Learning Outcomes 4 and 5). This is followed by a detailed discussion of the types of neurons and the relationships of the components of the neurons and the neuroglial cells specific to the central and peripheral nervous systems (Learning Outcomes 6–11). Finally, the processes of impulse conduction (Learning Outcomes 12–18) and impulse processing (Learning Outcome 19) conclude this chapter on the structure and function of the nervous system.

LEARNING OUTCOMES

After you have studied this chapter, you should be able to
10.1   Overview of the Nervous System
   1.   Describe the general functions of the nervous system.
   2.   Identify the two types of cells that compose nervous tissue.
   3.   Identify the two major groups of nervous system organs.
10.2   General Functions of the Nervous System
   4.   List the functions of sensory receptors.
   5.   Describe how the nervous system responds to stimuli.
10.3   Description of Cells of the Nervous System
   6.   Describe the parts of a neuron.
   7.   Describe the relationships among myelin, the neurilemma, and nodes of Ranvier.
   8.   Distinguish between the sources of white matter and gray matter.
10.4   Classification of Cells of the Nervous System
   9.   Identify structural and functional differences among neurons.
   10.   Identify the types of neuroglia in the central nervous system and their functions.
   11.   Describe the role of Schwann cells in the peripheral nervous system.
10.5   The Synapse
   12.   Explain how information passes from a presynaptic neuron to a postsynaptic cell.
10.6   Cell Membrane Potential
   13.   Explain how a cell membrane becomes polarized.
   14.   Describe the events leading to the generation of an action potential.
   15.   Explain how action potentials move down the axon as a nerve impulse.
   16.   Compare impulse conduction in myelinated and unmyelinated neurons.
10.7   Synaptic Transmission
   17.   Identify the changes in membrane potential associated with excitatory and inhibitory neurotransmitters.
   18.   Explain what prevents a postsynaptic cell from being continuously stimulated.
10.8   Impulse Processing
   19.   Describe the basic ways in which the nervous system processes information.

FOCUS QUESTION

Describe what happens in the time between deciding to sit down and open your book and doing the actions you decided. Think about what is happening on the cellular level and how it results in these actions and your abilities.

MASTERY TEST

Now take the mastery test. Do not guess. Some questions may have more than one correct answer. As soon as you complete the test, check your answers and correct any errors. Note your successes and failures so that you can reread the chapter to meet your learning needs.

   1.   The two basic types of cells found in neural tissue are _____ and _____ cells.

2. Nerves are bundles of
   a. axons.
   b. dendrites.
   c. axons and dendrites.
   d. neuroglial cells.

3. The purpose of the dendrites is
   a. to support the neurons.
   b. to receive input from other neurons.
   c. to transmit information from the cell body.
   d. to produce energy for the neuron.

4. The small spaces between neurons are called _____.

5. Electrochemical messages are carried across synapses by _____.

6. The nervous system is composed of two groups of organs called the _____ nervous system and the _____ nervous system.

7. Monitoring such phenomena as light, sound, and temperature is a _____ function of the nervous system.

8. The peripheral nervous system has two motor divisions: the _____ nervous system and the _____ nervous system.

9. What three features do all neurons have?

10. What do you call the cytoplasmic structures that consist mostly of rough endoplasmic reticulum?

11. There is always only one _____ in a neuron.
    a. nucleolus
    b. axon
    c. mitochondrion
    d. dendrite

12. Which of the following structures is *not* common to all nerve cells?
    a. neurofibrils
    b. axon
    c. chromatophilic substances
    d. Schwann cells

13. The structure that carries impulses towards the cell body of the neuron is the
    a. dendrite.
    b. neurofibril.
    c. axon.
    d. neurilemma.

14. The neurilemma is composed of
    a. Nissl bodies.
    b. myelin.
    c. the cytoplasm and nuclei of Schwann cells.
    d. neuron cell bodies.

15. The type of neuron that lies totally within the central nervous system is the
    a. sensory neuron.
    b. motor neuron.
    c. interneuron.
    d. unipolar neuron.

16. The supporting framework of the nervous system is composed of
    a. neurons.
    b. dendrites.
    c. neuroglial cells.
    d. myelin.

17. The neuroglial cells that can phagocytize bacterial cells and increase when there is inflammation of the brain or spinal cord are
    a. astrocytes.
    b. oligodendrocytes.
    c. microglia.
    d. ependyma.

18. Which of the following injuries to nervous tissue can be repaired?
    a. damage to a cell body
    b. damage to nerve fibers that have myelin sheaths
    c. damage to nerve fibers in the CNS
    d. nerve damage cannot be repaired

19. The neuron that brings an impulse to the synapse is a _____ neuron.

20. The difference in electrical charge between the inside and the outside of the membrane in the resting nerve cell is called the _____ _____.

21. The unequal distribution of positive and negative ions across the membrane results in a _____ _____.

22. The propagation of action potentials along a fiber is called
    a. a threshold potential.
    b. repolarization.
    c. a nerve impulse.
    d. a sensation.

23. The period of total depolarization of the neuron membrane when the neuron cannot respond to a second stimulus is called the _____ _____ period.

24. The refractory period acts to limit the
    a. intensity of nerve impulses.
    b. rate of conduction of nerve impulses.
    c. permeability of nerve cell membranes.
    d. excitability of nerve fibers.

25. In which type of fiber is conduction faster?

    a. myelinated   b. unmyelinated

26. A decrease in calcium ions below normal limits will

    a. facilitate the movement of sodium across the cell membrane.   c. facilitate the movement of potassium across the cell membrane.

    b. inhibit the movement of sodium across the cell membrane.   d. inhibit the movement of potassium across the cell membrane.

27. The neurotransmitter that stimulates the contraction of skeletal muscles is

    a. dopamine.   c. gamma-aminobutyric acid.

    b. acetylcholine.   d. encephalins.

28. The amount of neurotransmitter released at a synapse is controlled by

    a. calcium.   c. potassium.

    b. sodium.   d. magnesium.

29. Continuous stimulation of a neuron on the distal side of this junction is prevented by

    a. exhaustion of the nerve fiber.   c. enzymes within the neural junction.

    b. the chemical instability of neurotransmitters.   d. rapid depletion of ionized calcium.

30. Neuropeptides that are synthesized by the brain and spinal cord in response to pain are _____.

31. The process that allows coordination of incoming impulses that represent information from a variety of receptors is called _____.

32. The process by which an impulse from a single neuron may be amplified by spreading to other neurons is _____.

STUDY ACTIVITIES

Definition of Word Parts

Define the following word parts used in this chapter.

astr-

ax-

bi-

dendr-

ependym-

-lemm

moto-

multi-

oligo-

peri-

saltator-

sens-

syn-

uni-

100

10.1 Overview of the Nervous System

A.   When the nervous system detects changes in the body, it can stimulate _____ and _____ to respond.

B.   1.   Name the two types of cells that make up neural tissue.

2.   Structures that bring input to the cell bodies are _____; information is carried away from the neuron by (a/an) _____.

3.   Nerves are comprised of (axons/dendrites).

4.   The space between a neuron and the cell with which it communicates is a _____.

C.   Name the two divisions of the nervous system and list their component parts.

10.2 General Functions of the Nervous System

A.   What are the three general functions of the nervous system?

B.   1.   Where are sensory receptors located?

2.   What is the function of sensory receptors?

3.   In what part of the nervous system are sensory receptors integrated and interpreted?

C.   1.   Effectors are (inside/outside) the nervous system.

2.   Conscious control of activities is overseen by the _____ nervous system.

3.   Involuntary control of body activities is characteristic of the _____ nervous system.

10.3 Description of Cells of the Nervous System

A.   Label the structures in the following illustration of a motor neuron.

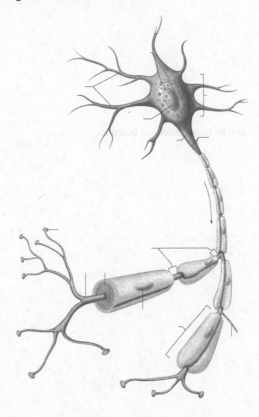

B.   Match the parts of a neuron in the first column with the correct description in the second column.

1.   neurofibrils

2.   Nissl bodies

3.   dendrites

4.   axon

5.   Schwann cells

a.   slender fiber that carries impulses away from the cell body; this fiber may give off collaterals

b.   membranous sacs in the cytoplasm associated with the manufacture of protein molecules

c.   cells of the myelin sheath

d.   network of fine threads that extend into nerve fibers

e.   highly branched to provide receptor surfaces to which processes from other neurons can communicate

C.   Describe how Schwann cells make up the myelin sheath and the neurilemma on the outsides of nerve fibers.

D.   What is the composition of white matter in the brain and spinal cord? What is the composition of gray matter?

10.4 Classification of Cells of the Nervous System

A.   What are two ways in which neurons are classified?

B.   Describe the structure and function of each kind of neuron.
bipolar

unipolar

multipolar

C.   Describe each kind of neuron by its location and function.
sensory neuron

interneuron

motor neuron

D.   Fill in the following table concerning the neuroglial cells.

Cell	Location	Characteristics	Function
Astrocytes			
Oligodendrocytes			
Microglia			
Ependyma			
Schwann cells			
Satellite cells			

E.   Describe the regeneration of nerve fibers, include a description of a neuroma.

10.5 The Synapse

A.   Label the structures in the accompanying drawing of a synapse.

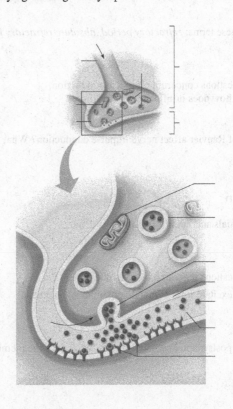

B. How does a neurotransmitter initiate depolarization? (Include the role of both the presynaptic and the postsynaptic neuron membranes.)

10.6 Cell Membrane Potential

A. Describe the ion distribution in a neuron at rest and during an action potential.

B. What is the resting potential? How is this difference maintained to ensure the excitability or development of an action potential?

C. Answer the following questions regarding the local potential changes.
1. How would hyperpolarization affect the resting potential?

2. What is meant by the term *depolarization*?

3. What is the threshold potential and what happens when it is reached?

D. Answer the following regarding the movements of ions during action potentials
1. What is the trigger zone and what happens here to initiate an action potential?

2. How will sodium and potassium ion distribution change along the length of the axon during the action potential?

E. What is meant by "all-or-none response"?

F. Define and distinguish these terms: *refractory period, absolute refractory period,* and *relative refractory period.*

G. Answer the following questions concerning impulse conduction.
1. What is myelin and how does it influence conduction?

2. How do the nodes of Ranvier affect nerve impulse conduction? What is this type of conduction called?

10.7 Synaptic Transmission

A. How do excitatory potentials and inhibitory potentials differ?

B. Answer the following questions regarding the synaptic potentials.
1. What happens if an excitatory postsynaptic potential is generated?

2. When an inhibitory postsynaptic potential occurs, what does the membrane become more permeable to?

C.	Answer the following questions regarding the neurotransmitters.

1.	What are neurotransmitters?

2.	What is the chemical make-up of most of the neurotransmitters?

3.	What influences do they have on the postsynaptic neurons?

4.	How are the actions of the neurotransmitters controlled? How do you destroy them or limit their effect?

D.	What are neuropeptides and what is their function?

10.8 Impulse Processing

A.	What is a neuronal pool? What is facilitation?

B.	Explain what happens in convergence.

C.	Explain what occurs in divergence.

D.	Address the following concepts concerning addiction and the role of receptors.

1.	Briefly describe the history of addiction.

2.	Define *addiction*.

3.	Describe the role of neurotransmitters and their receptors in the development of addiction.

Clinical Focus Questions

Jack, age 24, amputated his finger while doing some carpentry work. The amputated part was brought to the hospital and reattached using microsurgery techniques. Jack is quite traumatized by the incident and a bit confused as you meet him this morning. He explains that the surgeon informed him that the surgery was successful but he still has no sensation in the finger. What would you tell Jack?

When you have completed the study activities to your satisfaction, retake the mastery test. If there are still some areas you do not understand, repeat the appropriate study activities.

CHAPTER 11

NERVOUS SYSTEM II: DIVISIONS OF THE NERVOUS SYSTEM

OVERVIEW

This chapter continues your study of the nervous system. It includes a study of the general structure of the brain; its functions; the relationship among the brain, brain stem, and spinal cord; the reflex function of the spinal cord; the coverings of the brain and spinal cord; and the formation and function of cerebrospinal fluid (Learning Outcomes 1–10). The chapter continues with a discussion of the structure and function of the peripheral and autonomic nervous systems (Learning Outcomes 11–18). The chapter ends with a discussion of aging-associated changes in the nervous system (Learning Outcome 19).

LEARNING OUTCOMES

After you have studied this chapter, you should be able to

11.1   Overview of Divisions of the Nervous System
    1.   Describe the relationship among the brain, brain stem, and spinal cord.
11.2   Meninges
    2.   Describe the coverings of the brain and spinal cord.
11.3   Ventricles and the Cerebrospinal Fluid
    3.   Discuss the formation and function of cerebrospinal fluid.
11.4   Brain
    4.   Describe the development of the major parts of the brain and explain the functions of each part.
    5.   Distinguish among sensory, association, and motor areas of the cerebral cortex.
    6.   Discuss hemisphere dominance.
    7.   Explain the stages in memory storage.
    8.   Explain the functions of the limbic system and the reticular formation.
11.5   Spinal Cord
    9.   Describe the structure of the spinal cord and its major functions.
    10.   Describe a reflex arc and reflex.
11.6   Peripheral Nervous System
    11.   Distinguish between the major parts of the peripheral nervous system.
    12.   Describe the structure of a peripheral nerve and how its fibers are classified.
    13.   Identify the cranial nerves and list their major functions.
    14.   Explain how spinal nerves are named and their functions.
11.7   Autonomic Nervous System
    15.   Characterize the autonomic nervous system.
    16.   Distinguish between the sympathetic and the parasympathetic divisions of the autonomic nervous system.
    17.   Compare sympathetic and parasympathetic nerve pathway.
    18.   Explain how the different autonomic neurotransmitters affect visceral effectors.
11.8   Life-Span Changes
    19.   Describe aging-associated changes in the nervous system.

FOCUS QUESTION

It is noon, and you are just finishing an anatomy assignment. You hear your stomach growling and you realize you are hungry. You make a ham sandwich and pour a glass of milk. After eating, you decide you have been studying for three hours and you should go for a walk. How does the nervous system receive internal and external cues, process incoming information, and decide what action to take?

MASTERY TEST

Now take the mastery test. Do not guess. Some questions have more than one correct answer. As soon as you complete the test, check your answers and correct any errors. Note your successes and failures so that you can reread the chapter to meet your learning needs.

1. The organs of the central nervous system are the _____ and the _____ _____.

2. List the parts of the brain.

3. What part of the central nervous system provides two-way communication with the peripheral nervous system?
   a. brain stem
   b. cerebellum
   c. diencephalon
   d. spinal cord

4. The outer membrane covering the brain is composed of fibrous connective tissues and is called the
   a. dura mater.
   b. arachnoid mater.
   c. pia mater.
   d. periosteum.

5. Cerebrospinal fluid is found between the
   a. arachnoid mater and the dura mater.
   b. vertebrae and the meninges.
   c. pia mater and the arachnoid mater.
   d. the skull and the dura mater.

6. Meningitis is caused by
   a. bacteria.
   b. a virus.
   c. accumulation of blood in the membranes.
   d. a blockage in the central canal.

7. A series of four interconnected cavities located within the cerebral hemispheres and brain stem are the
   a. sulci.
   b. ventricles.
   c. gyri.
   d. nuclei.

8. Cerebrospinal fluid is secreted by the _____ _____.

9. The function(s) of cerebrospinal fluid (is/are) to
   a. supply information about the internal environment.
   b. act as a shock absorber.
   c. prevent infection.
   d. provide nutrition to central nervous system cells.

10. The spinal cord ends
    a. at the sacrum.
    b. between thoracic vertebrae 11 and 12.
    c. between lumbar vertebrae 1 and 2.
    d. at lumbar vertebra 5.

11. There are _____ pairs of spinal nerves.

12. Which of the following statements is/are true about the white matter in the spinal cord?
    a. A cross section of the cord reveals a core of white matter surrounded by gray matter.
    b. The white matter is composed of myelinated nerve fibers and makes up nerve pathways, called tracts.
    c. The white matter carries sensory stimuli to the brain; the gray matter carries motor stimuli to the periphery.
    d. The nerve fibers within spinal tracts arise from cell bodies located in the same part of the nervous system.

13. The knee-jerk reflex is an example of a
    a. reflex that controls involuntary behavior.
    b. pathological reflex.
    c. withdrawal reflex.
    d. monosynaptic reflex.

14. In the withdrawal reflex, which of the following is true?
    a. This involves contraction of extensor muscles on the ipsilateral side.
    b. This involves contraction of flexor muscles the ipsilateral side.
    c. Withdrawal occurs when pain is experienced.
    d. This involves contraction of flexor muscles on the contralateral side.

15. Damage to the corticospinal tract in an adult may result in a/an _____ reflex.
    a. biceps-jerk
    b. cremasteric
    c. ankle-jerk
    d. Babinski

108

16. Pain impulses are carried from the area stimulated to the brain along the
    a. fasciculus gracilis.
    b. spinothalamic tracts.
    c. fasciculus cuneatus.
    d. spinocerebellar tract.

17. An individual with injury to the spinocerebellar tract is likely to experience
    a. loss of a sense of touch.
    b. uncoordinated movements.
    c. involuntary muscle movements.
    d. severely diminished pain perception.

18. An individual suffering from flaccid paralysis has most likely sustained damage to the _____ tract.
    a. spinocerebellar
    b. corticospinal
    c. rubrospinal
    d. reticulospinal

19. Immediate, intensive treatment of spinal cord injuries is important to
    a. begin regeneration of severed nerve fibers.
    b. prevent extension of damage secondary to spinal shock.
    c. relieve the pain of the injury.
    d. maintain an electrolyte balance.

20. The cerebrum develops from a portion of the
    a. forebrain (prosencephalon).
    b. midbrain (mesencephalon).
    c. hindbrain (rhombencephalon).
    d. diencephalon.

21. A neural tube defect in the lower posterior portion of the tube results in _____.

22. The hemispheres of the cerebrum are connected by nerve fibers called the
    a. corpus callosum.
    b. falx cerebri.
    c. fissure of Rolando.
    d. tentorium.

23. The convolutions on the surface of the cerebrum are called
    a. sulci.
    b. fissures.
    c. gyri.
    d. ganglia.

24. Which of the following statements about the cerebral cortex is/are true?
    a. The cortex is the central white portion of the cerebrum.
    b. The cortex has sensory, motor, and association areas.
    c. The cortex is the outer gray area of the cerebrum.
    d. The cells in the right hemisphere of the cortex control the right side of the body.

25. Match the functions in the first column with the appropriate area of the brain in the second column.
    1. hearing
    2. vision
    3. recognition of printed words
    4. control of voluntary muscles
    5. pain
    6. complex problem solving

    a. frontal lobes
    b. parietal lobes
    c. temporal lobes
    d. occipital lobes

26. Centers for higher intellectual functions, such as planning and motivation, are located in the _____ lobes.

27. The primary motor centers of the cerebral cortex are located
    a. anterior to the precentral gyri.
    b. posterior to the lateral fissure.
    c. inferior to the lateral sulce.
    d. on the base of the brain near the optic chiasm.

28. Damage to the parietal lobes would impair an individual's ability to
    a. hear speech.
    b. understand speech.
    c. choose appropriate words in speaking.
    d. understand visual cues.

29. The general interpretive area or Wernicke's area is located
   a. near Broca's area.
   c. within the place where the temporal, parietal, and occipital lobes come together.
   b. in the frontal lobe.
   d. within areas common to the cerebrum and cerebellum.

30. In most people, the _____ hemisphere is dominant for verbal and computational skills.

31. Some investigators believe that intense, repetitive neuronal activity produces stable changes in nerve pathways to produce _____ memory.
   a. short-term
   c. collective
   b. long-term
   d. unconscious

32. Damage to Broca's area in the cerebral cortex may result in the inability to _____.

33. The function of basal nuclei is to
   a. inhibit emotional responses.
   c. aid in temperature control.
   b. facilitate motor functions.
   d. integrate hormonal function.

34. Which of the following structures is not part of the diencephalon?
   a. first and second ventricles
   c. optic chiasma
   b. thalamus
   d. posterior pituitary gland

35. The part of the brain that controls emotions such as happiness and anger is the
   a. thalamus.
   c. reticular system.
   b. limbic system.
   d. midbrain.

36. The cerebral aqueduct is located in the
   a. diencephalon.
   c. midbrain.
   b. red nucleus.
   d. pons.

37. A non-vital control center located in the brain stem is the
   a. cardiac center.
   c. respiratory center.
   b. sneezing center.
   d. vasomotor center.

38. The part of the brain that controls arousal and wakefulness is the
   a. hypothalamus.
   c. basal ganglia.
   b. red nucleus.
   d. reticular formation.

39. The red nucleus of the midbrain is the center for
   a. color vision.
   c. postural reflexes.
   b. eye reflexes.
   d. temperature control.

40. The relay station that receives all sensory impulses except smell is the
   a. pons.
   c. basal ganglia.
   b. medulla.
   d. thalamus.

41. The part of the brain responsible for the regulation of temperature and heart rate, control of hunger, and regulation of fluid and electrolytes is the
   a. thalamus.
   c. medulla oblongata.
   b. hypothalamus.
   d. pons.

42. The _____ _____ produces emotional reactions of fear, anger, and pleasure.

43. The area of the brain that contains control centers for vital visceral functions is the _____ _____.

44. REM sleep is also called _____ sleep.

110

45. With the eyes closed, a person can accurately describe the positions of the various body parts. Which of the following structures serve(s) in this function?

    a. proprioceptors

    b. pons

    c. frontal lobe of the cerebrum

    d. cerebellum

46. An individual who sustains damage to the cerebellum is likely to exhibit

    a. tremors.

    b. garbled speech.

    c. bizarre thought patterns.

    d. a loss of peripheral vision.

47. The peripheral nervous system has two divisions, the _____ nervous system and the _____ nervous system.

48. The nerve fibers that carry motor impulses to smooth muscle structures causing them to contract and to glands causing them to secrete are

    a. general somatic afferent fibers.

    b. general somatic efferent fibers.

    c. general visceral efferent fibers.

    d. general somatic afferent fibers.

49. There are _____ pairs of cranial nerves; all but two of these arise from the _____ _____.

50. The cranial nerve that raises the eyelid and focuses the lens of the eye is the

    a. optic nerve.

    b. oculomotor nerve.

    c. abducens nerve.

    d. facial nerve.

51. In shrugging the shoulders, the sternocleidomastoid and trapezius muscles are stimulated by

    a. the vagus nerve.

    b. the trigeminal nerve.

    c. the accessory nerve.

    d. the hypoglossal nerve.

52. Sensory fibers of spinal nerves that carry sensory impulses to the brain are found in

    a. the dorsal root of spinal nerves.

    b. the ventral root of spinal nerves.

    c. the anterior branch or rami of spinal nerves.

    d. complex nerve networks called plexuses.

53. The anterior branches of the lower four cervical nerves and the first thoracic nerve give rise to the _____ plexus.

54. Which of the following nerves arises from the lumbosacral plexus?

    a. musculocutaneous nerve

    b. femoral nerve

    c. common perineal nerve

    d. median nerve

55. The part of the nervous system that functions without conscious control is the _____ nervous system.

56. Neurons of the sympathetic division originate in the _____ _____ of the spinal cord found in the _____ and _____ segments.

57. Neurons of the parasympathetic division are found in the _____ and the _____ region of the spinal cord.

58. Match the parts in the first column with the appropriate division in the second column.

    1. collateral ganglia

    2. long preganglionic axons

    3. norepinephrine

    4. acetylcholine

    a. sympathetic division

    b. parasympathetic division

59. Which of the following are responses to stimulation by the sympathetic nervous system?

    a. increased heart rate

    b. increased blood glucose concentration

    c. increased peristalsis

    d. increased salivation

60. Which of the following are responses to stimulation of the parasympathetic nervous system?

    a.   dilation of the bronchioles   c.   contraction of the gallbladder

    b.   dilation of the coronary arteries   d.   contraction of the muscles of the urinary bladder

61. Control of the autonomic nervous system is in the _____ and _____ _____;
integration of autonomic function is in the _____.

STUDY ACTIVITIES

Definition of Word Parts

Define the following word parts used in this chapter.

cephal-

chiasm-

flacc-

funi-

gangli-

mening-

plex-

11.1 Overview of Divisions of the Nervous System

A.   Answer the following general questions about the central nervous system.

    1.   The central nervous system consists of the _____ and _____ _____.

    2.   List the parts of the brain.

    3.   The neurons found in the brain are _____ neurons.

    4.   The brain communicates with the spinal cord via the _____ _____.

    5.   What are the bony coverings of the central nervous system?

11.2 Meninges

A.   Fill in the following chart regarding the meninges

Layer	Location	Structure and Special Features	Function
Dura mater			
Arachnoid mater			
Pia mater			

B.   How is the structure of the dura mater related to the development of a subdural hematoma?

C.   How is venous blood from the brain returned to circulation?

D.   What is the cause of meningitis?

11.3 Ventricles and Cerebrospinal Fluid

A.   Describe the location of the four ventricles. Identify the largest of the ventricles.

B.   Where and by what tissues is cerebrospinal fluid secreted? What is its composition? How is this different from the composition of blood?

C.   Describe the circulation of cerebrospinal fluid.

D.   What are the functions of cerebrospinal fluid?

11.4 Brain

A.   Answer the following questions about the brain and its development.
1.   What is the function of the brain?

2.   Describe the development of the brain.

3.   How do anencephaly and spina bifida develop and what are the consequences of these abnormal developments?

B.   Answer the following questions concerning the structure of the cerebrum.
1.   List the five lobes of the cerebral hemispheres and describe the locations of each.

2. The "bridge" that connects the two hemispheres is the _____ _____.

3. The ridges of the hemispheres are called _____.

4. A shallow groove is a _____; a deeper groove is a _____.

C. Answer the following questions regarding the functions of the cerebrum.

1. What are the functions of the cerebrum?

2. List the various functional areas of the cortex.

3. a. What are the functions of the sensory areas of the cerebrum?

   b. Name the sensory areas of the cerebrum and identify their locations.

   c. The sensory area that is not bilateral is _____. What is its function?

4. a. What are the functions of the association areas of the brain?

   b. Where are the association areas located?

   c. The area responsible for concentrating, planning, and complex problem solving is found in which lobe?

   d. Memories of speech and reading, visual scenes, and other complex sensory patterns are stored in which lobe?

   e. Analyzing visual patterns is accomplished in the _____ _____.

5. a. Where are the primary motor areas of the brain located?

   b. Describe the function of the motor speech area or Broca's area. Where do you find this?

6. a. What is meant by hemisphere dominance? What traits or functions exhibit this?

   b. What are the functions of the nondominant hemisphere?

7. a. Describe the processes involved in short-term memory.

   b. What happens to create a long-term memory?

   c. What is the role of the hippocampus and the amygdala in memory consolidation?

D. Answer the following questions regarding the basal nuclei.
    1. Basal nuclei are located within the _____ _____.

    2. What structures are part of the basal nuclei?

    3. What is the inhibitory neurotransmitter produced by the nuclei?

    4. What is the function of the basal nuclei?

E. Answer these questions concerning the diencephalon.
    1. Locate the diencephalon and describe it.

    2. Name the structures which are found in the diencephalon and describe their locations.

    3. The thalamus is referred to as a messenger and an editor. Why is this an appropriate role for the thalamus?

    4. The hypothalamus is considered an important center for homeostatic function. What are mechanisms does the hypothalamus control or influence?

    5. What structures are part of the limbic system?

    6. How is the limbic system believed to help you with survival?

F. Answer the following questions about the brain stem.
    1. What is the brain stem and what are its component parts?

2. Fill in the following table concerning the components of the midbrain.

Structure	Location	Function
Cerebral aqueduct		
Cerebral peduncles		
Corpora quadrigemina		
Red nucleus		

3. Where is the pons located? What do you find in the pons?

4. a. Where is the medulla oblongata located? Describe its appearance.

    b. There are a number of nuclei found in the medulla. Name the nuclei that control vital visceral functions.

    c. There are a few nonvital reflexes controlled by the medulla. Please name these.

5. a. Describe the location of the reticular formation.

    b. What is the function of the ascending reticular activation system?

    c. What other functions will the reticular formation control because of its connections to the basal nuclei and motor cortex?

6. a. What are the two types of sleep?

    b. Describe what happens in non-REM sleep and how long it lasts.

    c. Why is REM sleep called "paradoxical sleep"?

G. Answer the following questions about the cerebellum.

1. Describe the location and structure of the cerebellum.

2. There are a number of features of the cerebellum. What is the *falx cerebelli*, the *arbor vitae*, the *dentate nucleus* and the *vermis*?

3. What are the functions of the cerebellum?

4. Compare the roles for the three cerebellar peduncles to assist the cerebellum in its "corrective function".

11.5 Spinal Cord

A. Answer the following questions about the structure of the spinal cord.
1. How many pairs of spinal nerves are there?

2. There are a number of features to the spinal cord. Fill in the following table regarding these features.

Structure	Description or Function
Cervical enlargement	
Lumbar enlargement	
Conus medullaris	
Cauda equine	
Filum terminale	
Posterior horns	
Anterior horns	
Lateral horns	
Central canal	
Gray commisure	

3. Label the accompanying drawing of a cross section of the spinal cord.

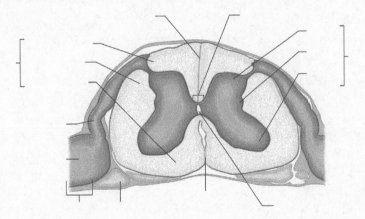

B.   Answer the following questions about the functions of the spinal cord.
1.   a.   What is a reflex?

      b.   Describe the reflex arc, what are the components and how do they work?

2.   a.   Label the parts of the patellar reflex shown in the following drawing.

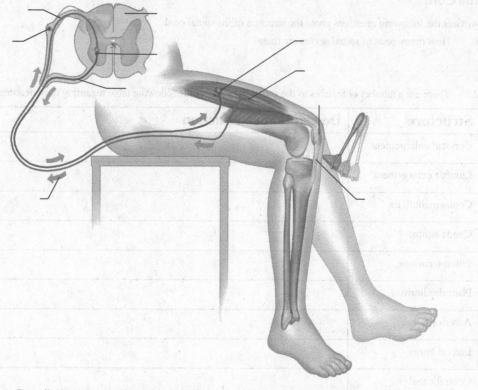

      b.   Describe how the patellar reflex actually keeps you in an upright position.

      c.   Describe the withdrawal reflex allows you to avoid harm.

3. Fill in the following table concerning the nerve tracts of the spinal cord.

Tract	Location	Function
Ascending Tracts		
Fasciculus gracilis		
Fasciculus cuneatus		
Spinothalamic tracts		
Spinocerebellar tracts		
Descending Tracts		
Corticospinal tracts		
Reticulospinal tracts		
Rubrospinal tracts		

11.6 Peripheral Nervous System

A.   1.   What are the parts of the peripheral nervous system?

2.   What is the function of the somatic nervous system?

3.   What is the function of the autonomic nervous system?

B.   Describe the structure of a peripheral nerve

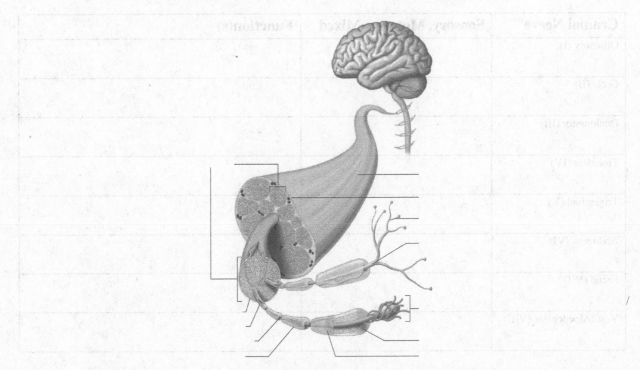

C.   What are the functions of each of the following peripheral nerve fibers?

     1.   general somatic efferent fibers

     2.   general visceral efferent fibers

     3.   general somatic afferent fibers

     4.   general visceral afferent fibers

     5.   What does the term "general" mean for these nerves?

     6.   What are the functions of the special nerve fibers?

D.   Fill in the following table regarding the cranial nerves. Note there are *many* mnemonic devices for learning the order of the cranial nerves and their functions. Please do an Internet search to find one that you relate to and can recall. Here is one example:

On old Olympus towering tops a Finn and German viewed some hops

    I   II   III   IV   V   VI   VII   VIII   IX   X   XI   XII

Note: The vestibulocochlear nerve (VIII) is also known as the acoustic nerve. You need to be able to identify the cranial nerves by both name and number.

Cranial Nerve	Sensory, Motor or Mixed	Function(s)
Olfactory (I)		
Optic (II)		
Oculomotor (III)		
Trochlear (IV)		
Trigeminal (V)		
Abducens (VI)		
Facial (VII)		
Vestibulocochlear (VIII)		

Glossopharyngeal (IX)		
Vagus (X)		
Accessory (XI)		
Hypoglossal (XII)		

E.　　Answer these questions regarding the spinal nerves.

1.　　Spinal nerves are not named individually but are grouped, please name the groups.

2.　　What is the dorsal root? What is the ventral root?

3.　　An area of skin in which a group of sensory nerves leads to a particular dorsal root is called _____.

4.　　What structures are innervated by the meningeal branch, the dorsal branch, and the ventral branch of a spinal nerve?

5.　　What nerves have a visceral branch?

6.　　What is a plexus?

7.　　Fill in the following table regarding the plexuses of the spinal nerves.

Name	Nerves Found Within	Structures Innervated
Cervical		
Brachial		
Lumbosacral		

8.　　Which spinal nerves are not found within a plexus and what do they innervate?

11.7 Autonomic Nervous System

A.   What structures make up the autonomic nervous system, and what is the function of this system?

B.   Identify the functional differences between the sympathetic and parasympathetic divisions of the autonomic nervous system.

C.   How are the nerve pathways of the autonomic division different from those of the somatic division?

D.   Describe the neural pathways of the sympathetic division.

E.   Describe the neural pathways of the parasympathetic division.

F.   Describe the differences in neurotransmitters used by these two divisions.

G.   1.   Describe the interaction between acetylcholine and muscarinic and nicotinic cholinergic receptors.

      2.   How does the action of norepinephrine and epinephrine depend on alpha and beta receptors?

H.   Describe the mechanisms of control of the autonomic nervous system.

11.8 Life-Span Changes

A.   1.   Describe the life-span changes that occur in the nervous system.

      2.   The expected loss in brain size over a lifetime is _____ %.

122

B.   What neural functions are most influenced by the aging process?

Clinical Focus Questions

A.   Your best friend has been hospitalized following a motor vehicle accident in which he sustained injuries to the left temporal and parietal areas. He is right-handed. What results of his injuries do you anticipate?

B.   Why is an injury to the first cervical vertebra fatal?

When you have completed the study activities to your satisfaction, retake the mastery test. If there are still some areas you do not understand, repeat the appropriate study activities.

OVERVIEW

This chapter will complete your study of the nervous system. You will focus on the sensory division exclusively to better understand how all the different encounters and experiences you have translate into an understanding of the world and survival. The chapter begins by describing the differences between the general senses and the special senses (Learning Outcome 1). It continues with a discussion of the different types of receptors including their locations, structures, and functions in maintaining homeostasis (Learning Outcomes 2, 5, and 7). It then examines how impulses are stimulated, how sensations are produced, and what adaptation is (Learning Outcomes 3, 4, and 6). The bulk of the chapter explores the special senses, noting the special anatomical features and explaining how stimuli result in sensation (Learning Outcomes 8–17). The chapter ends by describing aging-associated changes that diminish our sensory experiences (Learning Outcome 18).

An understanding of these senses is necessary to knowing how the nervous system receives input and responds to support life.

LEARNING OUTCOMES

After you have studied this chapter, you should be able to

12.1   Introduction to Sensory Function
    1.   Differentiate between general senses and special senses.
12.2   Receptors, Sensation, and Perception
    2.   Name the five types of receptors and state the function of each.
    3.   Explain how receptors trigger sensory impulses.
    4.   Explain sensation and sensory adaptation.
12.3   General Senses
    5.   Describe the differences among receptors associated with the senses of touch, pressure, temperature, and pain.
    6.   Describe how the sensation of pain is produced.
    7.   Explain the importance of stretch receptors in muscles and tendons.
12.4   Special Senses
    8.   Explain the relationship between the senses of smell and taste.
    9.   Describe how the sensations of smell and taste are produced and interpreted.
    10.   Name the parts of the ear and explain the function of each part.
    11.   Distinguish between static and dynamic equilibrium.
    12.   Describe the roles of the accessory organs to the eye.
    13.   Name the parts of the eye and explain the function of each part.
    14.   Explain how the eye refracts light.
    15.   Distinguish between rods and cones, and discuss their respective visual pigments.
    16.   Explain how the brain perceives depth and distance.
    17.   Describe the visual nerve pathways.
12.5   Life-Span Changes
    18.   Describe aging-associated changes that diminish the senses.

FOCUS QUESTION

When you began this chapter at 3:00 P.M., it was 32°F outside, but the sun was pouring into the room. It is now after 5:00 P.M. As you reach to turn on the light, you notice the room has become chilly, so you get a sweater. You smell the supper your roommate is preparing, and you realize that you are hungry. How have your somatic and special senses functioned to process and act on this sensory information?

MASTERY TEST

Now take the mastery test. Do not guess. Some questions may have more than one correct answer. As soon as you complete the test, check your answers and correct any errors. Note your successes and failures so that you can reread the chapter to meet your learning needs.

1. The function(s) of senses (is/are) to
   a. connect us to the outside world.
   b. perceive the world.
   c. help maintain homeostasis.
   d. respond to damaging stimuli.

2. Perception occurs in the _____ _____.

3. Sensory receptors are sensitive to stimulation by
   a. changes in the concentration of chemicals.
   b. temperature changes.
   c. tissue damage.
   d. mechanical forces.
   e. changes in the intensity of light.

4. The ability to ignore unimportant stimuli is called _____ _____.

5. The senses of touch, pressure, temperature, and pain are called _____ senses.

6. Match the sense in the first column with the appropriate receptor from the second column.
   1. touch and pressure
   2. light touch and texture
   3. heat
   4. cold
   5. deep pressure
   6. tension of muscle
   a. golgi tendon organs
   b. free nerve endings
   c. Pacinian corpuscles
   d. tactile corpuscles

7. Pain receptors are sensitive to all of the following *except*
   a. chemicals such as histamine, kinins, hydrogen ions, and others.
   b. electrical stimulation.
   c. extremes of pressure.
   d. extremes of heat and cold.

8. Heat relieves some kinds of pain by
   a. increasing the metabolism in injured cells.
   b. increasing blood flow to painful tissue.
   c. decreasing the membrane permeability of sensory nerve fibers.
   d. blocking pain sensation with heat sensation.

9. Pain perceived as located in a body part other than that part stimulated is
   a. chronic pain.
   b. referred pain.
   c. functional pain.
   d. acute pain.

10. Reflex sympathetic dystrophy is a form of _____ pain.

11. Pain perceived as a dull, aching sensation that is difficult to locate precisely is
    a. chronic pain.
    b. referred pain.
    c. functional pain.
    d. visceral pain.

12. Awareness of pain begins when pain impulses reach the
    a. spinal cord.
    b. medulla.
    c. thalamus.
    d. cerebral cortex.

13. The area of the body responsible for locating sources of pain or exerting control over emotional responses is the
    a. limbic system.
    b. thalamus.
    c. reticular formation.
    d. cerebral cortex.

14. Pain from the heart is likely to be experienced in the left shoulder. This is an example of _____ pain.

15. The impulses that create a pain sensation that seems sharp and localized to a specific area, and that seems to originate in the skin and to disappear when the stimulus is removed, are likely to be transmitted on (acute/chronic) pain fibers.

16. With the exception of impulses arising from tissues of the head, pain impulses are carried on _____ nerves.

17. A group of neuropeptides that have pain-suppressing activity and are released by the pituitary gland and the hypothalamus are _____.

18. Which of the sensory receptors are proprioceptors?
    a. stretch receptors
    b. pain receptors
    c. heat receptors
    d. pressure receptors

19. The senses of vision, taste, smell, hearing, and equilibrium are called _____ senses.

20. The receptors for taste and smell are examples of
    a. mechanical receptors.
    b. chemoreceptors.
    c. thermoreceptors.
    d. photoreceptors.

21. Olfactory receptors are located in
    a. the nasopharynx.
    b. the inferior nasal conchae.
    c. the superior nasal conchae.
    d. the lateral wall of the nostril.

22. Impulses that stimulate the olfactory receptors are transmitted along the _____ _____.

23. The sensitive part of a taste bud is the taste
    a. cell.
    b. pore.
    c. hair.
    d. papilla.

24. Saliva enhances the taste of food by
    a. increasing the motility of taste receptors.
    b. dissolving the chemicals that cause taste.
    c. releasing taste factors by partially digesting food.

25. The five primary taste sensations are _____, _____, _____, _____, and _____.

26. Sense of taste is strongly related to which of the other special senses? _____

27. In addition to the sense of hearing, the ear also functions in the sense of _____.

28. The waxy substance secreted by glands in the external ear is _____.

29. The functions of the small bones of the middle ear are to
    a. provide a framework for the tympanic membrane.
    b. protect the structures of the inner ear.
    c. transmit vibrations from the external ear to the inner ear.
    d. increase the force of vibrations transmitted to the inner ear.

30. The skeletal muscles in the middle ear function to
    a. maintain tension in the eardrum.
    b. move the external ear.
    c. equalize the pressure on both sides of the eardrum.
    d. protect the inner ear from damage from loud noise.

31. The function of the auditory tube is to
    a. prevent infection.
    b. intensify sound.
    c. equalize pressure.
    d. modify pitch.

32. Ear infections are more common in children than in adults because
    a. children have immature immune systems.
    b. blood supply to the middle ear is less in children than in adults.
    c. the auditory tube is shorter in children than in adults.
    d. young children are likely to suck their thumbs.

33. The inner ear consists of two complex structures called the _____ and the _____ _____.

34. Sound is transmitted in the inner ear via a fluid called _____.

35. Hearing receptors are located in the
    a. spiral organ.
    b. scala vestibuli.
    c. scala tympani.
    d. round window.

36. Impulses from hearing receptors are transmitted via the
    a. abducens nerve.
    b. facial nerve.
    c. cochlear branch of the vestibulocochlear nerve.
    d. trigeminal nerve.

37. Prolonged exposure to noise, tumors, and some antibiotics are causes of _____ deafness.

38. A cochlear implant may be used to treat _____ deafness.

39. The organs concerned with static equilibrium are located within the _____.

40. The hair cells of the crista ampullaris are stimulated by
    a. bending the head forward or backward.
    c. changes in the position of the body relative to the ground.
    b. rapid turns of the head or body.
    d. changes in the position of skeletal muscles.

41. The muscle that raises the eyelid is the
    a. orbicularis oculi.
    c. levator palpebrae superioris.
    b. superior rectus.
    d. ciliary muscle.

42. The lacrimal gland is located in the _____ of the orbit.
    a. superior lateral wall
    c. inferior lateral wall
    b. superior medial wall
    d. inferior medial wall

43. The conjunctiva covers the anterior surface of the eyeball, except for the _____.

44. The superior rectus muscle rotates the eye
    a. upward and toward the midline.
    c. away from the midline.
    b. toward the midline.
    d. upward and away from the midline.

45. The orbicularis oculi is innervated by the
    a. oculomotor nerve.
    c. abducens nerve.
    b. trochlear nerve.
    d. facial nerve.

46. The transparency of the cornea is due to
    a. the nature of the cytoplasm in the cells of the cornea.
    c. the lack of nuclei with these cells.
    b. the small number of cells and the lack of blood vessels.
    d. keratinization of cells in the cornea.

47. In the posterior wall of the eyeball, the sclera is pierced by the _____.

48. The anterior portion of the middle tunic or vascular tunic of the eye contains the
    a. choroid coat.
    c. iris.
    b. ciliary body.
    d. cornea.

49. The shape of the lens changes as the eye focuses on a close object in a process known as
    a. accommodation.
    c. reflection.
    b. refraction.
    d. strabismus.

50. The anterior chamber of the eye extends from the _____ to the iris.

51. The aqueous humor leaves the anterior chamber via the
    a. pupil.
    c. ciliary body.
    b. scleral venous sinus.
    d. lymphatic system.

52. The part of the eye that controls the amount of light entering it is the _____.

53. The color of the eye is determined by the amount and distribution of _____ in the iris.

54. The inner tunic of the eye contains the receptor cells of sight and is called the _____.

55. The region associated with the sharpest vision is the
    a. macula lutea.
    c. optic disk.
    b. fovea centralis.
    d. choroid coat.

56. The largest compartment of the eye, which is bounded by the lens, ciliary body, and retina, is filled with _____ _____.

57. The bending of light waves as they pass at an oblique angle from a medium of one optical density to a medium of another optical density is called _____.

58. The lens loses elasticity with aging, causing a condition called _____.

59. There are two types of visual receptors: one has long, thin projections that are called _____; the other has short, blunt projections that are called _____.

60. Match the type of vision in the first column with the proper receptor from the second column.
    1. vision in relatively dim light   a. rods
    2. color vision   b. cones
    3. general outlines
    4. sharp images

61. The light-sensitive pigment in rods is _____. In the presence of light, this pigment decomposes to form _____ and _____.

62. The pigments found in cones are_____, _____, and _____.

63. The absence of cone pigments leads to _____ _____.

64. If the visual cortex is injured, the individual may develop (complete/partial) blindness in (one eye/both eyes).

STUDY ACTIVITIES

Definition of Word Parts

Define the following word parts used in this chapter.

aud-

choroid

cochlea

corn-

iris

labyrinth

lacri-

lut-

macula

malle-

ocul-

olfact-

palpebral

photo-

scler-

therm-

tympan-

vitre-

12.1 General Aspects of Sensory Function

A. Contrast the general senses and the special senses.

B. What characteristics do all senses have in common, e.g., how do they function?

12.2 Receptors, Sensation, and Perception

A. 1. A feeling that occurs when sensory impulses are recognized by the brain is a _____.

    2. The way or ability of the receptors to send information to the brain is called _____.

B. List five groups of sensory receptors and identify the sensations with which they are associated.

C. Describe the generation and transmission of sensory impulses.

D. Answer the following about sensation, perception and sensory adaptation

    1. Distinguish between sensation and perception.

    2. What does *projection* allow you to do?

    3. What is it that determines what sensation you are experiencing and how can you experience a sensation such as pain from a stimuli such as sound or temperature?

    4. The process that makes a receptor ignore an unimportant stimulus unless the strength of that stimulus increases is known as _____.

12.3 General Senses

A. Answer the following regarding the general senses.

    1. With what structures are the general senses associated?

    2. Name and describe the three types of receptors.

B. Fill in the following table regarding the cutaneous receptors for touch, pressure, temperature, and pain.

Type of Receptor	Location	Sensation
Free nerve endings (mechanoreceptors)		
Tactile (Meissner's) corpuscles (mechanoreceptors)		
Lamellated (Pacinian) corpuscles		
Thermoreceptors		
Nociceptors		

C.   Answer the following concerning pain receptors.

1.   Where do you find pain receptors and what is their generalized purpose?

2.   What forms of stimuli will cause pain?

3.   What events trigger visceral pain?

4.   What is referred pain? Why does it happen?

5.   Compare the characteristics of fast pain fibers and slow pain fibers.

6.   How are pain impulses regulated?

7.   Neuropeptides secreted by the spinal cord that inhibit pain impulses are _____ and
      _____.

8.   Pain suppressants secreted by the pituitary gland are _____.

D.   Compare the actions of stretch receptors in the muscles (muscle spindles) and the tendons (Golgi tendon organs).

12.4 Special Senses

A.   Answer the following questions about the sense of smell.
      1.   The sense of smell supplements the sense of _____.
      2.   On the accompanying illustration, label the structures of the nasal epithelium.

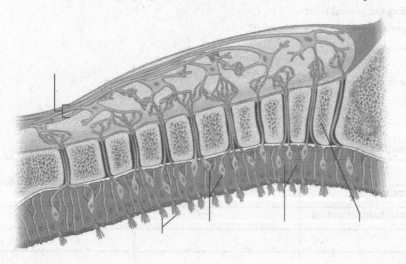
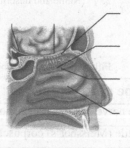

3. How do odors stimulate olfactory receptors?

4. What is synesthesia?

5. Describe the nerve pathways for the sense of smell.

6. How are the olfactory receptor neurons different from other neurons?

B. Answer the following questions about the sensation of taste.

1. Describe the structure of a taste receptor.

2. Why is saliva important to taste?

3. What are the five primary taste sensations?

4. Give examples of the chemical compounds that these taste receptors detect.

5. Describe the pathways for the sensation of taste.

6. What factors can influence or distort an individual's sense of smell and/or taste?

C. Answer the following questions regarding the sensation of hearing.

1. Describe the structures found in the external ear and the function of the external ear.

2. Within the middle ear, describe the vibration conduction pathway from the tympanic membrane to the round window. Name the structures and their roles in sound wave transmission.

3. What is the tympanic reflex and what kind of sounds will it protect you against?

4. How does the structure of the auditory tube and middle ear predispose the middle ear to infection?

5. How does chewing gum or yawning assist with equalizing pressure across the tympanic membrane?

6. The inner ear is composed of two distinct fluid filled tubes or chambers called labyrinths. Please name the parts of the inner ear and the fluids.

7. Name and locate the structures within the cochlea.

8. Trace a sound wave from the external ear to the spiral organ.

9. Once an action potential begins in the cochlear nerve where will it go to result in the perception of hearing?

D. Answer the following questions regarding the sense of equilibrium.
1. Distinguish between static and dynamic equilibrium.

2. Name and describe the parts of the vestibule.

3. Explain how gravity causes the gelatinous mass to move, for example, bending your head, and how this information is transmitted to the brain to help you maintain posture?

4. Name and describe the parts of the semicircular canals.

5. What other structures help you maintain equilibrium?

E. Answer the following questions concerning the sense of sight.
1. Answer the following concerning the visual accessory organs.
   a. Name the muscles that move the eyelids and describe their actions.

   b. Describe the lacrimal apparatus. How does it protect the eye?

   c. What do the tear glands secrete and what is its function?

   d. Identify the location and function of the following extrinsic eye muscles.

      superior rectus

      inferior rectus

      medial rectus

      lateral rectus

superior oblique

inferior oblique

2. Label the structures in the following illustration and state a function of each of the labeled structures.

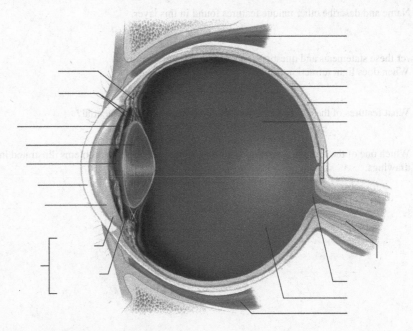

3. Answer the following regarding the outer tunic.
   a. What characteristics of the cornea contribute to the ease with which it is transplanted?

   b. Describe the features pertinent to this layer.

4. Answer the following questions about structures in or associated with the middle tunic.
   a. Name the parts of the middle tunic.

   b. Describe the structure and function of the lens.

   c. What happens in the process of accommodation?

   d. Trace the flow of aqueous humor through the anterior cavity.

   e. How does the iris control the size of the pupil?

5. Answer the following questions regarding the inner tunic.
   a. What is the retina?

   b. Name the five major groups of retinal neurons.

   c. Name and describe other unique features found in this layer.

6. Answer these statements and questions concerning refraction of light.
   a. When does light refraction occur?

   b. What features of the eye refract light? Which ones are most influential?

   c. Which one of the following illustrates normal vision? Identify the problems illustrated in the other two drawings.

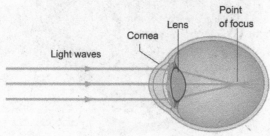

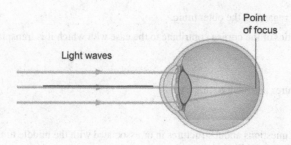

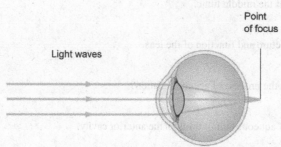

7. Answer the following questions regarding photoreceptors.
   a. How do the retinal pigment epithelium and the choroid coat assist with vision?

   b. What is the function of your rods?

   c. Describe the function of cones.

   d. Compare and contrast the locations of the rods and cones and how this affects vision.

8. Answer the following questions regarding visual pigments.
   a. What is rhodopsin and where is it found?

   b. What happens to this molecule in darkness?

   c. What occurs to rhodopsin in bright light?

   d. Why does vitamin A deficiency affect vision?

   e. What is the light sensitive pigment of the cones called?

   f. What does stereoscopic vision allow you to do?

9. Describe the visual pathways leading from the optic nerve to the visual cortex.

12.5 Life-Span Changes

Describe the effects of aging on the special senses.

Clinical Focus Questions

Based on your knowledge of the way in which the senses interact, explain why a blind person who has had bilateral amputations cannot learn to use artificial legs.

When you have completed the study activities to your satisfaction, retake the mastery test and compare your performance with your initial attempt. If there are still areas you do not understand, repeat the appropriate study activities.

OVERVIEW

The endocrine system, like the nervous system, regulates responses to maintain a relatively constant internal environment. However, the cellular mechanisms used by these two systems are different. The nervous system responds quickly to a perceived change using action potentials; and the endocrine system, using chemical messengers, responds more slowly but its effects are longer lasting. After studying this chapter, you will be able to describe the difference between endocrine and exocrine glands and locate the various glands of the endocrine system, the hormones they secrete, and how these secretions are regulated (Learning Outcomes 1 and 8–10). You will have mastered general information about how hormones function and be able to list the important functions of various hormones (Learning Outcomes 2 and 3). You will study how hormones are classified, how steroid and non-steroid hormones affect target cells, and how hormone secretion is controlled so that homeostasis is maintained (Learning Outcomes 2–7). Finally, you will understand different types of stress and their effects, the general stress response, and the impact of aging on the endocrine system (Learning Outcomes 11–13).

A knowledge of the function of the endocrine system is basic to the understanding of how metabolic processes are regulated to meet the changing needs of the body.

LEARNING OUTCOMES

After you have studied this chapter, you should be able to

13.1   General Characteristics of the Endocrine System
    1.   Distinguish between endocrine and exocrine glands.
    2.   Explain what makes a cell a target for a hormone.
    3.   List some important functions of hormones.
13.2   Hormone Action
    4.   Describe how hormones can be classified according to their chemical composition.
    5.   Explain how steroid and non-steroid hormones affect their target cells.
13.3   Control of Hormonal Secretions
    6.   Discuss how negative feedback mechanisms regulate hormone secretion.
    7.   Explain how the nervous system controls hormone secretion.
13.4–13.9   Pituitary Gland–Other Endocrine Glands
    8.   Name and describe the locations of the major endocrine glands and list the hormones that they secrete.
    9.   Describe the actions of the various hormones and their contributions to homeostasis.
    10.   Explain how the secretion of each hormone is regulated.
13.10   Stress and Its Effects
    11.   Distinguish between physical and psychological stress.
    12.   Describe the general stress response.
13.11   Life-Span Changes
    13.   Describe some of the changes of the endocrine system that are associated with aging.

FOCUS QUESTION

How does the endocrine system control homeostatic processes? How are endocrine secretions regulated?

MASTERY TEST

Now take the mastery test. Do not guess. Some questions may have more than one correct answer. As soon as you complete the test, check your answers and correct any mistakes. Note your successes and failures so that you can reread the chapter to meet your learning needs.

    1.   Potent chemicals secreted by a cell into interstitial fluid that eventually reaches the bloodstream and acts on target cells is a/an _____.

2. Glands that secrete substances into interstitial fluid and affect only neighboring cells are _____ glands; those that affect only their secretory cells are _____ glands.

3. Glands that release their secretions into ducts that lead to the outside of the body are _____ glands.

4. The nervous system releases neurotransmitters into synapses, while the endocrine system releases _____ into the _____.

5. List the functions of endocrine gland hormones.

6. Hormones belong to all of the following chemical families *except*
   a. amines.
   b. polysaccharides.
   c. proteins.
   d. steroids.

7. Steroid hormones are
   a. lipids.
   b. proteins.
   c. glycoproteins.
   d. carbohydrates.

8. Norepinephrine and epinephrine are examples of
   a. steroid hormones.
   b. amine hormones.
   c. peptide hormones.
   d. protein hormones.

9. An example of a protein hormone is that secreted by the
   a. anterior pituitary gland.
   b. thyroid gland.
   c. adrenal gland.
   d. parathyroid gland.

10. Prostaglandins are potent substances that act (locally/systemically).

11. Steroid hormones influence cells by
    a. altering the cell's metabolic processes.
    b. influencing the rate of cell reproduction.
    c. changing the nature of cellular protein.
    d. causing special proteins to be synthesized.

12. Combining with a cell membrane receptor and activating an activity site is characteristic of _____ hormones.

13. Which of the following substances is a common second messenger mediating the action of non-steroid hormones?
    a. adenosine diphosphate
    b. adenosine triphosphate
    c. cyclic adenosine monophosphate
    d. G protein

14. The physiological action of a hormone is determined by
    a. the conditions under which it is secreted.
    b. its chemical composition.
    c. type of membrane receptors present.
    d. protein substrate molecules in the cell.

15. Athletes may abuse _____ _____ to increase muscle size and improve athletic performance.

16. Prostaglandins have hormone-like effects and are thought to act by regulating
    a. the rate of mitosis.
    b. the production of cyclic AMP.
    c. cellular oxidation.
    d. the utilization of glucose.

17. The negative feedback systems that regulate hormone secretion result in the
    a. activation by nerve impulses.
    b. exertion of an inhibitory effect on the gland.
    c. exertion of a stimulating effect on the gland.
    d. tendency for levels of hormone to fluctuate around an average value.

18. The part of the brain most closely related to endocrine function is the _____.

19. The hormones secreted by the anterior lobe of the pituitary gland include
    a. thyroid-stimulating hormones.
    b. luteinizing hormone.
    c. antidiuretic hormone.
    d. oxytocin.

20. Nerve impulses from the hypothalamus stimulate the _____ lobe of the pituitary gland.

21. Which of the following are actions of pituitary growth hormone?
   a.   enhance the movement of amino acids through the cell membrane
   b.   increase the utilization of glucose by cells
   c.   increase the utilization of fats by cells
   d.   enhance the movement of potassium across the cell membrane

22. Which of the following conditions is/are likely to occur when the secretion of growth hormone is low during childhood?
   a.   mental retardation
   b.   short stature; well-proportioned appearance
   c.   small, short body; large head
   d.   failure to develop secondary sex characteristics

23. An adult who suffers from the oversecretion of growth hormone is said to have _____.

24. The pituitary hormone that stimulates and maintains milk production following childbirth is _____.

25. Thyroid-stimulating hormone secretion is regulated by
   a.   circulating thyroid hormones.
   b.   blood sugar levels.
   c.   the osmolarity of blood.
   d.   TRH secreted by the hypothalamus.

26. Which of the following does follicle-stimulating hormone produce?
   a.   growth of egg follicles
   b.   production of estrogen
   c.   production of progesterone
   d.   production of sperm cells

27. Which of the following pituitary hormones help(s) maintain fluid balance?
   a.   oxytocin
   b.   prolactin
   c.   antidiuretic hormone
   d.   luteinizing hormone

28. Antidiuretic hormone increases blood pressure by increasing calcium ion concentration, which stimulates the contraction, of the smooth muscle in blood vessels.
   a.   True
   b.   False

29. The thyroid hormones that affect the metabolic rate are _____ and _____.

30. Which of the following are functions of thyroid hormones?
   a.   control sodium levels
   b.   decrease rate of energy release from carbohydrates
   c.   increase protein synthesis
   d.   enhance the breakdown and mobilization of fats

31. The element necessary for normal function of the thyroid gland is _____.

32. The thyroid hormone that tends to increase calcium in the bone is _____.

33. A thyroid dysfunction characterized by exophthalmia, weight loss, excessive perspiration, and emotional instability is
   a.   simple goiter.
   b.   myxedema.
   c.   hyperthyroidism.
   d.   thyroiditis.

34. Which of the following statements about parathyroid hormone is/are true?
   a.   Parathyroid hormone enhances the absorption of calcium from the intestine.
   b.   Parathyroid hormone stimulates the bone to release ionized calcium.
   c.   Parathyroid hormone stimulates the kidney to conserve calcium.
   d.   Parathyroid hormone secretion is stimulated by the hypothalamus.

35. Injury to or removal of parathyroid glands is likely to result in
   a.   reduced osteoclastic activity.
   b.   Cushing's disease.
   c.   kidney stones.
   d.   hypocalcemia.

36. The hormones of the adrenal medulla are _____ and _____.

37. The adrenal hormone aldosterone belongs to a category of cortical hormones called
   a.   mineralocorticoids.
   b.   glucocorticoids.
   c.   sex hormones.
   d.   catecholamines.

38. The most important action(s) of cortisol in helping the body overcome stress is/are
   a.   inhibition of protein synthesis to increase the levels of circulating amino acids.
   b.   increasing the release of fatty acids and decreasing the use of glucose.
   c.   stimulation of gluconeogenesis.
   d.   conservation of water.

39. Adrenal sex hormones are primarily (male/female).

40. Masculinization of women, elevated blood glucose, decreases in tissue protein, and sodium retention are associated with
    a. Addison's disease.
    b. hypersecretion of adrenal cortical hormone.
    c. Cushing's disease.
    d. hyposecretion of adrenal cortical hormone.

41. The endocrine portion of the pancreas is made up of cells called _____ _____.

42. The hormone that responds to a low blood sugar by stimulating the liver to convert glycogen to glucose is _____.

43. The actions of insulin include
    a. enhancing glucose absorption from the small intestine.
    b. facilitating the transport of glucose across the cell membrane.
    c. promoting the transport of amino acids out of the cell.
    d. increasing the synthesis of fats.

44. Hypoinsulinism results in a disease called _____ _____.

45. The endocrine gland(s) that seem(s) to influence circadian rhythms is/are the
    a. thymus.
    b. pineal gland.
    c. gonads.
    d. adrenal cortex.

46. The only valid claim for the use of melatonin supplements is
    a. insomnia.
    b. autism.
    c. seizure disorders.
    d. jet lag.

47. Thymosin, the secretion of the thymus gland, affects the production of certain white blood cells known as
    _____.

48. Stressors stimulate which of the following endocrine glands?
    a. pancreatic islets
    b. parathyroid glands
    c. adrenal cortex
    d. adrenal medulla

49. A person experiencing emotional stress is (more/less) likely to develop an infection than an individual with a lower stress level.

50. The substance secreted by the kidney in response to stress is _____.

51. The most obvious change in endocrine function as we age involves
    a. thyroid function.
    b. declines in the ability of an athlete to handle stress.
    c. blood glucose regulation.
    d. sexual function.

STUDY ACTIVITIES

Definition of Word Parts

Define the following word parts used in this chapter.

cort-

-crin

diuret-

endo-

exo-

horm-

hyper-

hypo-

lact-

med-

140

para-

toc-

-tropic

vas-

13.1 General Characteristics of the Endocrine System

A. 1. The endocrine system secretes _____ into the _____, which carries this substance to specific cells called _____.

2. Exocrine glands secrete into _____ or _____ that lead to the body's _____.

3. List the two other types of glands that are not endocrine glands but also secrete substances that function similarly to endocrine glands but act locally.

B. Fill in the following table comparing the endocrine and nervous systems.

	Nervous System	**Endocrine System**
Cells		
Chemical Signal		
Specificity of Action		
Speed of Onset		
Duration of Action		

C. List the endocrine glands you are going to study in this chapter and some of their basic functions.

13.2 Hormone Action

A. Answer the following regarding the chemical composition of hormones.

1. Describe the chemical composition of steroid hormones.

2. Describe the chemical composition of non-steroid hormones.

3. What is the chemical composition of the prostaglandins and where are these produced?

B. Answer the following regarding the actions of hormones.

1. Explain the general action of hormones, including their interaction with receptors.

2. What is meant by *downregulation* or *upregulation*?

3. How do steroid hormones and thyroid hormones enter target cells?

4. How do they affect their target cells?

5. How do the non-steroid hormones influence their target cells? Briefly list the sequence of events that occur when cyclic AMP is involved.

6. What are some of the cellular responses to second messenger activation?

7. List the hormones that require cyclic AMP to function.

C. Answer the following regarding prostaglandins.
1. What is the role of prostaglandins in regulating a cell's response to hormonal stimulation?

2. How is the knowledge of prostaglandins used in current medical practice?

13.3 Control of Hormonal Secretions

A. What does the term *half-life* mean and what does this indicate about a hormone?

B. Answer the following questions regarding the control of secretions.
1. What are tropic hormones and how do they regulate certain hormone levels?

2. What endocrine glands are directly stimulated by the nervous system?

3. What endocrine glands respond to changes in the composition of the internal environment?

4. Explain how all of these methods for controlling secretions utilize negative feedback.

13.4 Pituitary Gland

A.   On the following illustration, identify the parts of the pituitary gland.

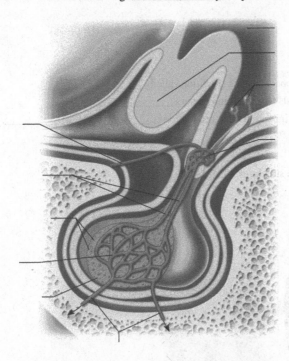
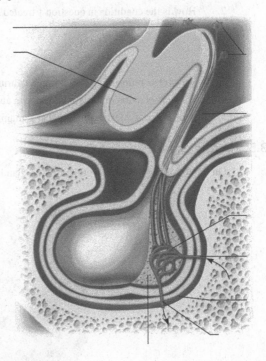

B.   Fill in the following table concerning the hormones of the pituitary gland.

Anterior Lobe	Action	Source of Control
Growth hormone (GH)		
Prolactin (PRL)		
Thyroid-stimulating hormone (TSH)		
Adrenocorticotropic hormone (ACTH)		
Follicle-stimulating hormone (FSH)		
Luteinizing hormone (LH)		
Posterior Lobe	**Action**	**Source of Control**
Antidiuretic hormone (ADH)		
Oxytocin (OT)		

C.   Answer the following questions on pituitary dysfunction.

1.   An insufficient amount of growth hormone in childhood is called _____.

2.   How is the condition in question 1 treated?

3.   An oversecretion of growth hormone during childhood leads to a condition called _____.

4.   An oversecretion of growth hormone in an adult leads to a condition called _____.

5.   A disorder of ADH regulation that is manifested by increased urine production is _____ _____.

13.5 Thyroid Gland

A.   On the following illustration of the thyroid gland, label the structures.

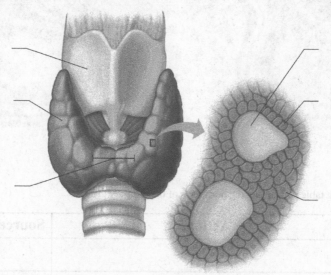

B.   Answer the following questions concerning thyroid hormones and their functions.

1.   Both thyroxine and triiodothyronine are synthesized by the _____ cells and require the element _____.

2.   What are the general functions of thyroxine and triiodothyronine and how do they influence metabolic processes?

3.   What happens to the thyroxine and triiodothyronine in circulation?

4.   When is calcitonin released and what does it do to restore homeostasis?

5.   During what physiological stages will calcitonin be most important?

C.   Fill in the following table concerning the disorders of the thyroid.

Condition	Mechanism or Symptom
Hyperthyroid	
Hyperthyroidism	
Grave's disease	
Hypothyroid	
Hashimoto	
Hypothyroidism (infantile)	
Hypothyroidism (adult)	
Simple goiter	

13.6 Parathyroid Glands

A.   Where are the parathyroid glands located?

B.   Answer the following concerning parathyroid hormones.

1.   Describe how parathyroid hormone affects blood levels of calcium and phosphorus. Include its effect on bone, the intestines, and the kidneys.

2.   How does parathyroid hormone cooperate with calcitonin to maintain blood calcium levels?

3.   What could hypocalcemia lead to? What does hypercalcemia cause?

13.7 Adrenal Glands

A.   Describe where the adrenal glands are located and their structure.

B.   Answer the following concerning hormones of the adrenal medulla.

    1.   Briefly describe the synthesis of epinephrine and norepinephrine.

    2.   What are the effects of these hormones?

C.   Fill in the following table concerning the hormones of the adrenal cortex.

Hormone	Action	Factors Regulating Secretion
Aldosterone		
Cortisol		
Adrenal androgens		

D.   Why is cortisol given to people suffering from autoimmune diseases, allergies, asthma, and preparing for tissue transplants? What other effects does cortisol have on the body?

E.   What are the symptoms of Addison's disease? What are the symptoms and treatment of Cushing's disease?

13.8 Pancreas

A.   Answer the following questions regarding the structure of the pancreas.

    1.   Where is the pancreas found in the body?

    2.   What secretory tissues are found in the pancreas?

    3.   Describe the endocrine portion of the pancreas.

B.   Fill in the following table concerning the hormones of the pancreas.

Hormone	Action	Source of Control
Glucagon		
Insulin		
Somatostatin		

C.   Compare insulin-dependent and non-insulin-dependent diabetes mellitus.

13.9 Other Endocrine Glands

A.   Where is the pineal gland located, and what is its function?

B.   Where is the thymus gland located, and what is its function?

C.   Match the following hormones to the organ that secretes it.
1.   estrogen   a. heart
2.   progesterone   b. testes
3.   atrial naturiuretic peptide   c. ovaries
4.   erythropoietin   d. stomach
5.   testosterone   e. kidneys

13.10 Stress and Its Effects

A.   Define *stress* and list the factors that lead to stress.

B.   Answer the following questions regarding types of stress.
1.   What causes physical stress?

2.   What causes psychological stress?

C.   Describe the body's response to stress. Be sure to include changes in hormone secretion during the alarm stage compared to the resistance stage.

13.11 Life-Span Changes

Describe the effect of life-span changes on each of the endocrine glands.

Clinical Focus Questions

Based on your knowledge of the endocrine system, what symptoms might an individual who had a tumor of the pituitary gland experience? What body systems and nutrients would be most affected if the tumor increased secretion of all the hormones?

When you have completed the study activities to your satisfaction, retake the mastery test and compare your performance with your initial attempt. If there are still areas you do not understand, repeat the appropriate study activities.

OVERVIEW

This chapter does not discuss an organ system but an important specialized connective tissue, blood. Blood cooperates with many of the systems that you have studied and will be studying in this course. It begins by describing the different cells and components of this tissue as well as the origins of the different cells found in blood (Learning Outcomes 1 and 2). The chapter then focuses on the most common cell, the erythrocyte. You will learn of the clinical use of red blood cell counts, the life cycle of red blood cells, and how the production of red blood cells is controlled (Learning Outcomes 3–5). The chapter continues with a discussion of the other important cells, the leukocytes and thrombocytes or platelets. You will learn how to distinguish the different types of leukocytes and what their functions are, as well as the characteristics of blood platelets and their functions (Learning Outcomes 6 and 7). You will be able to describe the matrix of blood (plasma), its components, and their functions (Learning Outcome 8). The chapter concludes with a discussion of hemostasis and coagulation (Learning Outcomes 9–11) and how to determine a person's blood type to perform a safe blood transfusion (Learning Outcomes 12 and 13).

Knowledge of the blood and its components expands the concept of how transport of vital components occurs in the body. This knowledge also helps in understanding how the body recognizes and rejects foreign protein.

LEARNING OUTCOMES

After you have studied this chapter, you should be able to

14.1   Characteristics of Blood
1.   Distinguish among the formed elements of blood and the liquid portion of blood.
14.2   Blood Cells
2.   Describe the origin of blood cells.
3.   Explain the significance of red blood cell counts and how they are used to diagnose disease.
4.   Discuss the life cycle of a red blood cell.
5.   Summarize the control of red blood cell production.
6.   Distinguish among the five types of white blood cells, and give the function(s) of each type.
7.   Describe a blood platelet, and explain its functions.
14.3   Blood Plasma
8.   Describe the functions of each of the major components of plasma.
14.4   Hemostasis
9.   Define *hemostasis*, and explain the mechanisms that help to achieve it.
10.   Review the major steps in blood coagulation.
11.   Explain how to prevent blood coagulation.
14.5   Blood Groups and Transfusions
12.   Explain blood typing and how it is used to avoid adverse reactions following blood transfusions.
13.   Describe how blood reactions may occur between fetal and maternal tissues.

FOCUS QUESTION

How do the physical and chemical characteristics of the blood components help to meet oxygenation needs, allow recognition and rejection of foreign protein, and control coagulation of the blood?

MASTERY TEST

Now take the mastery test. Do not guess. Some questions may have more than one correct answer. As soon as you complete the test, check your answers and correct any mistakes. Note your successes and failures so that you can reread the chapter to meet your learning needs.

1.   List the cellular and non-cellular components transported by plasma.

2.   Blood cells are primarily formed in _____ _____ _____.

3. What is the blood volume of an average-size adult?

4. The percentage of formed elements, especially red blood cells, in blood is called the _____.

5. What are the functions of blood?

6. Plasma represents approximately _____% of a normal blood sample.

7. Cellular components of the immune system and formed elements of blood originate from a common stem cell known as a hematopoietic stem cell.
    a. True
    b. False

8. The biconcave shape of red blood cells
    a. provides an increased surface area for gas diffusion.
    c. allows the cell to move through capillaries.
    b. moves the cell membrane closer to hemoglobin.
    d. prevents clumping of cells.

9. Red blood cells cannot reproduce because they lack a/an _____.

10. A normal red cell count is _____ for an adult female and _____ for an adult male.

11. Red blood cell counts are important clinically because they provide information about
    a. clotting ability.
    c. oxygen carrying capacity.
    b. bone marrow volume.
    d. dietary intake.

12. In the fetus, red blood cells are produced in
    a. the spleen.
    c. yellow marrow.
    b. red marrow.
    d. the liver.

13. Which of the following represents the correct order of appearance of cells in red blood cell production?
    a. erythrocytes, hemocytoblasts, erythroblasts
    c. hemocytoblasts, erythrocytes, erythroblasts
    b. erythroblasts, hemocytoblasts, erythrocytes
    d. hemocytoblasts, erythroblasts, erythrocytes

14. Red blood cell production is stimulated by the hormone _____ that is released from the kidney in response to low oxygen concentration.

15. Does statement a explain statement b? _____
    a. Vitamin B_{12} and folic acid are necessary for cell growth and reproduction.
    b. The rate of red blood cell production is particularly dependent on vitamin B_{12} and folic acid.

16. A lack of vitamin B_{12} is usually due to
    a. dietary deficiency.
    c. liver damage.
    b. a disorder of the stomach lining.
    d. kidney malfunction.

17. Damaged red blood cells are destroyed by which of the following cells?
    a. leukocytes
    c. neutrophils
    b. macrophages
    d. granulocytes

18. The heme portion of damaged red blood cells is decomposed into iron and
    a. biliverdin.
    c. bile.
    b. bilirubin.
    d. ferritin.

19. The most numerous type of white blood cell is the
    a. neutrophil.
    c. monocyte.
    b. eosinophil.
    d. lymphocyte.

20. The white blood cell that has the longest life span is the
    a. basophil.
    c. thrombocyte.
    b. lymphocyte.
    d. eosinophil.

21. The normal white blood cell count is _____ to _____ cells per microliter of blood.

22. The two most mobile and active types of phagocytic leukocytes are
    a.   eosinophils.
    b.   neutrophils.
    c.   monocytes.
    d.   basophils.

23. The blood element concerned with the control of bleeding and the formation of clots is the _____.

24. Match the functions and characteristics in the first column with the appropriate plasma proteins from the second column.
    1.   largest molecular size
    2.   significant in maintaining osmotic pressure
    3.   transport(s) lipids and fat-soluble vitamins
    4.   antibody(ies) of immunity
    5.   play(s) a part in blood clotting

    a.   albumins
    b.   globulins
    c.   fibrinogen

25. All of the following nutrients are present in plasma except
    a.   polysaccharides.
    b.   amino acids.
    c.   chylomicrons.
    d.   cholesterol.

26. List the plasma electrolytes.

27. The gases that are normally dissolved in plasma include
    a.   sulfur dioxide.
    b.   carbon dioxide.
    c.   oxygen.
    d.   nitrogen.

28. An increase in the blood level of non-protein nitrogen can indicate
    a.   positive nitrogen balance.
    b.   a kidney disorder.
    c.   pathological cell metabolism.
    d.   poor nutrition.

29. Which of these plasma electrolytes is responsible for maintaining blood pH?
    a.   calcium
    b.   sodium
    c.   potassium
    d.   bicarbonate

30. A platelet plug begins to form when platelets are
    a.   exposed to air.
    b.   exposed to a rough surface.
    c.   exposed to calcium.
    d.   crushed.

31. The basic event in the formation of a blood clot is the transformation of a soluble plasma protein, _____, to a relatively insoluble protein, _____.

32. Substances believed necessary to activate prothrombin are thought to include
    a.   calcium ions.
    b.   potassium ions.
    c.   phospholipids
    d.   glucose.

33. Prothrombin is a plasma protein that is produced by
    a.   the kidney.
    b.   the small intestine.
    c.   the pancreas.
    d.   the liver.

34. Once a blood clot begins to form, it promotes still more clotting. This is an example of a _____ feedback system.

35. Laboratory tests used to evaluate the blood coagulation mechanisms are the _____ _____, and the _____ _____ _____.

36. Retraction of the clot, pulling the edges of the severed vessel closer together, is due to the action of
    a.   serum formation.
    b.   actin.
    c.   vitamin K.
    d.   vitamin C.

37. An enzyme that may be used to dissolve blood clots is _____.

38. Factors that prevent coagulation in a normal vascular system include all of the following except
    a.   smooth, unbroken endothelium in blood vessels.
    b.   a blood plasma protein called antithrombin.
    c.   heparin.
    d.   vitamin K.

39. The application of medicinal leeches has been used as an adjunctive therapy to microsurgery to maintain the patency of small veins.
    a. True   b. False

40. The hereditary disease that is almost exclusively male and is due to the lack of one of several clotting factors is
    _____.

41. The clumping together of red blood cells when unlike types of blood are mixed is due to antibodies in the plasma and antigens on the
    a. thrombocytes.   c. basophils.
    b. erythrocytes.   d. eosinophils.

42. A person with type A blood has
    a. antigen A and antibody B.   c. antibodies A and B.
    b. antigens A and B.   d. neither antibody A nor antibody B.

43. Antibodies for Rh appear
    a. spontaneously as an inherited trait.   c. only in response to stimulations by Rh antigens.
    b. only rarely for poorly understood reasons.

44. An Rh-negative mother, carrying a fetus who is Rh-positive, may have an infant with a blood problem called _____
    _____.

45. An Rh-negative mother who delivers an Rh-positive baby is given _____ within 72 hours of delivery to prevent the condition in question 44.

46. Which of the following blood types is a universal donor?
    a. O   c. A
    b. AB   d. B

STUDY ACTIVITIES

Definition of Word Parts

Define the following word parts used in this chapter.

agglutin-

bil-

-crit

embol-

erythr-

hema-

hemo-

hepa-

leuko-

-lys

macro-

-osis

-poie

poly-

-stasis

thromb-

14.1 Characteristics of Blood

Answer the following concerning the volume and composition of blood.

1.   Describe blood in general and note its components.

2.   What factors influence a person's blood volume and what is the blood volume of an average adult?

3.   What is the hematocrit, note the percentages of the blood components?

4.   What do you find in the plasma?

14.2 Blood Cells

A.   Name and describe the process of blood cell formation.

B.   Answer the following questions concerning characteristics of red blood cells.
   1.   The shape of a red blood cell is a _____ _____.
   2.   How does their shape enhance the function of red blood cells?

   3.   How does the lack of a nucleus and other organelles affect red blood cell function?

C.   Answer these questions concerning red blood cell counts.
   1.   What are normal red blood cell counts for a man, a woman, and a child?

   2.   What factors may cause an increase in the red blood cell count?

D. Answer the following concerning red blood cell production and its control.

1. Where are red blood cells produced before and after birth?

2. Describe the process of red blood cell production.

3. How is the production of red blood cells controlled?

4. What factors can stimulate the release of erythropoietin?

E. Answer the following concerning dietary factors affecting red blood cell production.

1. What is the role of folic acid and vitamin B_{12} in red blood cell production?

2. Why is a B_{12} deficiency typically due to a disorder in the stomach lining?

3. What is the role of iron in red blood cell production?

4. List some of the different kinds of anemia as well as their causes

F. Answer the following concerning the destruction of red blood cells.

1. How are red blood cells damaged?

2. Damaged red blood cells are destroyed by cells called _____, located in the _____ and _____.

3. Describe how the body recycles hemoglobin.

G.   Fill in the following table regarding the types of white blood cells or leukocytes.

White Blood Cell (Leukocytes)	Description	Number Present	Function
Granulocytes			
Neutrophils			
Eosinophils			
Basophils			
Agranulocytes			
Monocytes			
Lymphocytes			

H.   Answer the following concerning the functions of white blood cells.

1.   What is diapedesis?

2.   The most mobile and active phagocytes are _____ and _____.

3.   Review and describe the inflammatory reaction. Include the role of histamine and the phenomenon of chemotaxis.

I.   Answer these questions concerning white blood cell counts.

1.   What is a normal white blood cell count?

2.   What is an excess of white blood cells called and what causes it?

3.   What is a deficiency in white blood cells called and what causes it?

4.   What is a differential white blood cell count and what can be diagnosed from this procedure?

J.   Answer these questions concerning platelets or thrombocytes.

1.   How are platelets formed?

2.   Describe the structure and function of platelets.

14.3 Blood Plasma

A.   1.   Fill in the following table regarding the plasma proteins.

Protein	Percentage of Total	Origin	Function
Albumins			
Globulin			
Alpha globulins			
Beta globulins			
Gamma globulins			
Fibrinogen			

2.   How does the concentration of plasma proteins affect water balance?

B.   Answer the following concerning nutrients and gases.

1.   List the gases found in plasma.

2.   What nutrients are found in plasma?

C.   Answer the following questions concerning the nonprotein nitrogenous substances.

1.   List the nonprotein nitrogenous substances found in plasma and explain where they come from.

2.   What factors can provoke an increase in these substances?

D.   Answer these questions concerning plasma electrolytes.

1.   What electrolytes are found in plasma?

2.   What are functions of the bicarbonate ions?

14.4 Hemostasis

A.   Answer the following concerning hemostasis and vascular spasm.

   1.   List the three mechanisms of hemostasis.

   2.   Are these mechanisms most likely to be successful in controlling blood loss from small or from large vessels?

   3.   What are the stimuli for vascular spasm?

B.   How is a platelet plug formed?

C.   Answer the following questions regarding the process of coagulation.

   1.   Describe the major events in the formation of a blood clot.

   2.   What triggers the extrinsic clotting mechanisms compared to the intrinsic clotting mechanisms?

   3.   What are some important components or factors for clotting to occur?

   4.   Fill in the following table comparing the extrinsic and intrinsic clotting mechanisms.

Steps	Extrinsic Clotting Mechanism	Intrinsic Clotting Mechanism
Trigger		
Initiation		
Series of reactions involving several clotting factors and calcium ions lead to the production of:		
Prothrombin activator and calcium ions cause the conversion of:		
Thrombin causes fragmentation, then joining of:		

   5.   What happens to a blood clot?

   6.   What factors allow the clot to dissolve?

   7.   A blood clot abnormally forming in a blood vessel is a/an_____. If it breaks off and is carried away in the blood, it is called a/an_____.

157

D.   Answer the following questions regarding the prevention of coagulation.
    1.   List the mechanisms that prevent coagulation and describe how they work.

    2.   What drug(s) can prevent clots in blood vessels?

14.5 Blood Groups and Transfusions

A.   Answer the following concerning antigens and antibodies.

    1.   What are antigens and antibodies?

    2.   The clumping of red blood cells when testing for compatability is called _____.

    3.   Antigens are present on the _____ _____ of red blood cells, antibodies are found in the _____.

B.   Answer the following concerning the ABO blood group.

    1.   Describe the basis for ABO blood types.

    2.   Fill in this table concerning blood types.

Blood Type	Antigen	Antibody
A		
B		
AB		
O		

    3.   What are the symptoms of mismatched blood transfusions?

    4.   Which blood type is considered the universal donor and which is the universal recipient?

C.   Answer the following concerning the Rh blood group.

    1.   What does it mean to be Rh positive or Rh negative?

    2.   How do anti-Rh antibodies develop in a person who is Rh negative?

    3.   Describe how erythroblastosis fetalis develops *in utero* or hemolytic disease following birth.

    4.   How can erythroblastosis fetalis be prevented?

Clinical Focus Questions

A.   Your uncle Bob is planning to have an elective hip replacement, and his surgeon has discussed the possibility of Uncle Bob storing several units of his blood in case he needs a transfusion during surgery. Your Uncle Bob asks you what you think about this. How would you respond?

B.   Based on your knowledge of blood and its functions, predict the symptoms of severe anemia (i.e., a hemoglobin of 6 g/dL).

When you have completed the study activities to your satisfaction, retake the mastery test and compare your performance with your initial attempt. If there are still areas you do not understand, repeat the appropriate study activities.

OVERVIEW

This chapter deals with the system that transports blood to and from the cells—the cardiovascular system (Learning Outcome 1). It identifies the location of the major organs of the cardiovascular system and explains the function of each organ (Learning Outcomes 2 and 9). You will be able to distinguish between the coverings of the heart and the layers of the heart, identify the structure and function of each part of the heart, and trace the pathway of blood through the heart (Learning Outcomes 3–5). You will be able to describe the cardiac cycle and the production of heart sounds, relate this information to the ECG pattern, and explain how the cardiac cycle is controlled (Learning Outcomes 6–8). You will be able to explain how blood pressure is produced and controlled to allow delivery of blood to the cells, how exchange of the fluids occurs in capillaries, and how venous blood is then returned to the heart (Learning Outcomes 10–12). You will be able to compare the pulmonary and systemic circuits of the cardiovascular system and identify the major arteries and veins (Learning Outcomes 13–15). Finally, you will be able to describe the life-span changes that affect the cardiovascular system (Learning Outcome 16).

Study of the cardiovascular system is essential for understanding how each part of the body is supplied with the materials it needs to sustain life.

LEARNING OUTCOMES

After you have studied this chapter, you should be able to
15.1   Overview of the Cardiovascular System
1.   Explain the roles of the heart and blood vessels in circulating the blood.
15.2   The Heart
2.   Describe the location of the heart within the body.
3.   Distinguish between the coverings of the heart and the layers that compose the wall of the heart.
4.   Identify and locate the major parts of the heart and discuss the function of each part.
5.   Trace the pathway of the blood through the heart and the vessels of coronary circulation.
6.   Describe the cardiac cycle and explain how heart sounds are produced.
7.   Identify the parts of a normal ECG and discuss the significance of this pattern.
8.   Explain control of the cardiac cycle.
15.3   Blood Vessels
9.   Compare the structures and functions of the major types of blood vessels.
10.   Describe how substances are exchanged between blood in the capillaries and the tissue fluid surrounding body cells.
15.4   Blood Pressure
11.   Explain how blood pressure is produced and controlled.
12.   Describe the mechanisms that aid in returning venous blood to the heart.
15.5   Paths of Circulation
13.   Compare the pulmonary and systemic circuits of the cardiovascular system.
15.6   Arterial System
14.   Identify and locate the major arteries.
15.7   Venous System
15.   Identify and locate the major veins.
15.8   Life-Span Changes
16.   Describe life-span changes in the cardiovascular system.

FOCUS QUESTION

As you run up the stairs from your laundry to your kitchen to answer the phone, your heart beats a little faster. How do your cardiovascular and respiratory systems work together to supply cells with enough oxygen and nutrients to meet your body's needs?

MASTERY TEST

Now take the mastery test. Do not guess. Some questions may have more than one correct answer. As soon as you complete the test, check your answers and correct any mistakes. Note your successes and failures so that you can reread the chapter to meet your learning needs.

1. The heart pumps approximately _____ liters of blood through the body daily.

2. Name the two circuits of the cardiovascular system.

3. The heart is a cone-shaped, muscular pump located within the _____ of the thoracic cavity.

4. The apex of the heart is located
   a. beneath the sternum, in the fifth intercostal space.
   b. in the second intercostal space, below the sternum.
   c. in the fourth intercostal space, in the midaxillary line.
   d. in the fifth intercostal space, about 3 inches left of the midline.

5. The visceral pericardium corresponds to the
   a. epicardium.
   b. myocardium.
   c. endocardium.
   d. exocardium.

6. Purkinje fibers are located in the
   a. epicardium.
   b. myocardium.
   c. endocardium.
   d. parietal pericardium.

7. The upper chambers of the heart are the right and left _____; the lower chambers are the right and left _____.

8. Small earlike projections are called _____ and can increase the atrial volume.

9. The vessels that empty into the upper right chamber of the heart are the
   a. inferior and superior venae cavae.
   b. pulmonary veins.
   c. pulmonary arteries.
   d. coronary sinuses.

10. The valve between the chambers of the right side of the heart is the _____ valve.
    a. semilunar
    b. bicuspid (mitral valve)
    c. tricuspid
    d. aortic

11. The structures that prevent the mitral and tricuspid valves from swinging into the atria during ventricular contraction are the
    a. chordae tendineae.
    b. papillary muscles.
    c. endocardia.
    d. Purkinje fibers.

12. Which of the following statements about the muscle walls of the right and left heart chambers is/are true?
    a. The muscle walls of the right and left heart are the same size.
    b. The muscle walls of the atria are thicker than those of the ventricles.
    c. The muscle walls of the right heart are thicker than those of the left heart.
    d. The muscle walls of the left ventricle are two to three times thicker than those of the right ventricle.

13. The valve that separates the left ventricle from the aorta is the _____ valve.

14. The pain that results when myocardial cells are deprived of oxygen is known as
    a. myocardial infarction.
    b. angina pectoris.
    c. endocarditis.
    d. myocardial ischemia.

15. Dense fibrous rings that surround the valves of the heart and the superior portion of the interventricular septum make up the _____ _____.

16. Trace a drop of blood through the heart beginning at the right atrium.

17. Blood is supplied to the heart by the right and left _____.

18. The branch of the left coronary artery that supplies the walls of both ventricles with blood is the _____ artery.
    a. circumflex
    b. anterior interventricular
    c. posterior interventricular
    d. marginal

19. Blood flow to cardiac muscle (increases/decreases) during ventricular contraction.

161

20. Blood from the myocardium is returned to the right atrium via the _____ _____.

21. Atrial contraction, while the ventricles relax, followed by ventricular contraction, while the atria relax, is known as the _____ _____.

22. Heart sounds heard with a stethoscope are produced by
    a. contraction of the muscle of the heart.
    b. the flow of blood through the heart.
    c. the opening and closing of the heart valves.
    d. changes in the velocity of blood flow through the heart.

23. A mass of merging cells that function as a unit is called
    a. smooth muscle.
    b. a functional syncytium.
    c. the sinoatrial node.
    d. the cardiac conduction system.

24. The cells that initiate the stimulus for contraction of the heart muscle are located in the
    a. sinoatrial node.
    b. atrioventricular node.
    c. Purkinje fibers.
    d. bundle of His.

25. The conduction impulse that starts in the right atrium travels to the _____.

26. The conduction system cells that are continuous with cardiac muscle cells are
    a. sinoatrial node cells.
    b. atrioventricular node cells.
    c. Purkinje fibers.
    d. cells of the bundle of His.

27. A recording of the electrical activity of the heart muscle is a/an _____.

28. The ECG wave or deflection that records atrial depolarization is the
    a. P wave.
    b. QRS wave.
    c. Q wave.
    d. ST segment.

29. The width of the QRS complex is an indication of the time needed for an impulse to travel through the
    a. atrium.
    b. AV node.
    c. AV bundle.
    d. ventricle.

30. An increase in vagus nerve stimulation on the heart (decreases/increases) the heart rate.

31. Abnormalities in the concentration of which of the following ions are likely to interfere with the contraction of the heart?
    a. chloride
    b. potassium
    c. calcium
    d. sodium

32. When a heart rate is 150 beats per minute, the rhythm is said to be
    a. bradycardia.
    b. flutter.
    c. fibrillation.
    d. tachycardia.

33. If an individual has a heart rate of 50 beats per minute, which of the following is probably the pacemaker?
    a. S-A node
    b. A-V node
    c. Purkinje fibers
    d. bundle branches

34. The vessel that participates directly in the exchange of substances between the cell and the blood is the
    a. arteriole.
    b. artery.
    c. capillary.
    d. venule.

35. The arterial wall layer that is made up of epithelial tissue and connective tissue rich in elastic and collagenous tissue is the
    a. tunica intima.
    b. tunica media.
    c. tunica adventitia.
    d. tunica interna.

36. Substances that inhibit platelet aggregation and cause vasodilation are secreted by the _____ of blood vessels.

37. The amount of blood that flows into capillaries is regulated by
    a. constriction and dilation of capillaries.
    b. arterioles and meta arterioles.
    c. the amount of intercellular tissue.
    d. precapillary sphincters.

38. Which of the following statements about capillaries is/are accurate?
    a. They connect the smallest arterioles and venules.
    b. They have more smooth muscle than venules in their walls.
    c. The openings in capillary walls are the largest in the liver, the red bone marrow, and the spleen.
    d. The blood-brain barrier exists in all parts of the brain.

39. The density of capillary networks varies with the metabolic activity of the tissues they serve.
    a. True
    b. False

40. The transport mechanisms used by the capillaries are _____, _____, and _____.

41. The method used to transport the oxygen in capillary blood to tissues is _____.

42. Why do plasma proteins remain in the blood?

43. What supplies the force for the process of filtration in the capillaries?

44. Blood pressure is highest in a/an
    a. artery.
    b. arteriole.
    c. capillary.
    d. vein.

45. Plasma proteins help retain water in the blood by maintaining
    a. osmotic pressure.
    b. hydrostatic pressure.
    c. a vacuum.
    d. surface tension.

46. Swelling occurs with tissue injury due to
    a. increased diastole in the heart.
    b. constriction of precapillary sphincters.
    c. increased permeability of capillary walls.
    d. increased pressure in venules.

47. Blood in veins is kept flowing in one direction by the presence of _____ in the endothelium.

48. Which of these structures is considered to be a blood reservoir?
    a. heart
    b. lungs
    c. capillaries
    d. veins

49. Increased venous pressure with dilation of superficial veins is characteristic of _____ _____.

50. The maximum pressure in the artery, occurring during ventricular contraction, is
    a. diastolic pressure.
    b. systolic pressure.
    c. mean arterial pressure.
    d. pulse pressure.

51. The amount of blood pushed out of the ventricle with each contraction is called _____ _____.

52. List the five factors that influence blood pressure.

53. The friction between blood and the walls of the blood vessels is (resistance/viscosity).

54. Cardiac output is calculated by multiplying _____ _____ by _____ _____.

55. Starling's law is related to which of the following cardiac structures?
    a. interventricular septum
    b. conduction system
    c. muscle fibers
    d. heart valves

56. When the baroreceptors in the aorta and carotid artery sense an increase in blood pressure, the medulla will relay (sympathetic/parasympathetic) impulses.

57. Peripheral resistance is maintained by increasing or decreasing the size of
    a. capillaries.
    b. arterioles.
    c. venules.
    d. veins.

58. Bradykinin, a chemical found in the blood, is a (vasoconstrictor/vasodilator).

59. When the underlying cause of high blood pressure is unknown, the individual is said to have_____ hypertension.

60. Blood flow in the venous system depends on
    a. contraction of the heart.
    b. venous compression by skeletal muscle contraction.
    c. constriction of veins.
    d. respiratory movements.

61. Angiotensin II directly increases blood pressure by
    a. promoting vasoconstriction.
    b. increasing blood volume.
    c. increasing cardiac output.
    d. increasing viscosity.

62. The central venous pressure is the pressure in the
    a. left atrium.
    b. right atrium.
    c. right ventricle.
    d. left ventricle.

63. Which of the following vessels carries deoxygenated blood?
    a. aorta
    b. innominate artery
    c. basilar artery
    d. pulmonary artery

64. The pulmonary veins enter the _____ _____ of the heart.

65. The aortic bodies containing chemoreceptors are located in the
    a. ascending aorta.
    b. aortic arch.
    c. carotid sinuses.
    d. descending aorta.

66. The ring of arteries at the base of the brain is called the _____ _____.

67. The veins that drain the abdominal viscera empty into a unique venous system called the _____ _____.

68. Coronary artery disease that begins early in life and remains asymptomatic until midlife or old age is due to deposition of _____ in arterial walls.

STUDY ACTIVITIES

Definition of Word Parts

Define the following word parts used in this chapter.

angio-

ather-

brady-

diastol-

edem-

-gram

lun-

myo-

papill-

phleb-

scler-

syn-

systol-

tachy-

15.1 Overview of the Cardiovascular System

Answer the following concerning the cardiovascular system.

1. The two circulatory circuits are the _____ circuit and the _____ circuit.

2. What is the function of each circuit?

15.2 The Heart

A. Answer the following regarding the size and location of the heart.

1. The heart is located in the _____ of the thoracic cavity and sits upon the
   _____.

2. Describe the average size of the heart as well as its precise location within the thoracic cavity.

3. Locate and describe the base and the apex of the heart.

B. Answer the following concerning the coverings of the heart.

1. The heart is enclosed by a double-layered _____.

2. What is the function of the fluid in the pericardial space?

3. What are the results of an inflammation of the pericardium?

4. What is the role of the fibrous pericardium?

C.   Answer the following concerning the wall of the heart.

1.   Label the parts of the wall of the heart.

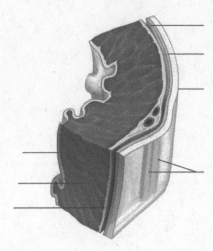

2.   Fill in this table regarding the layers of the heart.

Layer	Composition	Function
Epicardium (Visceral Pericardium)		
Myocardium		
Endocardium		

D.   Answer the following concerning heart chambers and valves.

1.   List the chambers of the heart.

2.   Why is the muscle wall of the right side of the heart smaller than that of the left side of the heart?

166

3. Label the structures of the heart in the accompanying drawing.

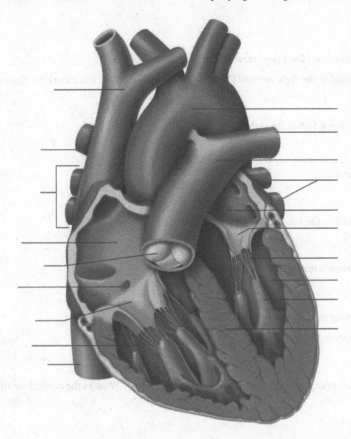

4. Fill in the following table regarding the valves of the heart.

Valve	Location	Function
Tricuspid Valve		
Pulmonary Valve		
Mitral Valve		
Aortic Valve		

5. What features of the heart anchor and control the valves opening and closing?

6. When the cusps of the mitral valve stretch and bulge upward into the atrium during ventricular contraction, the individual is said to have _____ _____.

E.   Describe the skeleton of the heart.

F.   Answer the following concerning the blood flow through the heart.
       1.   What vessels deliver blood to the right atrium? Describe the quality of blood that enters the right atrium.

       2.   Where does blood go when it leaves the right ventricle?

       3.   What happens in the lungs?

       4.   What vessels return blood to the left atrium? Describe this blood.

       5.   Where does blood go when it leaves the left ventricle?

G.   Answer the following concerning the blood supply to the heart.
       1.   Describe the blood supply to the heart.

       2.   Is the blood flow to the myocardium greatest during systole or diastole? What is the clinical significance of this fact?

       3.   What is the result when the heart is deprived of a blood supply?

H.   Answer the following concerning the cardiac cycle.
       1.   Contraction of the heart is known as _____, whereas relaxation is called _____.
       2.   When the atria contract, are the ventricles contracting as well?

       3.   Do both atria contract at the same time? How about the ventricles?

       4.   What causes the valves to open?

       5.   During ventricular diastole, which valves are open? Which valves are closed?

       6.   Would this be the same during ventricular systole?

I.   Answer these questions concerning heart sounds.
       1.   What produces the heart sounds heard with a stethoscope?

2.   What structures of the heart can be assessed by heart sounds?

3.   Where are the sounds related to the function of the following valves heard?

aortic valve

tricuspid valve

pulmonary valve

bicuspid (mitral) valve

J.   Answer the following regarding the cardiac muscle fibers.

1.   How do cardiac muscle fibers compare to skeletal muscle fibers?

2.   What is the functional syncytium?

K.   Answer the following concerning the cardiac conduction system.

1.   Identify the parts of the cardiac conduction system.

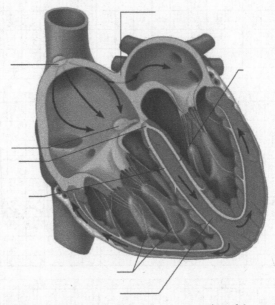

2.   Describe the conduction of an impulse from the S-A node to contraction of the myocardium.

3.   In what part of the ventricle does contraction begin? What effect does this have on the movement of blood through the ventricle?

L.   Answer the following concerning the electrocardiogram.

1.   What does an ECG actually measure?

2.   How is this recording obtained?

3. What events are represented by each of the following:
P wave

QRS complex

T wave?

4. What is the significance of a lengthened P-Q interval?

5. Identify each of the rhythms seen in the ECG strips below.

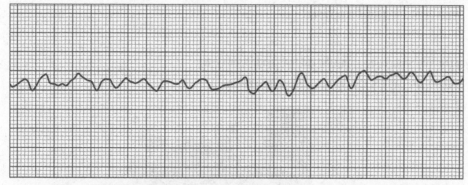

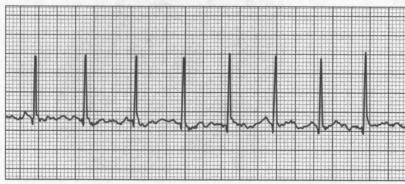

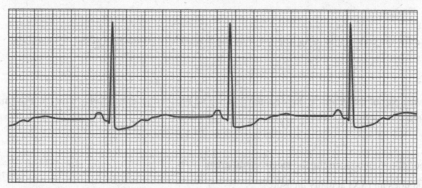

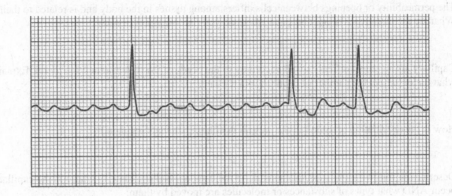

M.   Answer these questions concerning regulation of the cardiac cycle.

1.   How is the heart regulated by autonomic reflexes to meet the needs of the body? Name the sensors for the reflexes and the effect of the change in pressure on the heart function.

2.   How is the heart affected by the following ions: potassium and calcium?

3.   How does temperature affect the heart?

15.3 Blood Vessels

A.   Answer the following concerning the vascular system.

1.   What is meant by a closed circulatory system?

2.   Name the components of the system and give each one a function.

B.   Answer the following regarding the arteries and arterioles.

1.   What is the structure of the wall of arteries?

2.   How does the endothelium prevent blood clotting and contribute to the control of blood pressure?

3.   What is the role of the myocardium in control of blood pressure? How is the muscle controlled?

4.   How is the structure of arterioles different from that of arteries?

C.   Answer the following concerning capillaries.

1.   What is the structure of capillaries?

2. The permeability or openings between cells differs among tissues in the body and is related to their functions. What are the three types of openings and where do you find examples of each?

3. Capillary arrangement differs as well according to the needs of the tissues receiving blood. Explain in general what factors affect the number of capillaries in a tissue.

4. How is the distribution of blood in the various capillary pathways regulated?

5. Describe the following transport mechanisms in the capillary bed and identify where in the capillary bed they occur AND what types of substances or molecules are moved by them:

diffusion

filtration

osmosis.

6. Where does hydrostatic pressure come from and what does it cause to happen in the capillary bed?

7. Where does osmotic pressure come from and what does it cause to happen in the capillary bed?

D. Answer these questions concerning veins and venules.
1. Compare the structure of the walls of veins and arteries.

2. How do veins function as blood reservoirs?

E. Match the blood vessel disorders in the first column with the correct descriptions in the second column.
1. atherosclerosis   a. inflammation of a vein
2. arteriosclerosis   b. abnormal dilation of a superficial vein
3. varicose veins   c. characterized by an accumulation of fatty plaques
4. phlebitis   d. degenerative changes that lead to a loss of elasticity

15.4 Blood Pressure

A. Answer these questions concerning arterial blood pressure.
1. What cardiac events are related to systolic and diastolic arterial pressures?

2. How is blood pressure typically measured?

172

3. What is a pulse?

4. What are pulse pressure and mean arterial pressure?

B. Answer the following concerning the factors that influence arterial blood pressure.

   1. How is cardiac output calculated?

   2. How does cardiac output influence blood pressure?

   3. What factors influence blood volume?

   4. How does blood volume influence blood pressure?

   5. What is peripheral resistance measuring? What factors influence this?

   6. How does peripheral resistance influence blood pressure?

   7. What can change the viscosity of blood?

   8. How does blood viscosity affect the blood pressure?

C. Answer the following concerning the control of blood pressure.

   1. What does cardiac output depend on?

   2. How is stroke volume calculated?

   3. What effect does venous return have on cardiac output?

   4. What is the Starling law of the heart?

   5. What is contractility and how does it influence cardiac output?

   6. How are cardiac output and peripheral resistance regulated?

   7. Discuss the neural and chemical factors that affect cardiac output.

D.   Answer the following concerning hypertension.

1.   What causes hypertension?

2.   Why does arteriosclerosis lead to high blood pressure?

3.   What mechanism in kidney disease leads to high blood pressure?

4.   Discuss the results of high blood pressure.

E.   What factors help move blood through the venous system to return it to the heart?

F.   What is central venous pressure and what can cause it to increase or decrease?

15.5 Paths of Circulation

A.   Trace a drop of blood through the pulmonary circuit, noting where it is oxygenated and deoxygenated.

B.   What is the function of the systemic circuit?

15.6 Arterial System

A.   List the principal branches of the aorta in the order in which they arise, beginning with those that arise from the aortic arch.

B.   Describe the circulation to the head, neck, and brain.

C.   List the arteries that supply the shoulder and upper limb.

D.   List the arteries that supply the thoracic and abdominal walls.

E.   List the arteries that supply the pelvis and lower limbs.

15.7 Venous System

A.   Answer the following regarding characteristics of the venous pathways.

   1.   Describe the structure of the venous system.

   2.   The two major venous pathways that return blood to the right atrium are the _____ and the _____ _____ _____.

B.   List the veins from the brain, head, and neck.

C.   List the veins from the shoulders and arms.

D.   List the veins from the abdominal and thoracic walls.

E.   List the veins from the abdominal viscera.

F.   List the veins from the pelvis and lower limbs.

15.8 Life-Span Changes

A.   Why is it difficult to identify life-span changes in the cardiovascular system?

B.   List changes now thought to be due to aging.

Clinical Focus Questions

David is a 52-year-old overweight accountant who has had chest pain occasionally for several months, usually related to increased activity. His cardiologist has told him he has coronary artery disease.

A.   What are the risk factors for heart disease?

B.   What foods should David avoid?

C.   How might biofeedback be helpful to David?

When you have completed the study activities to your satisfaction, retake the mastery test and compare your performance with your initial attempt. If there are still areas you do not understand, repeat the appropriate study activities.

176

OVERVIEW

The lymphatic system has important roles in the maintenance of fluid balance, transport of fats, and the defense against infection. This chapter begins by describing how the lymphatic system assists the circulatory system (Learning Outcome 1). You will study the major lymph pathways, including how lymph forms, and circulates, along with the consequences of lymphatic obstruction (Learning Outcomes 2–4). You will study the major lymphatic organs, learning their locations and functions as they relate to defense (Learning Outcomes 5–7). You will differentiate between the non-specific and specific defenses, explaining the cells involved and the mechanisms and actions of these two divisions of the immune response (Learning Outcomes 8–12). Various types of immune responses, including primary and secondary responses, active and passive responses, allergic reactions, tissue rejection reactions, and immune changes across the life span are also explained in this chapter (Learning Outcomes 13–16).

The study of the lymphatic system completes your knowledge of how fluid is transported to and from tissues. Knowledge of the cellular and molecular mechanisms of the lymphatic system is the basis for understanding how the body defends itself against diverse pathogens.

LEARNING OUTCOMES

After you have studied this chapter, you should be able to

16.1   Lymphatic Pathways
1.   Describe the functions of the lymphatic vessels.
2.   Identify and describe the parts of the major lymphatic pathways.

16.2   Tissue Fluid and Lymph
3.   Describe how tissue fluid and lymph form, and explain the function of lymph.
4.   Explain how lymphatic circulation is maintained, and describe the consequence of lymphatic obstruction.

16.3   Lymphatic Tissues and Lymphatic Organs
5.   Describe a lymph node and its major functions.
6.   Identify the locations of the major chains of lymph nodes.
7.   Discuss the locations and functions of the thymus and spleen.

16.4   Body Defenses Against Infection (Immunity)
8.   Distinguish between innate (non-specific) and adaptive (specific) defenses.
9.   List seven innate body defense mechanisms, and describe the action of each mechanism.
10.   Explain how two major types of lymphocytes are formed and activated, and how they function in immune mechanisms.
11.   Identify the parts of an antibody molecule.
12.   Discuss the actions of the five types of antibodies.
13.   Distinguish between primary and secondary immune responses.
14.   Distinguish between active and passive immunities.
15.   Explain how hypersensitivity reactions, tissue rejection reactions, and autoimmunity arise from immune mechanisms.

16.5   Life-Span Changes
16.   Describe life-span changes in immunity.

FOCUS QUESTION

You have received a pretty nasty abrasion while playing a game of softball with some friends. Several days later, you notice that the area around your knee is swollen and that you have several enlarged lymph nodes in your groin. How are these signs related to the function of the lymphatic system in responding to injury and infection?

MASTERY TEST

Now take the mastery test. Do not guess. Some questions may have more than one correct answer. As soon as you complete the test, check your answers and correct any mistakes. Note your successes and failures so that you can reread the chapter to meet your learning needs.

1. List the major functions of the lymphatic system.

2. The lymphatic system returns fluid to the
   - a. cells.
   - b. tissues.
   - c. lacteals.
   - d. blood.

3. The lymphatic vessels in the villi of the small intestine, called _____, are involved in the absorption of _____.

4. The smallest vessels in the lymphatic system are called _____ _____.

5. The walls of lymphatic vessels are most similar to the walls of
   - a. arteries.
   - b. veins.
   - c. capillaries.
   - d. arterioles.

6. The largest lymph vessel(s) is/are the
   - a. lumbar trunk.
   - b. thoracic duct.
   - c. lymphatic duct.
   - d. intestinal trunk.

7. Lymph rejoins the blood and becomes part of the plasma in
   - a. lymph nodes.
   - b. the right and left subclavian veins.
   - c. the inferior and superior venae cavae.
   - d. the right atrium.

8. Tissue fluid originates from
   - a. the cytoplasm of cells.
   - b. lymph fluid.
   - c. blood plasma.
   - d. kidney filtrate.

9. Lymph formation is most directly dependent on
   - a. increasing osmotic pressure in tissue fluid.
   - b. a blood pressure of at least 100/60.
   - c. a sufficient volume of tissue fluid to create a pressure gradient between tissue and lymph capillaries.
   - d. diminished peripheral resistance in veins.

10. The function(s) of lymph is/are to
    - a. recapture protein molecules lost in the capillary bed.
    - b. form tissue fluid.
    - c. transport foreign particles to lymph nodes.
    - d. recapture electrolytes.

11. The mechanisms that move lymph through lymph vessels are similar to those that move blood through (arteries/veins).

12. The flow of lymph is greatest during periods of
    - a. physical exercise.
    - b. isometric exercise of skeletal muscle.
    - c. dream sleep.
    - d. REM sleep.

13. Obstruction of lymph circulation will lead to _____.

14. Lymph nodes contain
    - a. a hilum.
    - b. a medulla.
    - c. red pulp.
    - d. a bone.

15. Compartments within the node contain dense masses of
    - a. epithelial tissue.
    - b. cilia.
    - c. oocytes.
    - d. lymphocytes.

16. Inflammation of a lymph node is known as _____.

17. Clumps of lymph nodes in mucosa of the ileum are called _____ _____.

18. An infection in the toe would result in enlarged lymph nodes in the
    - a. axilla.
    - b. inguinal region.
    - c. pelvic cavity.
    - d. abdominal cavity.

19. Which of the following types of cells are produced by lymph nodes?
   a. leukocytes
   b. lymphocytes
   c. eosinophils
   d. basophils

20. The thymus is located in the
   a. posterior neck.
   b. mediastinum.
   c. upper abdomen.
   d. left pelvis.

21. Which of the following statements about the thymus is/are true?
   a. The thymus tends to increase in size with age, as glandular tissue is replaced by fat and connective tissue.
   b. The thymus is relatively large during infancy and childhood.
   c. The thymus produces a substance called thymosin that seems to stimulate the development of T lymphocytes.
   d. The thymus is a hard, multilobed structure.

22. The largest of the lymphatic organs is the _____.

23. Which of the following statements about the spleen is/are true?
   a. The spleen is located in the lower left quadrant of the abdomen.
   b. The spleen functions in the body's defense against infection.
   c. The structure of the spleen is exactly like that of a lymph node.
   d. Splenic pulp contains large phagocytes and macrophages on the lining of its venous sinuses.

24. Agents that enter the body and cause disease are called _____.

25. Examples of innate defenses are the
   a. skin.
   b. antibodies.
   c. acid environment of the stomach.
   d. lymphocytes.

26. The skin is an example of which of the following defense mechanisms?
   a. immunity
   b. inflammation
   c. mechanical barrier
   d. phagocytosis

27. Innate defensive mechanisms act (more rapidly/more slowly) than adaptive responses.

28. The enzyme lysozyme, which has antibacterial ability, is present in which of the following body fluids?
   a. sweat
   b. blood
   c. tears
   d. urine

29. Fever inhibits pathogen growth because
   a. bacterial cells lyse a higher temperatures.
   b. changes in body temperature affect the cell walls of microrganisms.
   c. it decreases the amount of iron in the blood.
   d. it causes T lymphocytes to proliferate.

30. List the four major symptoms of inflammation.

31. The accumulation of white blood cells, bacterial cells, and damaged tissue cells creates
   a. exudate.
   b. pus.
   c. a scab.
   d. lymph.

32. The most active phagocytes in the blood are _____ and _____.

33. Macrophages originated from which of these cells?
   a. neutrophils
   b. monocytes
   c. lymphocytes
   d. reticulocytes

34. Macrophages are located in the lining of blood vessels in the bone marrow, liver, spleen, and lymph nodes; they form the _____ _____ system.

35. The resistance to specific foreign agents in which certain cells recognize foreign substances and act to destroy them is _____.

36. Some undifferentiated lymphocytes migrate to the _____ where they undergo changes and are then called T lymphocytes.

37. Foreign proteins to which lymphocytes respond are called _____.

38. Lymphocytes seem to be able to recognize specific foreign proteins because
    a. of changes in the nucleus of the lymphocyte.
    b. the cytoplasm of the lymphocyte is altered.
    c. there are changes in the permeability of the cell membrane of the lymphocyte.
    d. of the presence of receptor molecules on lymphocytes, which fit the molecules of antigens.

39. B lymphocytes respond to foreign protein by
    a. phagocytosis.
    b. interacting directly with pathogens.
    c. producing antigens.
    d. producing antibodies.

40. T cells are responsible for _____ immunity.

41. The antibodies produced by B cells make up the _____ _____ fraction of plasma.

42. The immunoglobulin that crosses the placenta from the mother to the fetus is immunoglobulin
    a. A.
    b. G.
    c. M.
    d. Y.

43. Which of the following are actions of antibodies that protect the body against infection?
    a. agglutination
    b. precipitation
    c. activate complement
    d. neutralization

44. The most protective action of antibodies against antigens is activation of _____.

45. An accessory cell is necessary to activate (B cells/T cells/both).

46. In which of the following ways are primary and secondary immune responses different?
    a. Primary responses are more important than secondary responses.
    b. Primary responses produce more antibodies than secondary responses.
    c. A primary response is a direct response to an antigen; a secondary response is indirect.
    d. A primary response is the initial response to an antigen; a secondary response is all subsequent responses to that antigen.

47. A person who receives ready-made antibodies develops artificially acquired _____ immunity.

48. An immune response to a substance harmless to the body is a/an _____ _____.

49. The type of hypersensitivity reaction that occurs very quickly and can lead to death is a/an
    a. type I reaction.
    b. immune complex reaction.
    c. antibody-dependent cytotoxic reaction.
    d. delayed reaction.

50. Which of the following types of grafts are least likely to be rejected?
    a. isograft
    b. autograft
    c. allograft
    d. xenograft

51. Age-related decline in the competence of the immune system is due to the loss of _____.

52. The retrovirus that causes acquired immune deficiency syndrome is transmitted by
    a. the airborne route.
    b. contact with infected articles.
    c. inoculation with infected blood.
    d. unknown means.

53. When tolerance to self-substance is lost and the immune response is directed against the individual's own tissue, the individual is said to have an _____ disease.

54. The rational for giving influenza vaccine to people over 65 is because of
    a. increasing numbers of abnormal T cells.
    b. increasing size of the thymus gland.
    c. decreased effectiveness of the immune response.
    d. slower antibody response to antigens.

<u>STUDY ACTIVITIES</u>

Definition of Word Parts

Define the following word parts used in this chapter.

auto-

-gen

humor-

immun-

inflamm-

nod-

patho-

16.1 Lymphatic Pathways

A.   List the general components of the lymphatic system

B.   What are the functions of the lymphatic systems?

C.   Describe the lymph capillaries and explain their function.

D.   Compare the lymph vessels to veins.

E.   Answer the following regarding the lymphatic trunks and collecting ducts.
        1.   Label the following figure.

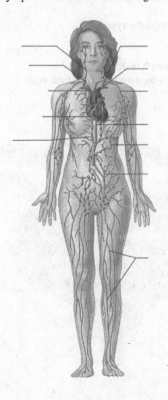

2. Compare and contrast the two main ducts regarding what regions of body they affect and identify the blood vessels they join to return lymph fluid to blood.

16.2 Tissue Fluid and Lymph

A. Where does tissue fluid come from? Include the composition of tissue fluid and the pressure gradients needed for it to form.

B. How is lymph formed?

C. How does the structure of the walls of lymph capillaries prompt the movement of fluid from tissue into lymph capillaries?

D. Describe the forces responsible for the transport of lymph.

E. What are the functions of lymph and how does the structure of the capillary wall assist with this?

16.3 Lymphatic Tissues and Lymphatic Organs

A. Name the organs and tissues of the lymphatic system.

B. Answer the following regarding the lymph nodes.
   1. Label the structures in the following drawing of a lymph node.

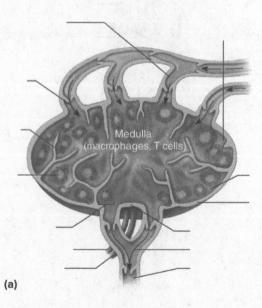

Medulla
(macrophages, T cells)

(a)

2. Match the following lymph node locations and areas they receive fluids from.

    a. cervical region   1. in the mediastinum along the trachea and bronchi
    b. thoracic cavity   2. receive from upper limbs, thorax, and mammary glands
    c. supratrochlear region   3. receive from skin of scalp, face, nasal cavity, and pharynx
    d. inguinal region   4. receive lymph from abdominal viscera
    e. axillary region   5. located superficially on the medial side of elbow
    f. pelvic cavity   6. receive lymph from the pelvic viscera
    g   abdominal cavity   7. receive from the lower limbs and external genitalia

3. Inflammation of lymph vessels is _____. Inflammation of a lymph node is _____.

4. What are the functions of lymph nodes?

C. Answer the following regarding the thymus gland.

1. Describe the location, structure, and function of the thymus gland.

2. What secretion of the thymus stimulates maturation of T lymphocytes?

D. Answer the following concerning the spleen.

1. Where is the spleen located?

2. Label the structures in the following diagram and explain the significance of red and white pulps.

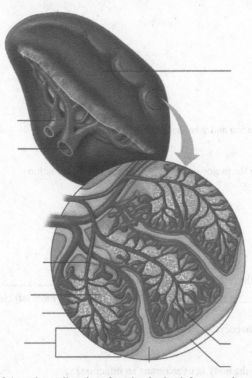

3. What characteristics of the spleen allow it to function in the defense against foreign protein?

16.4 Body Defenses Against Infection (Immunity)

A.   What kinds of agents cause disease?

B.   Name and describe the two major types of defense mechanisms that prevent disease.

C.   Answer the following regarding the innate or non-specific defenses.

     1.   What is species resistance?

     2.   What structures function as mechanical barriers?

     3.   What enzymes help resist infection by acting as chemical barriers?

     4.   Describe how the following chemical barriers function in defense.

          interferons

          defensins

          collectins

          complement

          perforins

     5.   What causes inflammation and what happens during inflammation?

     6.   Explain the reason for the major signs and symptoms of inflammation.
          redness

          swelling heat

          pain

     7.   Cells that assist with the inflammatory process are the _____ and the _____.
          The _____ are actually monocytes that have left circulation.

     8.   Describe the role of phagocytosis in defense.

     9.   How does fever assist the body in overcoming an infection?

D.   Answer these questions concerning the adaptive or specific defenses or immunity.

1.   What is immunity?

2.   A foreign substance to which lymphocytes respond is called a/an _____.

3.   What molecules make good antigens? How are haptens different from antigens?

4.   Fill in the following table regarding the comparison of the B and T lymphocytes.

Characteristic	T Cells	B Cells
Origin of Undifferentiated Cell		
Site of Differentiation		
Primary Locations		
Primary Functions		

5.   What are clones and WHY are these cells considered part of the specific defense?

6.   T cells are activated by _____ _____.

7.   How do T cells perform the cellular immune response, what are the roles for cytokines, especially interleukin-1 and -2 as well as colony-stimulating factors.

8.   Compare and contrast the functions of the following types of T cells:

      helper T cells

      memory T cells

      cytotoxic T cells

9.   Describe how the helper T cells assist with B cell activation and proliferation.

10.   Describe what happens once a B cell becomes activated to produce antibodies, include the formation of plasma cells and memory B cells.

11. Describe a typical antibody molecule.

12. Fill in the following table regarding the characteristics of immunoglobulins.

Type	Occurrence	Major Function
IgG		
IgA		
IgM		
IgD		
IgE		

13. Describe the following antibody actions.

agglutination

precipitation

neutralization

complement activation

opsonization

chemotaxis

lysis

inflammation

14. Compare the two immune responses regarding speed, production of antibodies, and likeliness of becoming ill.

15. Describe these practical classifications of immunity regarding how antigens are encountered and the body's response to the antigen and will you develop memory of the encounter.

naturally acquired active immunity

artificially acquired active immunity

artificially acquired passive immunity

naturally acquired passive immunity

16.   What are allergens and what is a hypersensitivity reaction?

17.   Describe the following types of hypersensitivity reactions regarding the immune cells that mediate the reaction, how quickly the reaction occurs and examples of these reactions.
Immediate reaction (type I)

antibody-dependent cytotoxic reaction (type II)

immune complex reaction (type III)

delayed reaction (type IV)

18.   What is a tissue rejection reaction and why does it occur?

19.   How do we reduce the recipient's rejection of a transplanted tissue?

20.   What are autoimmunity disorders? List a few of the more common ones.

21.   List some of the known causes for autoimmunity disorders.

16.5 Life-Span Changes

What are the underlying reasons for the lowered or less effective immune response in the elderly?

Clinical Focus Questions

Your 13-year-old daughter is at the correct age to receive the vaccine that protects against some strains of the human papillomavirus (HPV) that can lead to cervical cancer. Would you have her get it? What would be important for you to know about the vaccine before allowing your daughter to receive it? You have a 15-year-old son as well, what advantages would there be to him receiving the vaccine?

When you have completed the study activities to your satisfaction, retake the mastery test and compare your performance with your initial attempt. If there are still areas you do not understand, repeat the appropriate study activities.

OVERVIEW

This chapter is about the digestive system, which processes the food you eat so that nutrients can be absorbed and utilized by your cells. This chapter begins with a description of the processes involved in digestion and names the major organs of the digestive system (Learning Outcomes 1 and 2). It then takes a generalized look at the system by exploring the structures of the wall of the alimentary canal (Learning Outcome 3) along with the way mixing and movement occur along the canal (Learning Outcome 4). The role of the autonomic nervous system in the regulation of this movement and secretions of the cells is discussed (Learning Outcome 5) before you begin examining the specific regions. You will then compare and contrast the structures and the functions of each organ focusing on their specific contribution to the digestive process, and examine their secretions and the mechanisms that regulate those secretions (Learning Outcomes 6–28). The chapter then concludes with a description of age-related changes in the digestive system (Learning Outcome 29).

LEARNING OUTCOMES

After you have studied this chapter, you should be able to

17.1   General Characteristics of the Digestive System
1.   Which processes are carried out by the digestive system?
2.   Name the major organs of the digestive system.
3.   Describe the structure of the wall of the alimentary canal.
4.   Explain how the contents of the alimentary canal are mixed and moved.
5.   Discuss the general effects of innervation of the alimentary canal by the sympathetic and parasympathetic divisions of the autonomic nervous system.

17.2   Mouth
6.   Describe the functions of the structures associated with the mouth.
7.   Describe how different types of teeth are adapted for different functions, and list the parts of a tooth.

17.3   Salivary Glands
8.   Locate the salivary glands and describe their secretions.
9.   Identify the function of salivary amylase.
10.   Describe how saliva secretion is controlled.

17.4   Pharynx and Esophagus
11.   Locate the pharynx and esophagus, and describe their general functions.
12.   Describe the mechanism of swallowing.

17.5   Stomach
13.   Locate the stomach and explain its function.
14.   Describe the secretions of the stomach.
15.   Describe how stomach secretion is controlled.

17.6   Pancreas
16.   Locate the pancreas and describe its secretions.
17.   Identify the function of each enzyme secreted by the pancreas.
18.   Describe how pancreatic secretion is regulated.

17.7   Liver and Gallbladder
19.   Locate the liver and describe its structure.
20.   Explain the various liver functions.
21.   Locate the gallbladder and describe the release of bile.

17.8   Small Intestine
22.   Locate the small intestine and describe its structure.
23.   Identify the function of each enzyme secreted by the small intestine.
24.   Describe how small intestinal secretion is regulated.
25.   Explain how the products of digestion are absorbed in the small intestine.

17.9   Large Intestine
        26.   Locate the large intestine and describe its structure.
        27.   Identify the functions of the large intestine.
        28.   Describe the mechanism of defecation.
17.10   Life-Span Changes
        29.   Describe aging-related changes in the digestive system.

FOCUS QUESTION

How does your body make the nutrients found in food, such as the slice of supreme pizza you had at lunchtime, available for metabolic processes in your body?

MASTERY TEST

Now take the mastery test. Do not guess. Some questions may have more than one correct answer. As soon as you complete the test, check your answers and correct any mistakes you find. Note your successes and failures so that you can reread the chapter to meet your learning needs.

1.   The mechanical and chemical breakdown of food into forms that can be absorbed by cell membranes is _____.

2.   The mouth, pharynx, esophagus, stomach, small intestine, and large intestine make up the _____ _____ of the digestive system.

3.   The salivary glands, liver, gallbladder, and pancreas are considered _____ _____.

4.   List the layers of the alimentary canal beginning with the innermost layer.

5.   The vessels that nourish the structures of the alimentary canal are found in the

      a.   mucous membrane.   c.   muscular layer.
      b.   submucosa.   d.   serous layer.

6.   The two basic types of movement of the alimentary canal are _____ movements and _____ movements.

7.   Does statement a explain statement b? _____
      a.   Peristalsis is stimulated when the walls of the alimentary canal are stretched.
      b.   Peristalsis acts to move food along the alimentary canal.

8.   When the alimentary canal is being stimulated by the parasympathetic division,

      a.   the impulses arise in the brain and the thoracic   c.   the activity of the organs of the digestive
            segment of the spinal cord.   system is increased.
      b.   impulses are conducted along the vagus nerve to   d.   sphincter tone in the anus is increased.
            the esophagus, stomach, pancreas, gallbladder,
            small intestine, and parts of the large intestine.

9.   Which of the following is/are function(s) of the mouth?

      a.   speech   c.   perceiving pleasure
      b.   initiating digestion of protein   d.   altering the size of pieces of food

10.   The tongue is anchored to the floor of the mouth by a fold of membrane called the _____.

11.   During swallowing, muscles draw the soft palate and uvula upward to

      a.   move food into the esophagus.   c.   separate the oral and nasal cavities.
      b.   enlarge the area to accommodate a bolus of food.   d.   move the uvula from the path of the food bolus.

12.   The third set of molars is sometimes called the _____ _____.

13.   The teeth that bite off pieces of food are

      a.   incisors.   c.   canines.
      b.   bicuspids.   d.   molars.

14.   The material that covers the crown of the teeth is

      a.   cementum.   c.   enamel.
      b.   dentin.   d.   plaque.

15. Which of the following is *not* a function of saliva?
    a. cleansing of mouth and teeth
    b. dissolving chemicals necessary for tasting food
    c. helping in formation of food bolus
    d. beginning digestion of fats

16. Stimulation of salivary glands by parasympathetic nerves will (increase/decrease) the production of watery saliva.

17. The salivary glands that secrete amylase are the _____ glands.
    a. submaxillary
    b. parotid
    c. sublingual
    d. pharyngeal

18. When food enters the esophagus, it is transported to the stomach by a movement called _____.

19. A chronic condition that replaces squamous epithelium with columnar epithelium is known as _____ _____.

20. The area of the stomach that acts as a temporary storage area is the _____ region.
    a. cardiac
    b. fundic
    c. body
    d. pyloric

21. Forceful vomiting after feeding in a newborn is a sign of _____ _____ _____.

22. The chief cells of the gastric glands secrete
    a. mucus.
    b. hydrochloric acid.
    c. digestive enzymes.
    d. potassium chloride.

23. The digestive enzyme pepsin, secreted by gastric glands, begins the digestion of
    a. carbohydrate.
    b. protein.
    c. fat.
    d. nucleic acids.

24. The intrinsic factor secreted by the stomach aids in the absorption of _____ from the small intestine.

25. The release of the hormone somatostatin (increases/decreases) the release of hydrochloric acid by parietal cells.

26. The release of gastrin is stimulated by
    a. the sympathetic nervous system.
    b. the parasympathetic nervous system.
    c. histamine.
    d. somatostatin.

27. The presence of food in the small intestine eventually (stimulates/inhibits) gastric secretions.

28. The semifluid paste formed in the stomach by mixing food and gastric contents is _____.

29. The foods that stay in the stomach the longest are high in
    a. fat.
    b. protein.
    c. carbohydrate.
    d. caffeine.

30. The substances absorbed from the stomach include
    a. water.
    b. alcohol.
    c. carbohydrate.
    d. protein.

31. The enterogastric reflex (stimulates/inhibits) peristalsis of the stomach.

32. The vomiting center is located in the _____ _____.

33. Pancreatic enzymes travel along the pancreatic duct and empty into the
    a. duodenum.
    b. jejunum.
    c. ileum.
    d. stomach.

34. Which of the following enzymes is present in the secretions of the mouth and pancreas?
    a. amylase
    b. lipase
    c. trypsin
    d. lactase

35. Which of the following is secreted by the pancreas in an inactive form and is activated by a duodenal enzyme?
    a. nuclease
    b. trypsin
    c. chymotrypsin
    d. carboxypeptidase

36. The secretions of the pancreas are (acidic/alkaline).

37. What stimulates the release of secretin?
    a. a decrease in the pH of the chyme
    b. an increase in the fat content of chyme
    c. an increase in sympathetic impulses
    d. an increase in gastrin production

38. The majority of the liver is located in the _____ _____ quadrant of the abdomen.

39. The most vital functions of the liver are those that are related to metabolism of
    a. carbohydrates.
    b. fats.
    c. proteins.
    d. vitamins.

40. Extra iron is stored by the liver in the form of _____.

41. Nutrients are brought to the liver cells via the
    a. central vein.
    b. liver capillaries.
    c. hepatic sinusoids.
    d. connective tissue of the lobes of the liver.

42. The type(s) of hepatitis that is/are blood borne is/are
    a. hepatitis A.
    b. hepatitis B.
    c. hepatitis C.
    d. hepatitis D.
    e. hepatitis E.

43. The function of the gallbladder is to _____ bile.
    a. store
    b. secrete
    c. produce
    d. concentrate

44. The hepatopancreatic sphincter is located between the
    a. pancreatic duct and the common bile duct.
    b. hepatic duct and the cystic duct.
    c. common bile duct and the duodenum.
    d. pancreatic duct and the duodenum.

45. Which of the following is/are the function(s) of bile?
    a. emulsification of fat globules
    b. absorption of fats
    c. increase the solubility of amino acids
    d. absorption of fat-soluble vitamins

46. List the three portions of the small intestine: _____, _____, _____.

47. The velvety appearance of the lining of the small intestine is due to the presence of
    a. cilia.
    b. villi.
    c. mucus secreted by the small intestine.
    d. capillaries.

48. The intestinal enzyme that breaks down fats is
    a. sucrase.
    b. maltase.
    c. lipase.
    d. intestinal amylase.

49. Lactose intolerance leads to an inability to digest
    a. red meat.
    b. eggs.
    c. leafy vegetables.
    d. milk and dairy products.

50. Which of the following transport mechanisms is/are not used by the small intestine?
    a. diffusion
    b. osmosis
    c. filtration
    d. active transport

51. Diarrhea results from an intestinal movement called _____ _____.

52. Cholesterol is delivered to tissues by _____; cholesterol is removed from tissues and delivered to the liver by _____.

53. The small intestine joins the large intestine at the _____.

54. The only significant secretion of the large intestine is
    a. potassium.
    b. mucus.
    c. chyme.
    d. water.

55. The only nutrients normally absorbed in the large intestine are _____ and _____.

56. Which of the following are synthesized by the bacteria of the colon?
    a. gas
    b. electrolytes
    c. vitamin K
    d. ascorbic acid

57. The most noticeable signs of aging on digestion appear in the
    a. mouth.
    b. accessory organs.
    c. small intestine.
    d. large bowel.

STUDY ACTIVITIES

Definition of Word Parts

Define the following word parts used in this chapter.

aliment-

cari-

cec-

chym-

decidu-

frenul-

gastr-

hepat-

hiat-

lingu-

peri-

pyl-

rect-

sorpt-

vill-

17.1 Overview of the Digestive System

A.   Define *digestion*.

B.   Which structures are belong to the alimentary canal and which are the accessory organs?

C.   Label the structures and give their functions on this diagram of the digestive system.

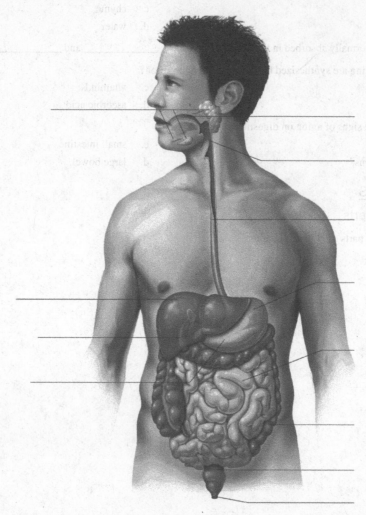

D.   Answer the following regarding the generalized characteristics of the alimentary canal.

   1.   Fill in the following table regarding the structure and function of the wall of the alimentary canal.

Layer	Composition	Function
Mucosa		
Submucosa		
Muscularis		
Serosa		

   2.   Describe the two types of generalized movement through the alimentary canal.

3. Parasympathetic stimulation provokes a/an _____ in the activity of the tube; sympathetic stimulation provokes a/an _____ in the activity of the tube.

4. Where do parasympathetic impulses originate and what structures do they innervate?

5. Where do the sympathetic impulses originate and what do they do?

17.2 Mouth

A. What structures do you find in the mouth and what are the functions of the mouth?

B. Describe the structure of the cheeks and lips.

C. Answer the following concerning the tongue.
1. Describe the structure and features of the tongue.

2. What is the function of the tongue?

3. Which pair of tonsils is associated with the tongue?

D. Answer these questions concerning the palate.
1. What are the parts of the palate?

2. What is the function of the palate?

3. Which sets of tonsil are found associated with palates?

E. Answer the following concerning the teeth.
1. Use yourself or a partner to locate the central incisors; lateral incisors; canines; first premolars; second premolars; and the first, second, and third molars. Which of these teeth are known as the "wisdom teeth?"

2. Describe the development of teeth.

3. Identify the functions of the following kinds of teeth.
incisors

canines (cuspids)

premolars and molars

4. In the following illustration of a tooth, label the parts.

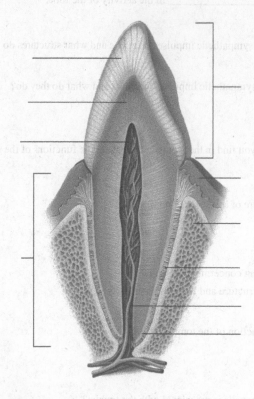

17.3 Salivary Glands

A.   Name the salivary glands and describe their functions.

B.   Answer the following regarding salivary secretions.
    1. What chemicals are found in the secretions and what are their functions?

    2. What regulates the secretions and what stimulates the process?

C.   Fill in the following table concerning the major salivary glands.

Gland	Location	Duct	Type of Secretion
Parotid Glands			
Submandibular Glands			
Sublingual Glands			

17.4 Pharynx and Esophagus

A. Describe the nasopharynx, oropharynx, and laryngopharynx. In the description, include the muscles in the walls that assist with swallowing.

B. List the events of swallowing and note whether they are voluntarily controlled or involuntary reflexes.

C. Answer the following regarding the esophagus.
1. Describe the structure of the esophagus.

2. Describe the movement through the esophagus.

3. The esophagus passes through the diaphragm via an opening called the _____.

4. What are the features of the esophagus that assist with its function?

17.5 Stomach

A. Describe the stomach.

B. Name the features and regions of the stomach.

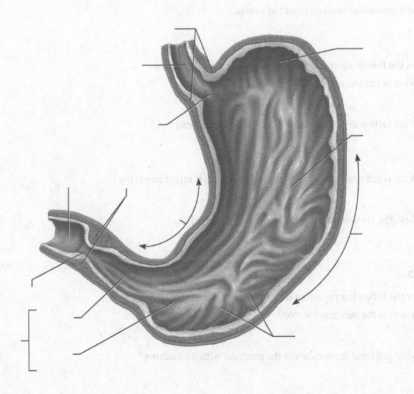

C.   Fill in the following table regarding the compounds found in gastric secretions.

Component	Source	Function
Pepsinogen		
Pepsin		
Hydrochloric Acid		
Mucus		
Intrinsic Factor		

D.   Answer the following regarding regulation of gastric secretions.

1.   How are gastric secretions regulated, and address the role for somatostatin, parasympathetic impulses, gastrin, and histamines in controlling the secretions?

2.   Describe the three phases of gastric secretion, note how each phase is initiated or stimulated, and what the effect is on the stomach.

3.   What is the "alkaline tide," and when does it occur?

E.   List the substances absorbed from the stomach.

F.   Answer the following concerning mixing and emptying actions.

1.   What is chyme, and how is it produced?

2.   What factors affect the rate at which the stomach empties?

3.   What is the enterogastric reflex, and how does it affect emptying?

4.   Describe vomiting, include the stimuli for this reflex.

17.6 Pancreas

A.   Answer the following regarding the structure of the pancreas.

1.   Where is the pancreas located?

2.   What cells and features assist the pancreas with its function?

B.   Answer the following concerning pancreatic juice.
1.   Describe the action of the following pancreatic enzymes:

amylase

lipase

trypsin

chymotrypsin

carboxypeptidase

2.   What activates the protein digesting enzymes, and how does this protect the pancreas?

3.   Describe acute pancreatitis.

4.   What substance makes the pancreatic juice alkaline, and why is this important?

C.   Answer the following regarding the regulation of pancreatic secretions.
1.   Describe the neural mechanisms that regulate pancreatic secretion, include when stimulation occurs.

2.   What stimulates the release of cholecystokinin, and how does it affect pancreatic juice?

3.   What triggers release of secretin?

17.7 Liver

A.   Answer the following concerning the structure of the liver.
1.   Describe the location and structure of the liver.

2.   Describe circulation through the liver.

B. Fill in the following table regarding the liver's functions.

General Function	Specific Function
Carbohydrate Metabolism	
Lipid Metabolism	
Protein Metabolism	
Storage	
Blood Filtering	
Detoxification	
Secretion (Digestion)	

C. Describe the six types of hepatitis. Be sure to include the mode of transmission of each type.

D. Answer the following questions concerning the composition of bile.
    1. What all is found in bile? Which substances have digestive functions?

    2. Bile pigments, bilirubin, and biliverdin are the breakdown products of _____.
    3. What causes jaundice?

E. Answer the following questions about the gallbladder.
    1. Where is the gallbladder located and what is its function?

    2. Describe the ducts between the gallbladder and the duodenum. Include a discussion of the sphincters.

    3. How are gallstones formed?

F. How is the release of bile regulated?

G. What are the functions of bile salts, and how do they assist with fat absorption?

200

17.8 Small Intestine

A. Answer the following regarding the small intestine and its parts.

1. Name and locate the three portions of the small intestine.

2. Describe the differences in the three regions.

3. The peritoneal membrane that forms a membranous apron over abdominal contents is the _____.

B. Answer the following regarding the structures of the small intestinal wall.

1. Label the structures in the following illustration.

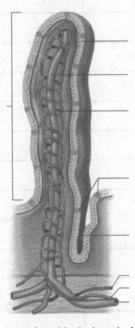

2. Assign functions to the cells and features found in the intestinal wall.

C. Answer the following regarding the secretions of the small intestines.

1. Describe the fluid released by the intestinal glands.

2. Name the enzymes produced by the cells of the intestinal mucosa.

D. Answer the following regarding the regulation of small intestinal secretions.

1. What are the stimuli for the release of secretions?

2. What controls the secretions of the small intestines?

E. Fill in the following table of the major digestive enzymes.

Enzyme	Source	Digestive Action
Salivary Enzyme		
Salivary Amylase		
Gastric Enzymes		
Pepsin		
Gastric Lipase		
Pancreatic Enzymes		
Pancreatic Amylase		
Pancreatic Lipase		
Trypsin and Chymotrypsin		
Carboxypeptidase		
Nucleases		
Intestinal Enzymes		
Peptidase		
Sucrase, Maltase and Lactase		
Intestinal Lipase		
Enterokinase		

F. Answer the following concerning absorption in the small intestine.
   1. Fill in the following table regarding intestinal absorption of nutrients.

Nutrient	Absorption Mechanism	Means of Circulation
Monosaccharides		
Amino Acids		
Fatty Acids and Glycerol		
Electrolytes		
Water		

2. Describe fat absorption. Begin with the role of chylomicrons and describe their fate in the bloodstream.

3. Name some of the causes of malabsorption and describe what happens.

G. Answer the following concerning the movements of the small intestine.
   1. a. The normal movements of the small intestine are _____ and _____ movements.
      b. The major mixing movement is _____.
   2. How are these movements regulated?

   3. The result of peristaltic rush is _____.
   4. What separates the small and large intestines? How is this structure controlled?

17.9 Large Intestine

A. Label the parts of the large intestine.

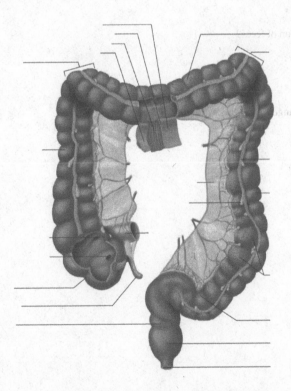

B. How does the structure of the large intestine differ from that of the small intestine?

C. Answer these questions concerning the functions of the large intestine.
   1. What are the digestive functions of the large intestines?

   2. How is the rate of mucus secretion controlled?

3. What is the function of mucus?

4. What substances are absorbed in the large intestine, and what transport mechanisms are used?

5. What is the function of the bacteria in the colon?

D. Answer the following concerning the movements of the large intestine.
1. Describe the movements of the large intestine.

2. List the events of the defecation reflex.

E. What is the composition of feces?

17.10 Life-Span Changes

A. Describe life-span changes in the following parts of the digestive system.

mouth

esophagus

stomach

small intestine

large intestine

pancreas

liver

gallbladder

Clinical Focus Questions

Your grandmother is 80 years old, and both she and your grandfather describe themselves as being in excellent health. Your grandmother runs the household for the two of them as she has always done, including preparing all the meals. Your grandmother tells you that both your grandparents have had some bowel "irregularity" lately and asks you to recommend a laxative. Based on your knowledge of the alimentary tube, what information would you need from your grandparents and what advice would you give them?

When you have completed the study activities to your satisfaction, retake the mastery test and compare your performance with your initial attempt. If there are still areas you do not understand, repeat the appropriate study activities.

OVERVIEW

We begin this chapter by discussing the fate of all the nutrients that have been absorbed after the digestive process. You will learn of common dietary sources for carbohydrates, lipids, and proteins and what the fates of these macronutrients are when they enter the body (Learning Outcomes 1–6). You will learn the meaning of nitrogen balance and what causes imbalances (Learning Outcome 7). You will learn about energy balance, energy value of food, factors that affect individual energy requirements, desirable weight, and how your consumption of nutrients is regulated (Learning Outcomes 8–12). You will also examine the role for micronutrients in your diet, being able to distinguish between the different classes of vitamins and what bodily processes they influence (Learning Outcome 13). You should be able to distinguish between vitamins and minerals as well as learn the functions for major and trace minerals (Learning Outcomes 14 and 15). You will end the chapter by looking at what constitutes an adequate diet, what causes primary and secondary malnutritions, and what the influence of aging is on the processing of nutrients (Learning Outcomes 16–18).

Knowledge of what foods to select and in what quantities provides a firm foundation for the study of nutrition and maintenance of health throughout your life.

LEARNING OUTCOMES

After you have studied this chapter, you should be able to
18.1 Carbohydrates
    1. List the major sources of carbohydrates.
    2. Describe how cells use carbohydrates.
18.2 Lipids
    3. List the major sources of lipids.
    4. Describe how cells use lipids.
18.3 Proteins
    5. List the major sources of proteins.
    6. Describe how cells use proteins.
    7. Identify examples of positive and negative nitrogen balances.
18.4 Energy Expenditures
    8. Explain how energy values of foods are determined.
    9. Explain the factors that affect an individual's energy requirements.
    10. Contrast the physiological impact of positive and negative energy balances.
    11. Explain what *desirable weight* means.
18.5 Appetite Control
    12. Explain how hormones control appetite.
18.6 Vitamins
    13. List the fat-soluble and water-soluble vitamins and summarize the general functions of each vitamin.
18.7 Minerals
    14. Distinguish between a vitamin and a mineral.
    15. List the major minerals and trace elements, and summarize the general functions of each.
18.8 Healthy Eating
    16. Describe an adequate diet.
    17. Distinguish between primary and secondary malnutritions.
18.9 Life-Span Changes
    18. List the factors that may lead to inadequate nutrition later in life.

FOCUS QUESTION

What factors would you need to measure or know about so you could design a diet that will meet but not exceed a person's requirements for energy, growth, and repair?

MASTERY TEST

Now take the mastery test. Do not guess. Some questions may have more than one correct answer. As soon as you complete the test, check your answers and correct any mistakes. Note your successes and failures so that you can reread the chapter to meet your learning needs.

1. List the macronutrients.

2. List the micronutrients.

3. Nutrients, such as amino acids and fatty acids, that are necessary for health but cannot be synthesized in adequate amounts by the body are called _____ _____.

4. A protein hormone secreted by adipocytes that regulates fatty acid catabolism is _____.

5. The hypothalamic substance that regulates the sensations of satiety and hunger is
   a. cholecystokinin.
   b. neuropeptide Y.
   c. ghrelin.
   d. leptin.

6. Carbohydrates are ingested in foods such as
   a. meat and seafood.
   b. bread and pasta.
   c. butter and margarine.
   d. bacon.

7. A carbohydrate that cannot be broken down by human digestive enzymes and that facilitates muscle activity in the alimentary tube is _____.

8. Energy is released from glucose in a process called _____.

9. Glucose can be stored as glycogen in the
   a. blood plasma.
   b. muscles.
   c. adipose.
   d. liver.

10. The organ most dependent on an uninterrupted supply of glucose is the
    a. heart.
    b. liver.
    c. adrenal gland.
    d. brain.

11. The estimated daily amount of carbohydrate needed to avoid utilization of fats and proteins for energy sources is
    a. 30–50 grams.
    b. 125–175 grams.
    c. 50–275 grams.
    d. 300–350 grams.

12. The most common dietary lipids are _____.

13. An essential fatty acid that cannot be synthesized by the body is _____ _____.

14. When there is an excess of acetyl CoA molecules formed from beta oxidation, what are they converted to?
    a. glucose
    b. ketones
    c. amino acids
    d. phospholipids

15. The primary physiological function of fats is to
    a. provide absorption of fat-soluble vitamins.
    b. conserve heat.
    c. provide material for the synthesis of hormones.
    d. supply energy.

16. A lipid that furnishes molecular components for the synthesis of sex hormones and some adrenal hormones is _____.

17. Although the amounts and types of fats needed for optimal health are unknown, it is generally believed that the average American diet contains (too much/too little) fat.

18. Proteins function as
    a. enzymes that regulate metabolic reactions.
    b. promoters of calcium absorption.
    c. energy supplies.
    d. structural materials in cells.

19. Proteins are absorbed and transported to cells as _____ _____.

20. A protein that contains adequate amounts of the essential amino acids is called a _____ protein.

21. Does statement a explain statement b?
    a. Carbohydrates are used before other nutrients as an energy source.
    b. Carbohydrates have a protein-sparing effect.

207

22. The balance between gain and loss of protein in the body is characterized by
    a. nitrogen balance.
    b. homeostasis.
    c. optimal nutrition.
    d. the amount used for cellular respiration.

23. Protein requirements are relatively high during
    a. pregnancy.
    b. young adulthood.
    c. nursing an infant.
    d. old age.

24. The amount of potential energy contained in a food is expressed as _____.

25. The rate the body at rest expends energy is called the _____ _____ _____.

26. The resting body's expenditure of energy is expected to increase in which of the following situations?
    a. rise in body temperature above 100°F
    b. decreased levels of thyroxine
    c. weight loss sufficient to affect body surface area
    d. increase in room temperature

27. To lose excess weight, a person must create a _____ energy balance.

28. Tables of desirable weights are based on
    a. longevity within a population.
    b. estimated muscle mass.
    c. average weight of people 25 to 30 years of age.
    d. computation of amount of adipose tissue.

29. Vitamins A, D, E, and K are _____ soluble.

30. Which of the following statements about vitamin A is *not* true?
    a. Vitamin A is found only in foods of animal origin.
    b. Children are less likely to develop vitamin A rhodopsin.
    c. Vitamin A can be synthesized by the body from carotenes.
    d. Vitamin A is essential for the synthesis of deficiency than adults.

31. Megadoses of vitamin A taken by pregnant women may cause birth defects.
    a. True
    b. False

32. Vitamin D₃ is produced by exposure of 7-dehydrocholesterol in the skin to _____.

33. Exposure to excessive amounts of vitamin D will cause
    a. rickets.
    b. osteomalacia.
    c. calcification of soft tissue.
    d. osteopenia.

34. Vitamin E is found in highest concentrations in the
    a. bone.
    b. muscle.
    c. central nervous system.
    d. pituitary and adrenal glands.

35. The vitamin essential for normal blood clotting is
    a. vitamin C.
    b. vitamin K.
    c. vitamin E.
    d. vitamin B₁₂.

36. Which of the B-complex vitamins can be synthesized from tryptophan by the body?
    a. niacin
    b. thiamine
    c. riboflavin
    d. pyridoxine

37. Which of the following B-complex vitamins is required for pyruvic acid to enter the citric acid cycle?
    a. B₁ or thiamine
    b. B₂ or riboflavin
    c. B₆
    d. B₁₂ or cyanobalamin

38. Which of the following statements are true of niacin?
    a. It can be synthesized from tryptophan.
    b. It is found only in vegetables and whole grains.
    c. Increased or excess amounts of niacin can cause a deep blush.
    d. It is unstable in heat and acids.

39. The requirement for B₆ varies in relation to the amounts of which of the following nutrients?
    a. carbohydrate
    b. protein
    c. fat
    d. cholesterol

40. The transport of which of the following is regulated by intrinsic factor and calcium?
    a. folic acid
    b. pantothenic acid
    c. cyanocobalamin
    d. biotin

41. A deficiency of which of the following vitamins can lead to a neural tube defect in a fetus?
    a. biotin
    b. ascorbic acid
    c. pantothenic acid
    d. folic acid

42. Which of the following is *not* a good source of vitamin C?
    a. potatoes
    b. tomatoes
    c. grains
    d. cabbage

43. The most abundant minerals in the body are _____ and _____.

44. Calcium is necessary for all but which of the following?
    a. blood coagulation
    b. muscle contraction
    c. color vision
    d. nerve impulse conduction

45. Which of the following is least likely to be a reason for potassium deficiency?
    a. diarrhea
    b. inadequate intake of potassium
    c. vomiting
    d. diuretic drugs

46. The blood concentration of sodium is regulated by the kidneys, which are influenced by the hormone _____.

47. Chlorine is usually ingested with _____.

48. The organelle most associated with magnesium is the
    a. cell membrane.
    b. Golgi apparatus.
    c. endoplasmic reticulum.
    d. mitochondrion.

49. Iron is associated with the body's ability to transport _____.

50. The best natural source(s) of iron is/are
    a. the liver.
    b. red meat.
    c. egg yolk.
    d. raisins.

51. What vitamin can increase the absorption of iron when ingested together?

52. A substance necessary for bone development, melanin production, and myelin formation is
    a. iron.
    b. iodine.
    c. copper.
    d. zinc.

53. The type of malnutrition that is due to poor food intake is _____ malnutrition.

54. Kwashiorkor is due to inadequate intake of
    a. calories.
    b. proteins.
    c. carbohydrates.
    d. fats.

55. Athletes should get the majority of their calories from
    a. proteins.
    b. carbohydrates.
    c. fats.
    d. vitamins.

STUDY ACTIVITIES

Definition of Word Parts

Define the following word parts used in this chapter.

bas-

calor-

carot-

lip-

mal-

-meter

nutri-

obes-

pell-

18.1 Carbohydrates

A.   Carbohydrates are _____ compounds that are used primarily to supply _____.

B.   Answer the following concerning carbohydrate sources.

   1.   In what forms are carbohydrates ingested?

   2.   In what forms are carbohydrates absorbed?

   3.   List the plant carbohydrates that provide fiber.

   4.   How do sugar substitutes sweeten with fewer calories?

C.   Answer the following concerning carbohydrate utilization.

   1.   Define *glycogenesis* and *glycogenolysis*. What happens to excess glucose that cannot be stored in the liver?

   2.   Why are carbohydrates essential to the production of nucleic acids?

   3.   What happens when the body is not supplied with its minimum carbohydrate requirement?

   4.   What cells are particularly dependent on a continuous supply of glucose?

D.   Answer the following concerning carbohydrate requirements.

   1.   What is the estimated daily requirement for carbohydrate?

   2.   What is the usual daily carbohydrate intake of Americans?

18.2 Lipids

A.   In what forms are lipids usually ingested?

B.   What are the sources of triglycerides, saturated and unsaturated fats, and cholesterol?

C.   Answer the following concerning the use of lipids.
1. Describe the process by which fatty acids are metabolized to produce energy.

2. Describe what happens when lipid molecules are synthesized by the liver.

3. Which fatty acid molecules cannot be made by the liver, and what are they needed for in the body?

4. Describe how the body uses and transports cholesterol and triglycerides.

D.   Answer these questions concerning lipid requirements.
1. What is the estimated daily requirement for lipids?

2. In the average American's diet, what amount of calories is supplied by fat?

18.3 Proteins

A.   Answer these questions concerning protein.
1. In what form is protein transported and utilized by cells?

2   How are proteins used by the body?

3. Describe deamination. What waste product is produced by this process?

B.   Answer the following questions concerning protein sources.
1. What is an essential amino acid? List the essential amino acids.

2. What is the difference between a complete protein and an incomplete protein?

3. Why must various sources of vegetable protein be combined in the diet?

C.   Answer the following regarding nitrogen balance.
        1.   An individual whose rate of protein synthesis equals his or her rate of protein breakdown is said to be in a state of
              _____ _____.

        2.   What is a negative nitrogen balance and what are the causes?

        3.   What is a positive nitrogen balance and what are some reasons for this?

D.   Answer these questions concerning protein requirements.
        1.   What factors influence protein requirements?

        2.   How is the protein requirement for a normal adult determined?

18.4 Energy Expenditures

A.   Answer these questions concerning the energy values of foods.
        1.   What are a calorie and a kilocalorie?

        2.   Compare the energy values of a gram of carbohydrate, protein, and fat.

B.   Answer the following concerning energy requirements.
        1.   What is the basal metabolic rate (BMR)?

        2.   What factors affect the BMR?

C.   When caloric intake in food equals caloric output in the form of energy, an individual is said to be in a state of
        _____ _____.

D.   Answer these questions concerning desirable weight.
        1.   What is desirable weight?

        2.   What factors are used to determine body mass index (BMI)?

        3.   How is obesity treated?

18.5 Appetite Control

A.   What is appetite and what can influence this?

B.   Fill in the table regarding the substances that control appetite.

Substance	Site of Secretion	Function
Insulin		
Leptin		
Neuropeptide Y		
Gherlin		

18.6 Vitamins

A.   Answer these questions concerning vitamins.

1.   What is a vitamin?

2.   What are the general characteristics of fat-soluble vitamins and which vitamins are fat-soluble?

3.   What are the general characteristics of water-soluble vitamins and which vitamins are water-soluble?

B.   Fill in the following table regarding the fat-soluble vitamins.

Vitamin	Characteristics	Functions	Sources and RDAs for Adults
Vitamin A			
Vitamin D			
Vitamin E			
Vitamin K			

C.   Fill in the following table regarding the water-soluble vitamins.

Vitamin	Characteristics	Functions	Sources and RDAs for Adults
Thiamine (Vitamin B₁)			
Riboflavin (Vitamin B₂)			
Niacin (Vitamin B₃ and Nicotinic Acid)			
Pantothenic Acid (Vitamin B₅)			
Vitamin B₆			
Biotin (Vitamin B₇)			
Folacin (Vitamin B₉ and Folic Acid)			
Cyanocobalamin (Vitamin B₁₂)			
Ascorbic Acid (Vitamin C)			

18.7 Minerals

A.   Describe the general characteristics of minerals.

B.   Fill in the following table regarding the major minerals.

Mineral	Distribution	Functions	Sources and RDAs for Adults
Calcium (Ca)			
Phosphorus (P)			
Potassium (K)			
Sulfur (S)			
Sodium (Na)			
Chorine (Cl)			
Magnesium (Mg)			

C.   Answer the following concerning trace elements.

   1.   What is a trace element?

   2.   Fill in the table regarding the trace elements.

Trace Element	Distribution	Functions	Sources and RDAs for Adults
Iron (Fe)			
Manganese (Mn)			
Copper (Cu)			
Iodine (I)			
Cobalt (Co)			
Zinc (Zn)			
Fluorine (F)			
Selenium (Se)			
Chromium (Cr)			

   3.   What substances are considered dietary supplements?

   4.   What might make taking dietary supplements dangerous?

18.8 Healthy Eating

A.   Answer the following regarding healthy eating in general.

   1.   What is an adequate diet?

   2.   What are the RDAs, and how are they determined?

   3.   Describe the food pyramid, and how does this help you understand nutrition?

B.   Answer the following regarding malnutrition.

1.   What is primary malnutrition, and what causes this?

2.   What is secondary malnutrition, and what causes this?

C.   Answer the following regarding starvation.

1.   Compare marasmus and kwashiorkor.

2.   Compare anorexia nervosa and bulimia.

18.9 Life-Span Changes

What factors contribute to a person's changing nutritional needs as he or she ages?

Clinical Focus Questions

A close friend is planning to conceive and she has a BMI of 27. What advice would you give her regarding weight management related to conception and what changes would she need to make to her diet and activities while pregnant?

When you have completed the study activities to your satisfaction, retake the mastery test and compare your performance with your initial attempt. If there are still areas you do not understand, repeat the appropriate study activities.

OVERVIEW

Your respiratory system comprises structures that take up oxygen from the atmosphere and excrete carbon dioxide from the body. This process of gas exchange is critical for cellular metabolism and therefore your survival. This chapter begins by describing the location and function of the organs of the respiratory system as well as explaining why we breathe (Learning Outcomes 1–4). You will identify and distinguish respiratory and nonrespiratory air movements, learn how to measure respiratory volumes, and calculate capacities and alveolar ventilation (Learning Outcomes 5–8). You should be able to explain how normal breathing is controlled and what factors affect this process (Learning Outcomes 9 and 10). You will read about the process of gas exchange in the lungs and the physical factors that drive it, you will read about how gas is transported in the blood, and you will reexamine the role of the pulmonary and systemic circuits in the efficient exchange and delivery of gases (Learning Outcomes 11–14). Lastly, as usual, you will note the life-span changes that occur in this system (Learning Outcome 15).

There are four events in respiration: (1) exchange of gas with the external environment, (2) diffusion of gas across the respiratory membrane, (3) transport of gas to and from the cell, and (4) diffusion of gas across the cell membrane for utilization of oxygen by the cell. An understanding of all these events and how they interact is basic to understanding how cells can capture energy necessary for life.

LEARNING OUTCOMES

After you have studied this chapter, you should be able to

19.1   Overview of the Respiratory System
    1.   Identify the general functions of the respiratory system.
    2.   Explain why respiration is necessary for cellular survival.
19.2   Organs of the Respiratory System
    3.   Name and describe the locations of the organs of the respiratory system.
    4.   Describe the functions of each organ of the respiratory system.
19.3   Breathing Mechanism
    5.   Explain how inspiration and expiration are accomplished.
    6.   Describe each of the respiratory air volumes and capacities.
    7.   Show how alveolar ventilation rate is calculated.
    8.   List several nonrespiratory air movements, and explain how each occurs.
19.4   Control of Breathing
    9.   Locate the respiratory areas, and explain control of normal breathing.
    10.   Discuss how various factors affect breathing.
19.5   Alveolar Gas Exchanges
    11.   Describe the structure and function of the respiratory membrane.
    12.   Explain the importance of partial pressure in diffusion of gases.
19.6   Gas Transport
    13.   Explain how the blood transports oxygen and carbon dioxide.
    14.   Describe gas exchange in the pulmonary and systemic circuits.
19.7   Life-Span Changes
    15.   Describe the effects of aging on the respiratory system.

FOCUS QUESTION

As you are taking laundry out of the dryer, you start to sneeze as dust from the dryer hits you in the face. How and why would this occur? What benefit is there to these types of reflexes? The phone rings in the kitchen and you run up a flight of stairs to answer it. How does the respiratory system extract oxygen from the atmosphere and give off waste gases from the body so that your body can adjust to such different levels of activity?

MASTERY TEST

Now take the mastery test. Do not guess. Some questions may have more than one correct answer. As soon as you complete the test, check your answers and correct any mistakes. Note your successes and failures so that you can reread the chapter to meet your learning needs.

1. The process of exchanging gases between the atmosphere and body cells is _____.

2. Exchange of carbon dioxide and oxygen by cells is part of
   a. ventilation.
   b. breathing.
   c. internal respiration.
   d. transport of gases.

3. The gas exchange made possible by respiration enables cells to capture some of the _____ in food molecules.

4. Carbon dioxide combines with water to form _____ _____. An excess of CO_2 will cause the blood pH to (increase/decrease).

5. Which of the following organs is/are part of the upper respiratory tract?
   a. lungs
   b. pharynx
   c. bronchi
   d. larynx

6. Match the functions in the first column with the appropriate part of the nose in the second column.
   1. warm incoming air
   2. trap particulate matter in the air
   3. prevent infection
   4. moisten air
   5. move nasal secretions to pharynx

   a. mucous membrane
   b. mucus
   c. cilia

7. Which of the following is/are the result of cigarette smoking?
   a. paralysis of respiratory cilia
   b. production of increased amounts of mucus
   c. easier access to respiratory tissue by pathogenic organisms
   d. loss of elasticity in the walls of respiratory passages

8. Does statement a explain statement b?
   a. The sinuses are air-filled spaces in bones of the skull and face.
   b. Inflammation of the nose can lead to fluid being trapped in the sinuses.

9. The pharynx is the cavity behind the mouth extending from the _____ _____ to the _____.

10. The portions of the larynx concerned with preventing foreign objects from entering the trachea are the
    a. arytenoid cartilages.
    b. glottis.
    c. epiglottis.
    d. hyoid bone.

11. The portion of the larynx visible in the neck as the Adam's apple is the _____ _____.

12. The pitch of the voice is controlled by
    a. changing the tension of the vocal cords.
    b. changing the force of the air passing through the larynx.
    c. opening the vocal cords.
    d. increasing the volume of air passing through the larynx.

13. The trachea is maintained in an open position by
    a. cartilaginous rings.
    b. the amount of collagen in the wall of the trachea.
    c. the tone of smooth muscle in the wall of the trachea.
    d. the continuous flow of air through the trachea.

14. A temporary opening in the trachea made to bypass an obstruction is a _____.

15. The right and left bronchi arise from the trachea at the
    a. suprasternal notch.
    b. manubrium of the sternum.
    c. fifth thoracic vertebra.
    d. eighth intercostal space.

16. The smallest branches of the bronchial tree are the _____.

17. As the lumen of the branches of the bronchial tree decreases, the amount of cartilage (increases/decreases).

18. The instrument used to examine the trachea and bronchial tree and to remove foreign objects aspirated into air passages is a _____ _____.

19. The type of epithelium found in the alveoli is
    a. simple squamous.
    b. ciliated columnar.
    c. pseudostratified.
    d. cuboidal.

20. Blood is pumped out of the body and across a gas-permeable membrane that adds oxygen and removes carbon dioxide in
    a. artificial respiration.
    b. extracorporeal membrane oxygenation.
    c. mechanical ventilation.
    d. intravascular oxygenation.

21. Each lung is entered on its medial surface by a bronchus and blood vessels in a region called the _____.

22. The _____ lung is composed of superior, inferior, and middle lobes.

23. The serous membrane covering the lungs is the _____ _____.

24. The serous membrane covering the inner wall of the thoracic cavity is the _____ _____.

25. Inspiration occurs after the diaphragm _____, thus (increasing/decreasing) the size of the thorax and (increasing/decreasing) the pressure within the thorax.

26. The other muscles that act to change the size of the thorax during normal respiration are the
    a. sternocleidomastoids.
    b. pectorals.
    c. external intercostals.
    d. latissimus dorsi.

27. Expansion of the lungs during inspiration is assisted by the surface tension of fluid in the _____ cavity.

28. The surface tension of fluid in the alveoli is decreased by a secretion, _____, that prevents collapse of the alveoli.

29. The force responsible for expiration comes mainly from
    a. contraction of intercostal muscles.
    b. change in the surface tension within alveoli.
    c. elastic recoil of tissues in the lung and thoracic wall.
    d. contraction of abdominal muscles to push the diaphragm upward.

30. The ease with which lungs can be expanded in response to pressure changes during breathing is called _____.

31. The pressure in the pleural cavity is
    a. greater than atmospheric pressure.
    b. less than atmospheric pressure.
    c. the same as atmospheric pressure.
    d. irrelevant to the process of respiration.

32. Respiratory air volumes are measured by an instrument called a/an _____.

33. The amount of air that enters and leaves the lungs during a normal, quiet respiration is the
    a. vital capacity.
    b. respiratory cycle.
    c. total lung capacity.
    d. tidal volume.

34. Respiratory volumes are used to calculate _____ _____.

35. The anatomical dead space is composed of the passageways of the _____, _____, and _____.

36. In a normal individual, the anatomical dead space and the physiological dead space are (equal/not equal).

37. The amount of new air that reaches the alveoli and is available for gas exchange is represented by the _____ _____ rate.

38. Coughing, laughing, and yawning are examples of _____ _____ _____.

39. Because of normal respiratory physiology, people with bronchial asthma will initially have difficulty with
    a. inspiration.
    b. expiration.
    c. inspiration and expiration.

40. The pathological events of emphysema include all of the following *except*
    a. loss of elasticity in alveolar tissue.
    b. loss of interalveolar walls, so that larger chambers form.
    c. narrowing of the lumen of the bronchi.
    d. loss of capillary network.

41. Normal breathing is controlled by the respiratory center located in the _____ _____.

42. Changes in the rate of breathing are controlled by the
    a. dorsal respiratory group.
    b. ventral respiratory group.
    c. pneumotaxic area.
    d. respiratory group of the pons.

219

43. Activation of the _____ _____ _____ controls the action of the internal intercostals and abdominal muscles.

44. The Hering-Breuer reflexes are activated by
   a. stretch receptors in bronchioles and alveoli.
   b. an increase in hydrogen ions.
   c. a decrease in oxygen saturation.
   d. a sudden fall in blood pressure.

45. The most potent stimulus to increase respiratory rate and depth is to increase the blood concentration of _____ _____.

46. Hyperventilation leads to dizziness because of
   a. an increase in blood pressure.
   b. a decrease in heart rate.
   c. generalized vasoconstriction in cerebral arterioles.
   d. a decrease in blood pH.

47. Exercise provokes an increase in respiratory rate due to
   a. increased CO_2 levels.
   b. generalized vasoconstriction.
   c. stimulation of proprioceptors in joints.
   d. stimulation of the respiratory center by the cerebral cortex.

48. A phagocyte that moves through alveolar pores is a _____ _____.

49. The respiratory membrane consists of a single layer of epithelial cells and basement membrane from a/an _____ and a/an _____.

50. The rate at which a gas diffuses from one area to another is determined by differences in _____ in the two areas.

51. The pressure of each gas within a mixture of gases is known as its _____ _____.

52. Pneumonia, tuberculosis, and atelectasis present similar problems in that they
   a. decrease the surface available for diffusion of gases.
   b. obstruct the flow of air into the lungs.
   c. diminish blood circulation to the lungs.
   d. destroy surfactant.

53. Oxygen is transported to cells by combining with _____.

54. Oxygen is released in greater amounts as carbon dioxide levels and temperature (increase/decrease).

55. Carbon monoxide interferes with oxygen transport by binding to _____.

56. The largest amount of carbon dioxide is transported
   a. dissolved in blood.
   b. combined with hemoglobin.
   c. as bicarbonate.
   d. as carbonic anhydrase.

57. As individuals age, the susceptibility to infection (increases/decreases).

STUDY ACTIVITIES

Definition of Word Parts

Define the following word parts used in this chapter.

alveol-

bronch-

carcin-

carin-

cric-

220

epi-

exhal-

hem-

inhal-

phren-

tuber-

19.1 Overview of the Respiratory System

Answer the following regarding the purpose and general functions of the respiratory system.

1.   What term is used for the entire process of exchanging gases between the atmosphere and body cells?

2.   List the events of respiration and define what happens in each.

3.   Why must we get oxygen from the atmosphere, what is it used for in the body?

4.   Where does the carbon dioxide come from? Why must we excrete it?

19.2 Organs of the Respiratory System

A.   In the accompanying drawing, label the respiratory structures.

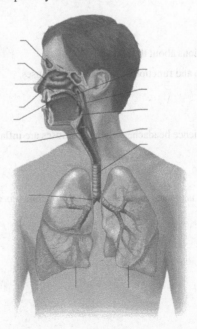

B.   Answer the following regarding the nasal cavity.

1.   Match the respiratory system functions in the first column with the appropriate terms in the second column.

1.   entrap dust   a.   mucous membrane

2.   supports membranes and increases surface area   b.   mucus

3.   warm and humidify air entering the nose   c.   nasal conchae

4.   provide movement to mucous layer   d.   cilia

2.   Label the following figure of the nasal cavity.

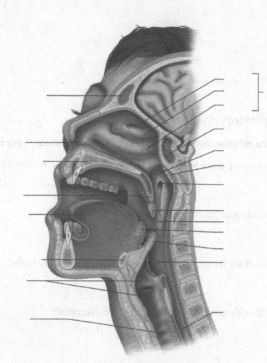

3.   What is the function of the cilia and what happens to all the mucus produced?

C.   Answer the following questions about the sinuses.

1.   Describe the structure and function of the paranasal sinuses.

2.   Why do people experience headaches when the sinuses are inflamed?

D.   Describe where the pharynx is located and name the three regions it is divided into?

E.   Answer the following concerning the larynx.

    1.   Label the structures in the accompanying drawings of the larynx.

Anterior View

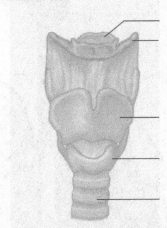

Posterior View

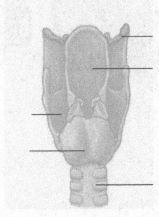

    2.   The structures of the larynx that help close the glottis during swallowing are the _____ and the _____ _____ _____.

    3.   The structures of the larynx that produce sound are the _____ _____ _____.

    4.   The _____ of the voice is due to the tension of the vocal cords.

    5.   The _____ of the voice is due to the force of the air passing over the vocal cords.

F.   Answer the following regarding the trachea.

    1.   The trachea is prevented from collapsing by the presence of _____ _____ that are C-shaped.

    2.   Why are these C-shaped instead of complete rings and what other tissues would you find in the trachea?

    3.   What is a tracheostomy?

Answer the following concerning the bronchial tree.

    1.   On the accompanying drawing, label the different structures.

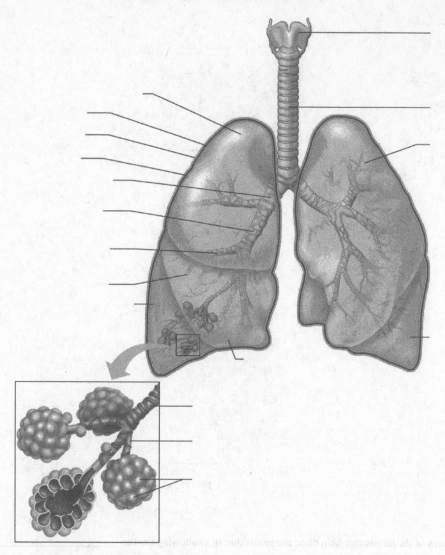

    2.   List the branches of the bronchial tree starting with the main or primary bronchi.

    3.   How do the structures of the bronchial tree change as the bronchi become smaller?

    4.   Differentiate between the functions of the alveoli and those of the respiratory tubes.

5. The trachea and bronchial tree can be seen with an instrument called a/an _____ _____.

6. List some of the ways to assist a person's survival when they have stopped breathing on their own.

H. Answer the following concerning the lungs.

1. The right lung has _____ lobes, the left lung has _____ lobes.

2. Describe the pleural membranes and what the role or significance of the pleural cavity is.

3. What does a lobule consist of?

4. The bronchi enter the right and left lungs at the _____.

19.3 Breathing Mechanism

A. Answer the following concerning inspiration.

1. What is atmospheric pressure and how does this it compare to pressure inside the lungs at rest?

2. What does Boyle's law state?

3. What muscles change the volume of the thoracic cavity and how does it change?

4. List the events of inspiration in order beginning with stimulation of the phrenic nerve.

5. Describe the role of surfactant in the alveoli.

6. What muscles can be used in forceful inspiration?

7. What is lung compliance?

B. Answer the following regarding the process of expiration.

1. What is the "driving force" for normal expiration and what is the diaphragm's role in expiration?

2. What effect do these actions have on pressure and how does this influence expiring?

3. What muscles can be used if forceful expiration is necessary?

C.   Match the terms regarding respiratory volumes and capacities.

1. inspiratory reserve volume

a. volume moved in or out of the lungs during quiet respiration

2. expiratory reserve volume

b. volume that can be inhaled during forced breathing in addition to tidal volume

3. residual volume

c. volume that can be exhaled in addition to tidal volume

4. vital capacity

d. volume that remains in the lungs at all times

5. total lung capacity

e. maximum air that can be exhaled after taking the deepest possible breath

6. tidal volume

f. maximum volume of air the lungs can hold

7. *Given the following volumes:*

inspiratory reserve 2,500 cc

expiratory reserve 1,000 cc

residual volume   1,100 cc

tidal volume   550 cc

Calculate the following lung capacities:

vital capacity

inspiratory capacity functional residual capacity

total lung capacity

8. Describe physiological dead space and anatomical dead space.

9. Under what circumstances are these values not the same?

D.   Answer the following questions concerning alveolar ventilation.

1. The volume of new atmospheric air moved into the respiratory passage each minute is called the _____ _____.

2. How do you calculate the alveolar minute volume?

3. Increasing the depth of breathing is more effective than increasing the rate of breathing, why is this true?

E.   Fill in the following table regarding the nonrespiratory air movements.

Air Movement	Mechanism	Function
Coughing		
Sneezing		
Laughing		
Crying		
Hiccuping		
Yawning		
Speech		

F.   How do the following disorders interfere with ventilation?

bronchial asthma

emphysema

19.4 Control of Breathing

A.   Answer the following concerning the respiratory areas.

1.   In what part of the brain are respiratory areas located?

2.   What are the general functions of these areas?

3.   Compare the dorsal respiratory group and the ventral respiratory group of the medullary respiratory center.

4.   What are the functions of the pontine respiratory center?

5.   Compare sleep apnea in infants and adults.

B.   Explain the concept of partial pressure of gas.

C.   Answer the following regarding the factors affecting breathing

1.   What chemical factors affect breathing?

2.   Describe the central chemoreceptors, include where they are found and what they are stimulated by.

3.   Describe the peripheral chemoreceptors, include where they are found and what they are stimulated by.

4.   How does the inflation reflex work and what does it protect against?

5.   List other factors that influence breathing rate and depth.

6.   What is hyperventilation and what does it cause?

D.   Answer these questions concerning exercise and breathing rate.

1.   What factors influence the breathing rate during exercise?

2.   What systems must respond to the cells' need for oxygen?

19.5 Alveolar Gas Exchanges

A.   Answer the following regarding the alveoli.

1.   What is the function of alveolar pores?

2.   What is the function of alveolar macrophages?

B.   Identify the layers of cells that make up the respiratory membrane.

C.   Answer the following concerning diffusion through the respiratory membrane.

    1.   What determines the direction and rate at which gases diffuse from one area to another?

    2.   Describe the diffusion of oxygen into the blood and carbon dioxide into the alveoli.

D.   Describe the effects of pneumonia, tuberculosis, atelectasis, and adult respiratory distress syndrome on alveolar gas exchange.

E.   How and why does high altitude affect gas exchange?

19.6 Gas Transport

A.   Answer the following concerning oxygen transport.

    1.   Describe how oxygen binds to hemoglobin.

    2.   Why is oxygen released to the cell?

    3.   What factors affect how much oxygen is released from hemoglobin to tissues?

    4.   A gas that interferes with oxygen transport by forming a stable bond with hemoglobin is _____ _____.

B.   Answer the following concerning carbon dioxide transport.

    1.   Describe the three ways that carbon dioxide can be transported from the cells to the lungs.

    2.   The diffusion of bicarbonate ions out of red blood cells into plasma and the diffusion of chloride ions from plasma into red blood cells to maintain ionic balance are known as _____ _____.

    3.   In the lungs, what happens to cause the carbon dioxide to leave the blood and enter the alveoli?

19.7 Life-Span Changes

1.   Describe the effects of aging on the respiratory system.

2.   Describe the consequences of environmental factors on the respiratory system over a lifetime.

Clinical Focus Questions

George L. is a 60-year-old carpenter. He smoked two packs of cigarettes a day until one year ago when he stopped smoking. Following a hospitalization for pneumonia, George was told he had emphysema.

A.   How will George L.'s emphysema affect his lifestyle?

B.   What might you suggest to help him cope with these changes?

When you have completed the study activities to your satisfaction, retake the mastery test and compare your performance with your initial attempt. If there are still areas you do not understand, repeat the appropriate study activities.

OVERVIEW

In this chapter, you will learn about the urinary system, which plays a vital role in maintaining the internal chemistry by excreting nitrogenous waste products and any excess metabolites and by selectively excreting or retaining water and electrolytes. You will identify, locate, and describe the functions of the organs of the kidneys (Learning Outcomes 1–3). You will study the perfusion of this organ to understand its influence on the blood (Learning Outcome 4). You will study the structure and function of the nephron, which is the basic unit of function of the kidney (Learning Outcome 5). You will be able to explain how glomerular filtrate is produced and how its composition changes, discuss the role of tubular reabsorption in urine production, and identify the causes of changes in the osmotic concentration of glomerular filtrate in the renal tubule (Learning Outcomes 6–9). You will learn how urine composition is affected by tubular secretion and how urine formation and composition reflect the needs of the body (Learning Outcomes 10–12). You will then focus on what structures transport and store urine and how release of urine from the body is controlled (Learning Outcomes 13 and 14). You will complete your analysis by noting the changes in the components of the urinary system throughout life (Learning Outcome 15).

A study of the urinary system is basic to understanding how the body maintains its chemistry within very narrow limits.

LEARNING OUTCOMES

After you have studied this chapter, you should be able to

20.1 Overview of Urinary System
1. Name the organs of the urinary system and list their general functions.
20.2 Kidneys
2. Describe the locations of the kidneys and the structure of the kidney.
3. List the functions of the kidneys.
4. Trace the pathway of blood flow through the major vessels within a kidney.
5. Describe a nephron and explain the functions of its major parts.
20.3 Urine Formation
6. Explain how glomerular filtrate is produced and describe its composition.
7. Explain how various factors affect the rate of glomerular filtration and identify ways this rate is regulated.
8. Explain tubular reabsorption and its role in urine formation.
9. Identify the changes in the osmotic concentration of the glomerular filtrate as it passes through the renal tubule.
10. Explain tubular secretion and its role in urine formation.
11. Identify the characteristics of a countercurrent mechanism, and explain its role in concentrating the urine.
12. Explain how the final composition of urine contributes to homeostasis.
20.4 Storage and Elimination of Urine
13. Describe the structures of the ureters, urinary bladder, and urethra.
14. Explain how micturition occurs, and how it is controlled.
20.5 Life-Span Changes
15. Describe how the components of the urinary system change with age.

FOCUS QUESTION

It is 90°F and a perfect day for the beach. You spend most of the day on the beach, swimming and relaxing. You drink two liters of lemonade in the course of the day. This evening, you will be meeting friends at a local pub for sandwiches and beer. How do the kidneys help maintain the internal environment under such varied conditions?

MASTERY TEST

Now take the mastery test. Do not guess. Some questions may have more than one correct answer. As soon as you complete the test, check your answers and correct any mistakes. Note your successes and failures so that you can reread the chapter to meet your learning needs.

1. The organ(s) of the urinary system whose primary function is transport of urine is/are the
   a. kidney.
   b. urethra.
   c. ureters.
   d. bladder.

2. The kidneys are located
   a. within the abdominal cavity.
   b. between the twelfth thoracic and third lumbar vertebrae.
   c. posterior to the parietal peritoneum.
   d. just directly below the diaphragm.

3. The superior end of the ureters is expanded to form the funnel-like _____.

4. The small elevations that project into the minor calyx are called
   a. renal pyramids.
   b. the renal medulla.
   c. renal calyces.
   d. renal papillae.

5. The granular shell around the medulla of the kidney is the _____.

6. Which of the following are regulatory functions of the kidney?
   a. excretion of metabolic wastes from the blood
   b. control of red blood cell production
   c. regulation of blood pressure
   d. regulation of calcium absorption by activation of vitamin D

7. The direct blood supply to the nephrons is via the
   a. renal artery.
   b. interlobar artery.
   c. arcuate artery.
   d. afferent arterioles.

8. The structure of the renal corpuscle consists of the
   a. glomerulus.
   b. glomerular (Bowman's) capsule.
   c. descending limb of the nephron loop.
   d. proximal convoluted tubule.

9. Inflammation of the glomeruli is
   a. nephritis.
   b. glomerulonephritis.
   c. pyelonephritis.
   d. cystitis.

10. Blood leaves the capillary cluster of the renal corpuscle via the
    a. afferent arteriole.
    b. efferent arteriole.
    c. peritubular capillary system.
    d. renal vein.

11. The renal vein carries blood from the kidney and returns blood to the general circulation via the
    a. superior vena cava.
    b. internal iliac vein.
    c. inferior vena cava.
    d. portal vein.

12. The distal convoluted tubule empties urine into a/an _____.

13. The tall, densely packed cells at the end of the nephron loop that regulate glomerular filtration rate are known as
    _____.

14. The relatively high pressure in the glomerulus is due to
    a. the small diameter of the glomerular capillaries.
    b. the increased size of the smooth muscle in the venules that receive blood from the glomerulus.
    c. the large volume of blood that circulates through the kidney relative to other body parts.
    d. the smaller diameter of the efferent arteriole in comparison with the afferent arteriole.

15. The end product of kidney function is _____.

16. The transport mechanism used in the glomerulus is
    a. filtration.
    b. osmosis.
    c. active transport.
    d. diffusion.

17. The juxtaglomerular apparatus is important in the regulation of _____ _____ _____.

18. The filtrate formed in the glomerular capsule of the nephron is the same as blood plasma except for the presence of
    a. glucose.
    b. larger molecules of protein in plasma.
    c. bicarbonate ions.
    d. creatinine.

232

19. Pressures within in the blood are responsible for urine formation because _____ _____ _____ and _____ _____ are necessary for filtration to occur in the glomerulus.

20. Sympathetic nerve impulses can be expected to (increase/decrease/maintain) glomerular filtration rate when there is a slight decrease in blood pressure.

21. A significant fall in blood pressure, as during shock, causes an/a (increase/decrease) in glomerular filtration.

22. An increase in glomerular capsular hydrostatic pressure will (increase/decrease) the filtration rate.

23. Does statement a explain statement b? _____
    a. An increase in glomerular capsular hydrostatic pressure causes a decrease in the glomerular filtration rate.
    b. An enlarged prostate gland tends to decrease the amount of urine produced.

24. How much fluid filters through the glomerulus in a 24-hour period?
    a. 1.5 liters   c. 180 liters
    b. 200 mL   d. 10 liters

25. Which of the following substances is present in glomerular filtrate but not normally in urine?
    a. urea   c. potassium
    b. sodium   d. glucose

26. Which of the following substances is/are transported by osmosis throughout most of the renal tubule?
    a. glucose   c. plasma proteins
    b. water   d. amino acids

27. Substances such as creatinine, lactic acid, sodium, and potassium ions are reabsorbed in the
    a. proximal convoluted tubule.   c. descending limb of the nephron loop.
    b. distal convoluted tubule.   d. ascending limb of the nephron loop.

28. About 70% of the water, sodium, and other ions in glomerular filtrate are reabsorbed by the time the filtrate reaches the
    a. descending limb of the nephron loop.   c. distal convoluted tubule.
    b. proximal convoluted tubule.   d. renal pyramid.

29. The reabsorption of sodium and chloride ions in the distal convoluted tubules and the collecting duct is influenced by
    _____.

30. The mechanism that acts to continue sodium reabsorption from tubular fluid in the nephron loop and at the same time causes the fluid to become hypotonic to its surroundings is the _____ mechanism.

31. The permeability of the distal segment of the tubule to water is regulated by
    a. blood pressure.   c. aldosterone.
    b. antidiuretic hormone (ADH).   d. renin.

32. Urea is a by-product of _____ catabolism.

33. The mechanism by which greater amounts of a substance may be excreted in urine than were filtered from the plasma in the glomerulus is
    a. tubular absorption.   c. pinocytosis.
    b. active transport.   d. tubular secretion.

34. Which of the following substances enter(s) the urine using tubular secretion?
    a. lactic acid   c. amino acids
    b. hydrogen ions   d. potassium

35. Which of the following is/are not (a) normal constituent(s) of urine?
    a. urea   c. creatinine
    b. uric acid   d. ketones

36. The normal output of urine for an adult in one hour is _____ mL.
    a. 20–30   c. 40–50
    b. 30–40   d. 50–60

37. Tests of renal clearance of inulin and creatinine are used to provide information about
    a. renal blood flow.   c. tubular reabsorption.
    b. glomerular filtration.   d. tubular secretion.

38. Urine is conveyed from the kidney to the bladder via the _____.

233

39. Urine moves along the ureters via
    a. hydrostatic pressure.
    b. gravity.
    c. peristalsis.
    d. segmentation.

40. The ureterorenal reflex will (increase/decrease) urine production in situations in which urine flow from the kidney to the bladder is impeded.

41. The internal floor of the bladder has three openings in a triangular area called the _____.

42. The third layer of the bladder is composed of smooth muscle fibers and is called the _____ muscle.
    a. micturition
    b. detrusor
    c. urinary
    d. sympathetic

43. When stretch receptors in the bladder send impulses along the parasympathetic paths, the individual experiences a sensation known as _____.

44. The usual amount of urine in the bladder that will trigger a desire to urinate, is about _____ mL.

45. Which of the following structures is under conscious control?
    a. external urethral sphincter
    b. internal urethral sphincter
    c. detrusor muscle
    d. ureter muscle

46. In the female, the external urethral orifice is located anterior to the _____ and posterior to the _____.

STUDY ACTIVITIES

Definition of Word Parts

Define the following word parts that are used in this chapter.

af-

calyc-

cort-

cyst-

detrus-

glom-

juxta-

mict-

nephr-

papill-

prox-

ren-

trigon-

20.1 Overview of the Urinary System

A.   List the functions of the urinary system.

B.   Identify the parts of the urinary system in the accompanying drawing.

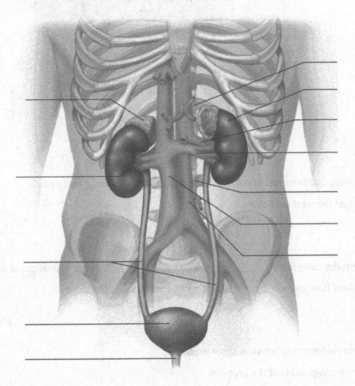

20.2 Kidneys

A.   Describe the precise locations of the kidneys.

B.   What are the functions of the kidney?

C.   Label the all the structures identified by lines in this drawing.

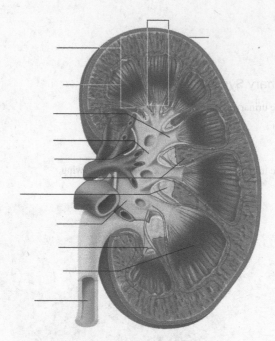

D.   Address the following questions and missing information regarding the renal blood vessels.

1.   From where do the renal arteries arise?

2.   The renal arteries carry from _____ % to _____ % of cardiac output at rest.

3.   Trace the blood flow through the arterial and venous pathways in the kidney.

E.   Provide answers to the following questions about nephrons.

1.   Name the two components of the nephron.

2.   Describe the structures of a renal corpuscle.

3.   What are the components of the renal tubule?

4.   What is the difference between cortical and juxtamedullary nephrons?

5. What is the juxtaglomerular apparatus? What two structures are considered part of this?

20.3 Urine Formation

A. Answer these following questions concerning urine formation.

1. How does urine formation begin?

2. What allows nephrons to filter so much fluid?

3. What is the process of returning fluids to the body called?

4. How would you calculate the amount of urine excreted?

B. Answer these questions concerning glomerular filtration.

1. What is glomerular filtration?

2. What would you normally find in glomerular filtrate?

3. What plasma substances increase when kidney function is compromised?

C. Answer the following questions regarding the filtration pressure.

1. What is the main force that moves substances out of the plasma?

2. What is the significance of two arterioles surrounding the glomerular capillaries?

3. What is the difference between the afferent and efferent arterioles that helps regulate filtration pressure?

4. What are the forces that oppose filtration in the glomerular corpuscle?

5. What then is net filtration pressure?

D. Answer the following questions concerning filtration rate.

1. What factors affect the glomerular filtration rate? Which of these is most important?

2. What is the normal or average glomerular filtration rate and how much blood is then filtered in a 24-hour period?

3. List the factors which could cause an increase in glomerular filtration rate.

4. List the factors which could cause a decrease in glomerular filtration rate.

E. Answer the following questions concerning control of filtration rate.

1. What is autoregulation?

2. What is the influence of sympathetic stimulation on this?

3. What is the renin-angiotensin system? What activates this?

4. What do the macula densa and the juxtaglomerular cells sense?

5. What is the role of angiotensin II, aldosterone and antidiuretic hormone in this process?

6. What causes the release of atrial and ventricular natriuretic peptide?

F. Answer the following questions regarding the process of tubular reabsorption.

1. What is tubular reabsorption and why do we say it is selective?

2. How do the peritubular capillaries assist with this process?

3. Describe the reabsorption of glucose, amino acids, and albumin.

4. What is meant by the term *renal plasma threshold?* How can this lead to glucosuria?

5. What is the nephrotic syndrome?

6. List the substances that are reabsorbed by the epithelium of the proximal convoluted tubule.

G. Answer the following questions regarding the reabsorption of sodium and water.

1. How are sodium and water reabsorption related and how does the movement of sodium ions influence other ions?

2. What hormones have the greatest influence on these two substances?

H. Answer these questions about tubular secretion.

1. What is tubular secretion?

2. How are hydrogen ions secreted and why?

3. How are potassium ions secreted?

4. What other substances may be secreted in the tubules of the nephron?

I. Answer the following concerning regulation of urine concentration and volume.

1. What is the role of ADH in water balance?

2. Is the permeability of water the same throughout the tubule? How does this change?

3. How does the countercurrent mechanism regulate the concentration and volume of urine?

4. How do the vasa recta help sustain the concentration gradient in the medulla?

J. Describe urea and uric acid excretion.

K. Answer the following questions concerning the composition of urine.
1. What is the composition of normal urine?

2. What is the normal output of urine?

3. What factors affect urinary output?

L. Answer the following concerning renal clearance.
1. What is renal clearance? How is it used to diagnose kidney disease?

2. How does kidney function differ in children and adults?

3. Describe ways to test renal clearance.

20.4 Elimination of Urine

A. Answer the following about the ureters.
1. Describe the location and structure of the ureters.

2. What are the three layers of this structure?

3. How is urine moved through the ureter?

4. What happens when a ureter is obstructed by a kidney stone?

B. Answer the following questions concerning the urinary bladder.

1. How does the bladder change as it fills with urine?

2. Describe the structure of the bladder wall include the four layers and features to assist.

C. Address the following regarding the urethra.

1. Describe the urethra.

2. What are the differences between the male and female urethra?

D. Describe the process of micturition. Be sure to include both autonomic and voluntary events.

E. How does the composition of urine help to identify the state of an individual's health?

20.5 Life-Span Changes

Describe the effects of aging on the organs in the urinary system.

Clinical Focus Questions

A.   Urinary tract infections are common problems seen by health care providers. Based on your knowledge of anatomy and physiology, would the incidence of such infections be higher in men or women? Explain your answer.

B.   How do you think one could differentiate between a bladder infection and a kidney infection?

When you have completed the study activities to your satisfaction, retake the mastery test and compare your performance with your initial attempt. If there are still areas you do not understand, repeat the appropriate study activities.

OVERVIEW

This chapter presents the interdependence of several body systems in maintaining proper concentrations of water and electrolytes. It begins with a discussion of balance and its application to water and electrolyte balance (Learning Outcomes 1–2). It continues with a description of body fluid compartments, how fluid composition varies within each compartment, and how fluids move from one compartment to another (Learning Outcomes 3 and 4). It then explains how the water and electrolytes enter and leave the body, which changes the balance (Learning Outcomes 5 and 7). You will then study the body's ability to reestablish this balance (Learning Outcomes 6 and 8). The chapter continues with an explanation of acid–base balance that includes the concept of pH, the major sources of hydrogen ions, the difference between strong and weak acids and bases, and the buffer systems that keep pH stable (Learning Outcomes 9–13). Finally, the chapter discusses the consequences of pH imbalances in body fluid (Learning Outcome 14) and how the renal and respiratory systems can compensate for these pH problems (Learning Outcome 15).

Water and electrolyte balance affects and is affected by the various chemical interactions of the body. A knowledge of the mechanisms that control fluid and electrolyte concentrations is essential to understand the nature of the internal environment.

LEARNING OUTCOMES

After you have studied this chapter, you should be able to

21.1   The Balance Concept
1.   Explain the balance concept.
2.   Explain the importance of water balance and electrolyte balance.

21.2   Distribution of Body Fluids
3.   Describe how body fluids are distributed in compartments.
4.   Explain how fluid composition varies among compartments and how fluids move from one compartment to another.

21.3   Water Balance
5.   List the routes by which water enters and leaves the body.
6.   Explain the regulation of water input and water output.

21.4   Electrolyte Balance
7.   List the routes by which electrolytes enter and leave the body.
8.   Explain the regulation of the input and output of electrolytes.

21.5   Acid–Base Balance
9.   Explain acid–base balance.
10.   Identify how pH number describes the acidity and alkalinity of a body fluid.
11.   List the major sources of hydrogen ions in the body.
12.   Distinguish between strong acids and weak acids.
13.   Explain how chemical buffer systems, the respiratory center, and the kidneys keep the pH of body fluids relatively constant.

21.6   Acid–Base Imbalances
14.   Describe the causes and consequences of increase or decrease in body fluid pH.

21.7   Compensation
15.   For each of the four main types of acid–base imbalances, explain which physiological system(s)—renal, respiratory, or both–would help to return blood pH toward normal.

FOCUS QUESTION

Which body systems must be coordinated to maintain normal concentrations of fluids and electrolytes?

MASTERY TEST

Now take the mastery test. Do not guess. Some questions may have more than one correct answer. As soon as you complete the test, check your answers and correct any mistakes. Note your successes and failures so that you can reread the chapter to meet your learning needs.

1. Fluid and electrolyte balance implies that the quantities of these substances entering the body _____ the quantities leaving the body.

2. Which of the following statements about fluid and electrolyte balance is/are true?
   a. Fluid balance is independent of electrolyte balance.
   b. The concentration of an individual electrolyte is the same throughout the body.
   c. Water and electrolytes occur in compartments in which the composition of fluid varies.
   d. Water is evenly distributed throughout the tissues of the body.

3. About 63% of the total body fluid in an adult occurs within the cells in a compartment called the _____ fluid compartment.

4. Blood and cerebrospinal fluid occur in the _____ fluid compartment.

5. Which of the following electrolytes is/are most concentrated within the cell?
   a. sodium
   b. bicarbonate
   c. chloride
   d. potassium

6. Plasma leaves the capillary at the arteriole end and enters interstitial spaces because of _____ pressure.

7. Fluid returns from the interstitial spaces to the plasma at the venule ends of the capillaries because of _____ pressure.

8. The most important source of water for the normal adult is
   a. in the form of beverages.
   b. from moist foods such as lettuce and tomatoes.
   c. from oxidative metabolism of nutrients.
   d. from the air you breathe.

9. Thirst is experienced when
   a. the mucosa of the mouth begins to lose water.
   b. salt concentration in the cell increases.
   c. the hypothalamus is stimulated by the increasing osmotic pressure of extracellular fluid.
   d. the cortex of the brain is stimulated by shifts in the concentration of sodium.

10. The primary regulator of water output is through
    a. loss in the feces.
    b. evaporation as sweat.
    c. urine production.
    d. loss via respiration.

11. Chemicals that promote urine production are collectively called _____.

12. As dehydration develops, water is lost first from the _____ _____ compartment.

13. In treating dehydration, it is necessary to replace
    a. amino acids.
    b. glucose.
    c. water.
    d. electrolytes.

14. In water intoxication, excess water (enters/leaves) the cell.

15. Which of the following are at increased risk of dehydration because of the inability of the kidneys to concentrate urine?
    a. neonates
    b. school-age children
    c. young adults
    d. elderly people

16. Edema is a likely development in people suffering from starvation because lack of adequate protein leads to (increased/decreased) plasma (osmotic/hydrostatic) pressure.

17. The primary sources of electrolytes are _____ and _____.

18. List three routes by which electrolytes are lost.

19. Sodium and potassium ion concentration are regulated by the kidneys and the hormone _____.

20. Parathyroid hormone regulates calcium ion concentration in the plasma by
    a. freeing calcium from bones.
    b. influencing the renal tubule to conserve calcium.
    c. stimulating the absorption of calcium from the intestine.
    d. freeing calcium from muscle tissue.

21. Prolonged diarrhea is likely to result in
    a. low sodium (hyponatremia).
    b. high sodium (hypernatremia).
    c. low potassium (hypokalemia).
    d. high potassium (hyperkalemia).

22. Acid–base balance is mainly concerned with regulating _____ _____ concentration.

23. A pH of 8.5 is said to be
    a. acid.
    b. neutral.
    c. alkaline.

24. The pH of arterial blood is normally _____.

25. Normal metabolic reactions produce (more/less) acid than base.

26. Anaerobic respiration of glucose produces
    a. carbonic acid.
    b. lactic acid.
    c. acetoacetic acid.
    d. ketones.

27. The strength of an acid depends on the
    a. number of hydrogen ions in each molecule.
    b. nature of the inorganic salt.
    c. degree to which molecules ionize in water.
    d. concentration of water molecules.

28. A base is a substance that will _____ _____ hydrogen ions.

29. A buffer is a substance that
    a. returns an acid solution to neutral.
    b. converts acid solutions to alkaline solutions.
    c. converts strong acids or bases to weak acids or bases.
    d. returns an alkaline solution to neutral.

30. The most important buffer system in plasma is the _____ buffer.
    a. bicarbonate
    b. phosphate
    c. protein
    d. sulfate

31. The respiratory center controls hydrogen ion concentration by controlling the _____ and _____ of respiration.

32. The slowest acting of the mechanisms that control pH is the
    a. chemical buffer system.
    b. respiratory system.
    c. kidney.

33. When the blood pH decreases, there is an increase in the _____ ions excreted in the urine.

34. The accumulation of dissolved carbon dioxide is known as
    a. respiratory acidosis.
    b. respiratory alkalosis.
    c. metabolic acidosis.
    d. metabolic alkalosis.

35. Light-headedness, agitation, dizziness, and tingling sensations are symptoms of
    a. respiratory acidosis.
    b. respiratory alkalosis.
    c. metabolic acidosis.
    d. metabolic alkalosis.

STUDY ACTIVITIES

Definition of Word Parts

Define the following word parts used in this chapter.

de-

edem-

-emia

extra-

im- (or in-)

intra-

neutr-

-osis

-uria

21.1 The Balance Concept

Answer the following regarding the general concepts of this chapter.

1. Define *balance* in the context of water and electrolytes.

2. What happens to the concentration of electrolytes as the amount of water increases?

21.2 Distribution of Body Fluids

A. Answer the following regarding the fluid compartments.

1. Where are intracellular fluids found and what percentage of your fluids are found here?

2. What fluids make up the extracellular compartments?

3. Where do you find the transcellular compartments?

4. Why is there a difference in males and females regarding the percentage of body fluids?

B. Answer these questions about the composition of body fluids.

1. What is the composition of intracellular fluid?

2. What is the composition of extracellular fluid?

C. Describe the major mechanisms for moving water and electrolytes from one compartment to another.

21.3 Water Balance

A.   Answer these questions concerning water intake.

      1.   What is the usual water intake for an adult in a moderate climate?

      2.   From what sources is this water derived?

B.   Answer the following regarding regulation of water intake.

      1.   Describe the mechanisms that regulate the intake of water.

      2.   What does the term *osmolarity* describe?

      3.   What happens to osmotic pressure as the body loses water? What sensors detect this?

C.   Answer the following questions about water output.

      1.   By what routes is water lost from the body?

      2.   What happens during heatstroke?

D.   Answer the following questions regarding regulation of water output.

      1.   What is the primary means of regulating water output?

      2.   What triggers the release of antidiuretic hormone (ADH)?

      3.   Explain the osmoreceptor-ADH (antidiuretic hormone) mechanism.

      4.   What are diuretics and how do they work?

E.   Answer these questions concerning water balance disorders.

      1.   Define *dehydration.*

      2.   What conditions may lead to dehydration?

      3.   How does age influence the development of dehydration?

4.   What is the treatment for dehydration?

5.   What is water intoxication?

6.   What group of individuals is most susceptible to water intoxication?

7.   What is edema?

8.   List four causes of edema.

21.4 Electrolyte Balance

A.   Define *electrolyte balance*.

B.   Answer these questions concerning electrolyte intake.

    1.   List the electrolytes that are important to cellular function.

    2.   What are the sources of these electrolytes?

C.   Ordinarily, sufficient amounts of fluid and electrolytes are obtained as an individual responds to _____ and
_____.

D.   List three routes by which electrolytes are lost.

E.   Answer these questions concerning the regulation of electrolyte balance.

    1.   What is the role of aldosterone in electrolyte regulation?

    2.   What is the role of parathyroid hormone in electrolyte regulation?

    3.   What is the role of the kidney in electrolyte regulation?

    4.   How is the concentration of negatively charged ions regulated?

F.   Describe the causes and symptoms of the following electrolyte imbalances.

    1.   high calcium concentration (hypercalcemia)

    2.   low calcium concentration (hypocalcemia)

    3.   low sodium concentration (hyponatremia)

    4.   high sodium concentration (hypernatremia)

    5.   low potassium concentration (hypokalemia)

    6.   high potassium concentration (hyperkalemia)

21.5 Acid–Base Balance

A.   Answer these questions concerning acid–base balance.

    1.   What is an acid?

    2.   What is a base?

    3.   How is the concentration of hydrogen ions expressed?

    4.   What is the normal pH of the internal environment?

B.   List and describe the metabolic processes that produce hydrogen ions.

C.   What is the difference between a strong acid or base and a weak acid or base?

D.   Answer these questions concerning the regulation of hydrogen ion concentration.

1.   Normally you produce more acids and balance is accomplished through the elimination of acids. What are the three ways that acids can be eliminated?

2.   What is the basis or mechanisms of the chemical buffer systems?

3.   What are the three chemical buffer systems?

4.   Where are these systems most effective, what body compartments?

5.   Why are these systems only temporary solutions to the imbalances?

6.   How does the respiratory center regulate hydrogen ion concentration?

7.   How do the kidneys help regulate hydrogen ion concentration?

8.   How do these mechanisms differ from each other, especially with respect to speed of action and variety of chemicals that can be buffered?

21.6   Acid–Base Imbalances

A.   Answer the following general questions regarding acid–base imbalance.

1.   What is the normal arterial blood pH, what values indicate acidosis, and what values indicate alkalosis?

2.   At what point will survival be compromised?

B.   Answer the following regarding acidosis.

1.   What are the causes of respiratory acidosis?

2.   What are the causes of metabolic acidosis?

3.   What are the symptoms of acidosis?

C.   Answer the following regarding alkalosis.

1.   What are the causes of respiratory alkalosis?

2. What factors lead to metabolic alkalosis?

3. What are the symptoms of alkalosis?

21.7 Compensation

Answer the following regarding the ways the body can prevent death from acid–base imbalances.

1. If metabolic acidosis occurs from diabetes mellitus due to an increase in ketone bodies, how would your body compensate?

2. If metabolic alkalosis occurs from abuse of antacids, how would compensation occur?

3. If the pH imbalance is due to the kidney failure, how would compensation occur?

4. If the pH imbalance is due to a respiratory illness, how could the body compensate?

Clinical Focus Questions

Your family is planning a day excursion to the seashore. The age range of your group is from your sister's 2-month-old daughter to your 75-year-old grandparents. The temperature is expected to be in the 90s. In helping your mother plan the food and beverages to bring, what suggestions would you make to maintain everyone's fluid and electrolyte balances?

When you have completed the study activities to your satisfaction, retake the mastery test and compare your performance with your initial attempt. If there are still areas you do not understand, repeat the appropriate study activities.

OVERVIEW

This chapter explains the reproductive system—a unique system because it is essential for the survival of the species rather than for the survival of the individual. Your study begins with a description of the general functions of the male and female reproductive systems and how meiosis mixes up parental genes creating the gametes (Learning Outcome 1). The specific process of meiosis in males and females which results in viable gametes is presented to help you understand how you become fertile and remain so post-pubescence (Learning Outcomes 3 and 8). The structures and functions of the male and female reproductive systems that deliver and nurture the gametes are then explained (Learning Outcomes 2, 4, 5, and 7). Hormonal control of the process of gamete development in the male and female reproductive systems and the development of male and female secondary sex characteristics are described (Learning Outcomes 6, 9, and 10), and the structure of the mammary glands is reviewed (Learning Outcome 11). Finally, the mechanisms and effectiveness of birth control and the symptoms of common sexually transmitted infections are discussed (Learning Outcomes 12 and 13).

Knowledge of the anatomy and physiology of the male and female reproductive systems is basic to the study of human sexuality and the process of reproduction.

LEARNING OUTCOMES

After you have studied this chapter, you should be able to

22.1 Meiosis and Sex Cell Production
   1. Outline the process of meiosis, and explain how it mixes up parental genes.
22.2 Organs of the Male Reproductive System
   2. Describe the structure and function(s) of each part of the male reproductive system.
   3. Outline the process of spermatogenesis.
   4. Describe semen production and exit from the body.
   5. Explain how tissues of the penis produce an erection.
22.3 Hormonal Control of Male Reproductive Functions
   6. Explain how hormones control the activities of the male reproductive organs and the development of the male secondary sex characteristics.
22.4 Organs of the Female Reproductive System
   7. Describe the structure and function(s) of each part of the female reproductive system.
   8. Outline the process of oogenesis.
22.5 Hormonal Control of Female Reproductive Functions
   9. Explain how hormones control the activities of the female reproductive organs and the development of female secondary sex characteristics.
   10. Describe the major events during a menstrual cycle.
22.6 Mammary Glands
   11. Review the structure of the mammary glands.
22.7 Birth Control
   12. Describe several methods of birth control, including relative effectiveness of each method.
22.8 Sexually Transmitted Infections
   13. List the general symptoms of disease associated with sexually transmitted infections.

FOCUS QUESTION

How do the male and female reproductive systems differ and complement each other?

MASTERY TEST

Now take the mastery test. Do not guess. Some questions may have more than one correct answer. As soon as you complete the test, check your answers and correct your mistakes. Note your successes and failures so that you can reread the chapter to meet your learning needs.

1. The male and female reproductive systems
   - a. produce sex hormones.
   - b. produce and nurture sex cells.
   - c. transport sex cells to the site of fertilization.
   - d. ensure the development of appropriate secondary sex characteristics.

2. The type of cell produced by the second meiotic division is a _____ cell.

3. The number of chromosomes in each sex cell is _____.

4. The primary organ(s) of the male reproductive system is/are the _____.

5. In the fetus, the testes originate
   - a. in the scrotum.
   - b. posterior to the parietal peritoneum.
   - c. within the abdominal cavity.
   - d. in the pelvis.

6. The descent of the testes into the scrotum is stimulated by
   - a. increasing pressure within the abdominal cavity.
   - b. the male hormone testosterone.
   - c. shortening of the gubernaculum.
   - d. shifts in core temperature of the fetus.

7. The testes are suspended in the scrotum by the _____ _____.

8. The structure that guides the descent of the testes into the scrotum is the _____.

9. In order to descend into the scrotum, the testes must travel through the _____.
   - a. peritoneum.
   - b. vas deferens.
   - c. abdominal wall.
   - d. inguinal canal.

10. When a testis fails to descend into the scrotum, the condition is known as _____.

11. The fetal structure that can lead to the development of an indirect hernia is the
    - a. scrotal sac.
    - b. vaginal process.
    - c. tunica albuginea.
    - d. omentum.

12. The complex network of channels derived from the seminiferous tubules is the
    - a. rete testis.
    - b. tunica albuginea.
    - c. mediastinum testis.
    - d. epididymis.

13. Prior to adolescence, the undifferentiated spermatogenic cells in the testes are called _____.

14. The process by which the number of chromosomes in a sex cell is reduced from 46 to 23 and that ensures genetic variety is
    - a. mitosis.
    - b. crossing over.
    - c. mutation.
    - d. meiosis.

15. A small protrusion on the anterior portion of the head of the sperm containing enzymes that aid the sperm in penetrating the zona pellucida of the ovum is the _____.

16. Spermatogenesis occurs (continuously/episodically) in men after puberty until about age 65.

17. The energy needed for the lashing tail or flagellum of the sperm is provided by the _____ located in the _____ of the sperm.

18. The function of the epididymis is to
    - a. produce sex hormones.
    - b. provide the sperm with mobile tails.
    - c. store sperm as they mature.
    - d. supply some of the force needed for ejaculation.

19. The ductus deferentia unites with the duct of the _____ _____ just before emptying into the urethra.

20. Which of the following substances is/are added to sperm cells by the seminal vesicle?
    - a. acid
    - b. fructose
    - c. glucose
    - d. prostaglandins

21. The secretions of the prostate gland help to _____ secretions from the vagina.

253

22. The function of the bulbourethral glands is to
    a. neutralize the acid secretions of the vagina.
    b. nourish sperm cells.
    c. lubricate the penis.
    d. increase the volume of semen.

23. The external organs of the male reproductive system include the
    a. penis.
    b. testes.
    c. prostate gland.
    d. scrotum.

24. The smooth muscle in the scrotum is the _____ muscle.

25. Erection of the penis depends on
    a. contraction of the perineal muscles.
    b. filling of the corpus cavernosum with arterial blood.
    c. enlargement of the glans penis.
    d. peristaltic contractions of the vas deferens.

26. Hormones that control male reproductive functions are secreted by the
    a. hypothalamus.
    b. testes.
    c. posterior pituitary gland.
    d. anterior pituitary gland.

27. The pituitary hormone that stimulates the testes to produce testosterone is
    a. gonadotropin-releasing hormone.
    b. follicle-stimulating hormone (FSH).
    c. luteinizing hormone (LH).
    d. adrenocorticotropic hormone (ACTH).

28. In the male, the growth of body hair, especially in the axilla, face, and pubis, and increased muscle and bone development are examples of _____ _____ characteristics.

29. Oversecretion of LH is prevented by secretion of the hormone _____.

30. The primary organs of the female reproductive system are the _____.

31. In the ovary, the primary germinal epithelium is located
    a. in the medulla.
    b. between the medulla and cortex.
    c. in the cortex.
    d. on the free surface of the ovary.

32. The primary oocyte produces _____ mature egg cell(s).

33. At puberty, the primary oocyte begins maturing within the _____ _____.

34. The formation of polar bodies during oogenesis is a rare example of wasted energy and cellular material.
    a. True
    b. False

35. The egg cell is nourished by the
    a. theca interna.
    b. theca externa.
    c. zona pellucida.
    d. corona radiata.

36. The egg is released by the ovary in a process called _____.

37. Which of the following statements is/are true about the uterine (fallopian) tubes?
    a. The end of the uterine tube near the ovary has many fingerlike projections called fimbriae.
    b. The fimbriae are attached to the ovaries.
    c. The inner layer of the ovarian tube is cuboidal epithelium.
    d. There are cilia in the lining of the uterine tube that help move the egg toward the uterus.

38. The inner layer of the uterus is the _____.

39. The upper portion of the vagina that surrounds the cervix is the
    a. fornix.
    b. rectouterine pouch.
    c. vestibule.
    d. hymen.

40. Which of the following statements about the vagina is/are *true*?
    a. The mucosal layer contains many mucous glands.
    b. The bulbospongiosis is primarily responsible for closing the vaginal orifice.
    c. The mucosa is drawn into many longitudinal and transverse ridges.
    d. The hymen is a membrane that covers the mouth of the cervix.

41. The organ of the female reproductive system that is analogous to the penis is the
    a. vagina.
    b. mons pubis.
    c. clitoris.
    d. labia majora.

42. Which of the following tissues become engorged and erect in response to sexual stimulation?
    a. clitoris
    b. labia minora
    c. outer third of the vagina
    d. upper third of the vagina

43. The primary female sex hormones are _____ and _____.

44. Which of the following secondary sex characteristics in the female seem to be related to androgen concentration?
    a. breast development
    b. growth of axillary and pubic hair
    c. female skeletal configuration
    d. deposition of adipose tissue over hips, thighs, buttocks, and breasts

45. A female's first reproductive cycle is called _____.

46. Which of the following is *not* a source of female sex hormones?
    a. posterior pituitary gland
    b. placenta
    c. ovary
    d. adrenal medulla

47. During the menstrual cycle, the event that seems to provoke ovulation is
    a. increasing levels of progesterone.
    b. a sudden increase in concentration of LH.
    c. decreasing levels of estrogen.
    d. a cessation of secretion of FSH.

48. After the release of an egg, the follicle forms a _____ _____.

49. As the above structure develops, the level of which of the following hormones increases?
    a. estrogen
    b. progesterone
    c. FSH
    d. LH

50. As the hormone levels change in the part of the cycle before and immediately after ovulation, which of the following changes is/are seen in the uterus?
    a. growth of the endometrial tissue and blood vessels
    b. increase in adipose cells of the perimetrium
    c. thickening of the endometrium
    d. decrease in uterine gland activity

51. Breasts overlie the _____ muscle of the chest wall.

52. Methods of contraception that utilize mechanical barriers are
    a. coitus interruptus.
    b. the condom.
    c. the diaphragm.
    d. the IUD.

53. The method of contraception that is thought to interfere with ovulation is
    a. the rhythm method.
    b. the oral contraceptive (the pill).
    c. chemical foams.
    d. the IUD.

54. The commonly used surgical technique to sterilize the male is the _____.

55. The contraceptive method that is also effective in preventing the spread of sexually transmitted diseases (STDs) is the
    a. pill.
    b. coitus interruptus.
    c. condom.
    d. IUD.

56. Sexually transmitted infections are not treated promptly primarily because
    a. patients are embarrassed to consult a physician.
    b. there is a perception that they can be effectively treated with home remedies.
    c. many of the symptoms of these diseases are similar to symptoms of diseases or allergies that are not sexually related.
    d. of ignorance of how they are transmitted.

STUDY ACTIVITIES

Definition of Word Parts

Define the following word parts used in this chapter.

andr-

contra-

crur-

ejacul-

fimb-

follic-

-genesis

gubern-

labi-

mamm-

mast-

mens-

mons-

oo-

prim-

puber-

zon-

22.1 Meiosis and Sex Cell Production

A.   Answer the following questions regarding the process of meiosis in humans.

1.   Male sex cells are _____; female sex cells are _____.

2.   What does the word diploid mean? _____

3.   Why do we call your chromosomes homologous?

4.   When are the cells haploid?

B.   Answer the following questions regarding the first meiotic division.

1.   What happens in prophase I which leads to genetic variation?

2.   How is metaphase I different from mitosis and how does this result in genetic variation?

3.   What happens to the homologues by the end of meiosis I?

C.   What happens in meiosis II?

22.2 Organs of the Male Reproductive System

A. Describe the functions of the male reproductive system and name the primary sex organ(s).

B. Label the structures in the accompanying diagram.

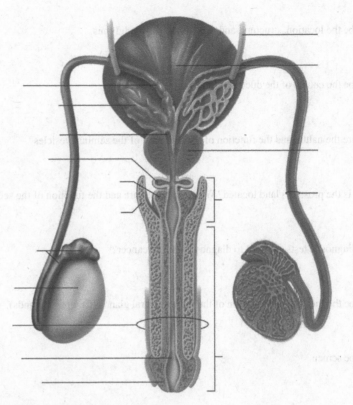

C. Answer the following questions concerning the testes.

1. Where do the testes originate during fetal life?

2. How do the testes descend into the scrotum?

3. What is cryptorchidism? How does this produce sterility?

4. Describe the structure of the testes.

5. Describe the cells you find in the testes which are involved in sperm formation.

6. What happens at puberty to the cells undergoing sperm formation? What is this process called?

7. Describe the structures of a sperm cell and explain how they assist with function.

D. Answer the following concerning male internal accessory reproductive organs.
   1. List the internal accessory organs of the male reproductive system.

   2. Describe the location, structure, and function of the epididymis.

   3. Describe the course of the ductus deferens.

   4. What are the nature and the function of the secretion of the seminal vesicles?

   5. Where is the prostate gland located? What are the nature and the function of the secretions of the prostate gland?

   6. What diagnostic tests are used to diagnose prostate cancer?

   7. Describe the location and function of the bulbourethral glands (Cowper's glands).

   8. Describe semen.

E. Answer the following concerning male external reproductive organs.
   1. Describe the scrotum and detail its role in sperm production.

   2. Label the following structures on the drawing of a cross section of a penis.

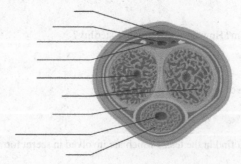

3. What is removal of the prepuce called?

4. Describe the events of erection and ejaculation. Be sure to distinguish between emission and ejaculation.

5. List the possible causative factors for male infertility and describe the diagnostic procedures used to diagnose male infertility.

22.3 Hormonal Control of Male Reproductive Functions

A. What glands secrete hormones that control male reproductive functions?

B. Answer the following regarding the hypothalamic and pituitary hormones.

1. The hormone secreted by the hypothalamus is _____. What is its function?

2. What is the function of FSH and LH?

C. Answer the following concerning the male sex hormones.

1. Where is testosterone produced?

2. What is the function of testosterone?

3. When does the secretion of testosterone begin?

D. What are the actions of testosterone?

E. Describe the regulation of sex hormones in the male.

22.4 Organs of the Female Reproductive System

A.   Label the structures in the accompanying drawing of the female reproductive organs.

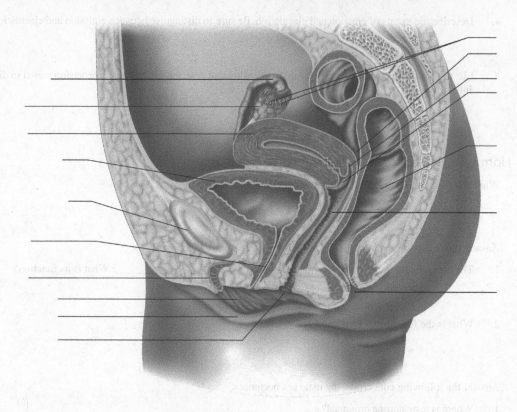

B.   What is the function of the female reproductive system and what are the primary sex organs of the female reproductive system?

C.   Answer the following questions concerning the ovaries.

1.   Describe the ovaries including their general location.

2.   Regarding ovary attachments, list the ligaments that hold the ovaries in place.

3.   Describe the formation and descent of the ovaries.

4.   Describe the structure of the ovary.

5.   What are primordial follicles and what do they contain?

6. Answer the following questions concerning oogenesis.
   a. Describe the development of female sex cells.

   b. How is this different from the development of male sex cells?

7. Answer the following questions concerning follicle maturation.
   a. What stimulates the maturation of a primary follicle?

   b. What changes occur in the follicle as a result of maturation?

   c. What is a dominant follicle and how long does maturation take?

8. Answer the following questions concerning ovulation.
   a. What provokes ovulation?

   b. What happens to the egg after it leaves the ovary?

D. Answer the following concerning female internal accessory organs.
   1. Label the structures identified in the accompanying drawing of the female reproductive accessory organs.

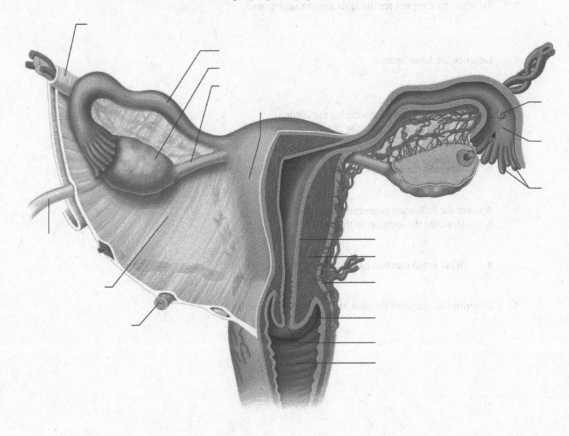

2. How does the structure of the uterine tube assists in the movement of the egg toward the uterus?

3. Describe the structure of the uterus; include location, regions, and layers.

4. What is a Pap smear?

5. Answer the following concerning the vagina.
   a. What is the function of the vagina?

   b. What are the fornices and the hymen?

   c. Describe the structure of the vagina.

E. Answer the following questions concerning female external reproductive organs.
   1. To what male organs are the labia majora analogous?

   2. Describe the labia minora.

   3. Answer these questions concerning the clitoris.
      a. To what male organ is the clitoris analogous?

      b. Where is the clitoris located?

   4. Answer the following concerning the vestibule.
      a. Describe the location of the vestibule.

      b. What is the function of the vestibular glands (Bartholin's glands)?

   5. Describe the events of erection and orgasm in the female.

22.5 Hormonal Control of Female Reproductive Functions

A.   Answer these questions concerning female sex hormones.

      1.   What hormone appears to initiate sexual maturation in the female?

      2.   What pituitary hormones influence sexual function in the female?

      3.   What are the sources of female sex hormones?

      4.   What is the function of estrogen?

      5.   What is the function of progesterone?

      6.   Female athletes and dancers can suffer from amenorrhea or may experience a disturbance of the menstrual cycle. This seems to be due to a loss of adipose which leads to decreased leptin. How does this influence the reproductive cycle?

B.   Answer the following concerning female reproductive cycles.
      1.   What is menarche?

      2.   Describe the events of the menstrual cycle. Include shifts in hormone levels, uterine changes, and ovarian changes.

C.   Answer these questions concerning menopause.

      1.   What is menopause and when does it occur?

      2.   What seems to be the cause of menopause?

22.6 Mammary Glands

A.   What is the location of the mammary glands?

B.   Describe the structure of the mammary glands.

22.7 Birth Control

Describe each of the following methods of birth control, and identify the advantages and disadvantages of each method.

A.   coitus interruptus

B.   rhythm method

C.   mechanical barriers:
        1.   condom (male and female)

        2.   diaphragm

        3.   cervical cap

D.   chemical barriers
        1.   combined hormone contraceptives

        2.   injectable contraceptive

E.   intrauterine devices

F.   surgical methods:
        1.   vasectomy

        2.   tubal ligation

22.8 Sexually Transmitted Infections

List the common symptoms of sexually transmitted infections.

Clinical Focus Questions

Your local school board is embroiled in a controversy related to when and if sex education should be offered in the school system and, if offered, when it should begin and what the goals of such education should be. Based on your knowledge of the male and female reproductive systems and on your own value system, develop a personal position on these questions.

When you have completed the study activities to your satisfaction, retake the mastery test and compare your performance with your initial attempt. If there are still areas you do not understand, repeat the appropriate study activities.

CHAPTER 23
PREGNANCY, GROWTH, AND DEVELOPMENT

OVERVIEW

In this chapter, you will study the outcome of successful reproduction. The chapter starts by following the events leading up to fertilization (Learning Outcome 1) and examining the events which lead to the formation of the zygote followed by the rapid cell division that produces a blastula within five days after fertilization (Learning Outcomes 2 and 3). You will study how implantation occurs in the endometrium (Learning Outcome 4) followed by a discussion regarding the processes of growth and development in the embryonic and fetal periods with a specific emphasis on studying the fetal cardiovascular system (Learning Outcomes 7–9). You will study the development of the membranes which enclose, protect and even help nourish the developing embryo (Learning Outcome 5). You will learn how these membranes change and contribute to the placenta and what the placenta's role is in the pregnancy (Learning Outcome 6). You will also focus on the changes occurring in the mother. You will study the hormonal changes necessary to sustain the pregnancy (Learning Outcome 10), and examine the hormonal processes that lead to birth and lactation (Learning Outcome 11). You will continue following the individual that results from fertilization by exploring postnatal adjustments which occur in the neonate (Learning Outcomes 13) and the major events in the other physiological stages of postnatal development (Learning Outcome 12), including the dying process (Learning Outcome 14). The chapter concludes by discussing the contrast between active and passive aging as well as between lifespan and life expectancy (Learning Outcomes 15 and 16).

LEARNING OUTCOMES

After you have studied this chapter, you should be able to
23.1   Fertilization
    1.   Trace the movement of sperm toward an egg.
    2.   Describe, in detail, fertilization.
23.2   Pregnancy and the Prenatal Period
    3.   List and provide details of the major events of cleavage.
    4.   Describe implantation.
    5.   Describe the extraembryonic membranes.
    6.   Describe the formation and function of the placenta.
    7.   Explain how the primary germ layers originate, and list the structures each layer produces.
    8.   Define *fetus,* and describe the major events of the fetal stage of development.
    9.   Trace the path of blood through the fetal cardiovascular system.
    10.   Discuss the hormonal and other changes in the maternal body during pregnancy.
    11.   Explain the role of hormones in the birth process and milk production.
23.3   Postnatal Period
    12.   Describe the major cardiovascular and physiological adjustments in the newborn.
    13.   Name the postnatal stages of development of a human, and indicate the general characteristics of each stage.
    14.   Describe the dying process.
23.4   Aging
    15.   Distinguish between passive and active aging.
    16.   Contrast lifespan and life expectancy.

FOCUS QUESTION

As you have completed your studies of the organ systems, can you relate the formation of these in early development to your current understanding of their anatomy? What organ systems will be functional before birth and which ones will not become functional until after birth?

MASTERY TEST

Now take the mastery test. Do not guess. Some questions may have more than one answer. As soon as you complete the test, check your answers and correct any mistakes. Note your successes and failures so that you can reread the chapter to meet your learning needs.

1. An increase in size is called _____.

2. The process by which an individual changes throughout life is _____.

3. The period of life that begins with fertilization and ends at birth is known as the _____ period.

4. The period of life from birth to death is known as the _____ period.

5. The nature of the secretions from the cervix and uterus during the first part of the reproductive cycle is
   a. thick and viscous.
   b. thin and watery.
   c. thick and sticky.
   d. thin and pale yellow.

6. Fertilization of the egg by the sperm takes place in the
   a. vagina.
   b. cervix.
   c. uterus.
   d. uterine (fallopian) tube.

7. Which of the following is thought to be the mechanism by which the sperm enters the egg?
   a. An antigen-antibody reaction briefly alters the cell membrane of the egg.
   b. The structure of the cell membrane of the egg allows entry of the sperm.
   c. The head of the sperm has an enzyme that permits digestion through the corona radiata and zona pellucida.
   d. The mechanism is unknown.

8. Intercourse that takes place during which time period is most like to result in fertilization?
   a. during menstuation
   b. no earlier than 48 hours prior to ovulation
   c. 72 hours after ovulation
   d. within 24 hours after ovulation

9. The period of cleavage ends with forming a _____.

10. After fertilization, the zygote divides into smaller and smaller cells forming a solid ball called the
    a. blastomere.
    b. blastocyst.
    c. morula.
    d. embryo.

11. Which of the following statements is/are true about implantation?
    a. Implantation is complete by one month after fertilization.
    b. Implantation marks the end of the period of cleavage.
    c. The fertilized egg adheres to the wall of the uterus, and the endometrium then grows over it.
    d. The trophoblast produces fingerlike projections that penetrate the endometrium.

12. The hormone produced by the trophoblast is _____ _____ _____.

13. The cells that form the new embryo arise in the _____ _____ _____.

14. The hormone that maintains the corpus luteum is
    a. LH.
    b. hCG.
    c. progesterone.
    d. FSH.

15. The primary source of hormones needed to maintain a pregnancy after the first three months is the _____.

16. Which of the following will *not* increase during pregnancy?
    a. blood volume
    b. hematocrit
    c. cardiac output
    d. urine production

17. The ectoderm, mesoderm, and endoderm are _____ _____ layers.

18. From which of the layers of the embryonic disk do the hair, nails, and glands of the skin arise?
    a. endoderm
    b. ectoderm
    c. mesoderm
    d. periderm

19. Which of the following structures arises from the mesoderm?
    a. lining of the mouth
    b. muscle
    c. lining of the respiratory tract
    d. epidermis

20. At what time does the embryonic disk become a cylinder?
    a. four weeks of development
    b. six weeks of development
    c. eight weeks of development
    d. four days of development

21. The chorion in contact with the endometrium becomes the _____.

22. The membrane covering the embryo is called the _____.

23. The number of blood vessels in the umbilical cord is
    a. one artery and one vein.
    b. one artery and two veins.
    c. two arteries and one vein.
    d. two arteries and two veins.

24. The embryonic structure(s) that form(s) fetal blood cells is/are the
    a. amnion.
    b. placenta.
    c. allantois.
    d. yolk sac.

25. The embryonic stage ends at _____ weeks.

26. Factors that cause congenital malformations by affecting the embryo are called _____.

27. A defect that can occur on day 28 in development is a _____ defect.

28. Fetal skeletal muscles are active enough to permit the mother to feel fetal movements starting in month
    a. four.
    b. five.
    c. six.
    d. seven.

29. Brain cells of the fetus rapidly form networks during the
    a. first trimester.
    b. second trimester.
    c. third trimester.
    d. all three trimesters.

30. Which of the following factors indicate(s) that the respiratory system is mature enough to allow survival when a baby is born prematurely?
    a. gestational age of seven months
    b. thinness of the respiratory membrane
    c. respiratory rate below 40 per minute
    d. sufficient amounts of surfactant

31. Oxygen and nutrient-rich blood reach the fetus from the placenta via the umbilical _____.

32. The ductus venosus shunts blood around the
    a. liver.
    b. spleen.
    c. pancreas.
    d. small intestine.

33. The structures that allow blood to avoid the nonfunctioning fetal lungs are the _____ and the
    _____.

34. The factor that decreases the effort required for an infant to breathe after the first breath is _____.

35. Labor is initiated by a decrease in _____ levels and the secretion of _____ by the posterior pituitary gland.

36. Bleeding following expulsion of the afterbirth is controlled by
    a. hormonal mechanisms.
    b. increased fibrinogen levels.
    c. contraction of the uterine muscles.
    d. sympathetic stimulation of arterioles.

37. Milk production following delivery is stimulated by the hormone _____.

38. The primary energy source(s) for the newborn is/are
    a. glucose.
    b. stored fat.
    c. protein.
    d. phospholipids.

39. An infant who is breast-fed usually receives milk
    a. immediately after birth.
    b. within 12 hours after birth.
    c. within 48 hours after birth.
    d. 3 days after birth.

40. An infant's urine is (more/less) concentrated than an adult's.

41. Which of the following fetal structures closes as a result of a change in pressure?
    a. ductus venosus
    b. ductus arteriosus
    c. umbilical vessels
    d. foramen ovale

42. The beginning of the ability to communicate is accomplished during _____.

43. Reproductive maturity occurs during _____.

268

44. The process of growing old is called _____.

45. Passive aging is a process of
    a. degeneration.
    b. programmed cell death.
    c. genetic breakdown.
    d. accelerated necrosis.

46. Lifespan and life expectancy are synonymous terms.
    a. True
    b. False

47. Which of the following changes is/are (a) part(s) of passive aging?
    a. loss of effective collagen and elastin
    b. lipofuscin accumulation
    c. an increase in mitochondrial function
    d. decrease in enzymes that inactivate free radicals

48. Programmed cell death is called _____.

STUDY ACTIVITIES

Definition of Word Parts

Define the following word parts used in this chapter.

allant-

chorio-

cleav-

ect-

lacun-

lanug-

mes-

morul-

nat-

ne-

post-

pre-

sen-

troph-

umbil-

23.1 Fertilization

A.   What is fertilization and where does it normally occur?

B.   Answer the following questions about the transport of the sex cell.

1.   Describe the factors that affect the movement of sperm from the vagina to the waiting ovum.

2.   Why are sperm described as inefficient?

3.   How do the secretions of the female reproductive tract change under the influence of estrogen and progesterone?

4.   How many sperm are found in a single ejaculate?

5.   a.   What is the survival time of ova and sperm following ovulation?

b.   Based on the answer to question 5a, and knowing how long sperm can survive in the female, when can conception occur?

C.   Answer these questions concerning a sperm cell uniting with a secondary oocyte.

1.   What must a sperm cell overcome to make contact with the oocyte cell membrane?

2.   What happens to the secondary oocyte when the sperm penetrates the cell membrane?

3.   What do you call the cell which results from the chromosomes of the oocyte and sperm cell and how many chromosomes should this cell have?

23.2 Pregnancy and the Prenatal Period

A.   Answer the following general questions about pregnancy and prenatal development.

1.   What does the term *pregnancy* refer to?

2.   How long does the prenatal period last?

270

3. How long does the embryonic stage last?

B. Answer the following questions concerning the period of cleavage during the embryonic stage of development.
1. When does cleavage begin and what is happening during this period?

2. What is the difference between a morula and a blastocyst?

3. Distinguish the inner cell mass from the trophoblast.

C. Answer the following regarding the process of implantation in the embryonic stage.
1. When and where does implantation occur?

2. Describe the process of implantation.

3. What hormone is secreted by the trophoblast and how does it affect pregnancy?

D. Answer the following regarding the formation of extraembryonic membranes and the placenta.
1. What is the chorion and how does it form?

2. What are the chorionic villi and the lacunae the result of and what do they allow to occur?

3. Describe the amnion and outline the purpose of amniotic fluid.

4. The flat disk that forms during the second week of pregnancy is the _____ _____.

5. Describe the formation of the umbilical cord.

6. What happens to the amnion as development continues?

7. Where does the yolk sac form and what structures or cells will come this?

8. What is the purpose of the allantois and what does it become?

9. Label the structures identified in the accompanying illustration of the placenta.

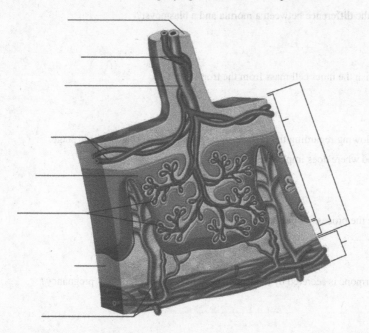

10. Describe the formation and appearance of the placenta.

11. What is the purpose of the placenta and what does it produce?

E. Answer the following regarding the processes of gastrulation and organogenesis.

1. What is gastrulation and when does it occur?

2. List the structures that form from the following germ layers:
ectoderm

mesoderm

endoderm

3.   Describe the events of the fourth week of pregnancy.

4.   What changes occur during the fifth through seventh weeks?

5.   Why is the embryonic stage described as the most critical period of development?

6.   What is a teratogen? List some common teratogens.

7.   Fill in the following table regarding the embryonic stage.

Stage	Time Period	Principal Events
Zygote		
Cleavage		
Morula		
Blastocyst		
Gastrula		

F.   Answer the following concerning the fetal stage.

1.   When does the fetal stage begin and end?

2.   Fill in the following table regarding the major events of the fetal stages of development.

Month	Major Events
Third	
Fourth	
Fifth	
Sixth	
Seventh	

3.   What does the fetus look like at full term and when does this occur?

4. Why is it stated that the birth of a healthy baby is "against the odds"?

G. Answer the following concerning fetal blood and circulation.

1. Compare fetal and adult hemoglobin.

2. Trace a drop of fetal blood from the placenta through the circulatory system. Identify the main differences between prenatal and postnatal circulation.

3. Fill in the following table regarding the cardiovascular adaptations in the fetus.

Adaptation	Function
Fetal blood	
Umbilical vein	
Ductus venosus	
Foramen ovale	
Ductus arteriosus	
Umbilical arteries	

H. Answer these questions concerning maternal changes during pregnancy.

1. How does human chorionic gonadotropin (hCG) prevent spontaneous abortions?

2. How long will hCG be secreted?

3. What hormones are secreted by the placenta? What are their roles in pregnancy?

4. What other hormonal changes occur during the pregnancy?

I. Describe the physical changes experienced by the mother as the fetus grows.

J. Answer the following questions concerning the birth process.

1. What events initiate the termination of pregnancy?

2.   What stimulates the secretion of oxytocin?

3.   Describe the events of labor.

4.   Describe involution.

K.   Answer the following regarding milk production and secretion.

1.   What hormones stimulate the development of the breasts?

2.   What hormone is responsible for milk production and how is this inhibited during the pregnancy?

3.   When does milk production begin and what will sustain the neonate until this happens?

4.   Describe how milk secretion is stimulated and what the baby's role in this is.

5.   Why does a breastfeeding mother not ovulate for several months after birth?

23.3 Postnatal Period

A.   Fill in the following table concerning the neonatal period.

Life Process	Adjustments Needed for Postnatal Life
Respiration	
Nutrition	
Urine formation	
Temperature control	
Circulation	

275

B.   When does infancy begin and what are the major growth and developmental events of infancy?

C.   When does childhood begin and what are the normal growth and developmental events of childhood?

D.   When does adolescence begin and what are the normal growth and developmental events of adolescence?

E.   Answer the following regarding adulthood.
        1.   What happens during the decade following adolescence?

        2.   What are hallmark changes that occur in the third decade?

        3.   What are notable changes in the fourth decade?

        4.   What happens in the fifth decade?

        5.   What do you have to look forward to when you reach age sixty?

F.   Describe senescence.

G.   Answer the following regarding the end of life.
        1.   Describe the events of pre-active dying.

        2.   Describe the events of active dying.

        3.   Note the important physiological changes that lead to or cause death.

23.4 Aging

A.   Describe passive aging processes.

B.   Describe the active aging processes.

C.   Compare the concepts of human lifespan and life expectancy.

Clinical Focus Questions

Your best friend has told you that she is about two weeks pregnant. She is quite sure because she has tested her urine using a home pregnancy kit. She tells you that there is little reason for her to seek prenatal care until she is four or five months pregnant. Based on your knowledge of prenatal growth and development, how would you respond?

When you have completed the study activities to your satisfaction, retake the mastery test and compare your performance with your initial attempt. If there are still areas you do not understand, repeat the appropriate study activities.

277

CHAPTER 24
GENETICS AND GENOMICS

OVERVIEW

This chapter is about genetics, a field of study that attempts to explain the similarities and differences between individuals at the level of DNA and how traits are inherited. The chapter begins with reminding you of the concepts presented in Chapter 4. These include distinguishing the sections of DNA, known as the gene, from the entire sequence, the genome, and examining how this chemical information is packaged in the nucleus (Learning Outcome 1). An explanation of how genetic information is passed from one generation to another, and what influence the environment has on genes are presented (Learning Outcomes 2 and 3). The chapter continues with a discussion of modes of inheritance, factors that affect the expression of single genes, and how traits determined by genes and environment are inherited (Learning Outcomes 4–9). The chapter then describes how and when sex is determined and the related concept of X-linked inheritance and the factors that affect how phenotypes may differ between the sexes (Learning Outcomes 10–12). The related topics of chromosome disorders and prenatal testing are discussed (Learning Outcomes 13 and 14). The chapter concludes with examining the value of information provided by gene sequencing and how this might improve the future of medicine regarding the possibility of personalized medicine (Learning Outcomes 15–17).

LEARNING OUTCOMES

After you have studied this chapter, you should be able to

24.1   Genes and Genomes
   1.   Distinguish among gene, chromosome, and genome.
   2.   Identify the two processes that transfer genetic information between generations.
   3.   Explain how the environment influences how genes are expressed.
24.2   Modes of Inheritance
   4.   Describe a karyotype, and explain what it represents.
   5.   Explain the basis of multiple alleles of a gene.
   6.   Distinguish between heterozygous and homozygous; genotype and phenotype; and dominant and recessive.
   7.   Distinguish between autosomal recessive and autosomal dominant inheritance.
24.3   Factors That Affect Expression of Single Genes
   8.   Explain how and why the same genotype can have different phenotypes among individuals.
24.4   Multifactorial Traits
   9.   Describe and give examples of how genes and the environment determine traits.
24.5   Matters of Sex
   10.   Describe how and when sex is determined.
   11.   Explain how X-linked inheritance differs from inheritance of autosomal traits.
   12.   Discuss factors that affect how phenotypes may differ between the sexes.
24.6   Chromosome Disorders
   13.   Describe three ways that chromosomes can be abnormal.
   14.   Explain how prenatal tests provide information about chromosomes.
24.7   Genomics and Health Care
   15.   State 3 clinical uses of DNA-based tests.
   16.   Discuss the scope of DNA testing.
   17.   Compare protein-based to DNA-based treatments of single-gene diseases.

FOCUS QUESTION

What value will be realized by individuals knowing and understanding their genetic composition?

MASTERY TEST

Now take the mastery test. Some questions may have more than one correct answer. As soon as you complete the test, check your answers and correct any mistakes. Note your successes and failures so that you can reread the chapter to meet your learning needs.

   1.   The instruction manual for the cells of our bodies is the _____ written in the language of _____.

2. The study of the inheritance of characteristics is _____.

3. The process(es) involved in transferring information from one generation to the next is/are
   a. mitosis.
   b. fertilization.
   c. meiosis.
   d. gene selection.

4. Somatic cells are _____ and have _____ chromosomes; sex cells (eggs and sperm) are _____ and have _____ chromosomes.

5. The portion of the DNA molecule that contains the information for producing particular types of protein is the
   a. allele.
   b. chromosome.
   c. gene.
   d. zygote.

6. A gene may have variant forms known as
   a. alleles.
   b. chromosomes.
   c. haploids.
   d. mutants.

7. In a heterozygote, the gene that determines the phenotype is the _____ gene.

8. An illness transmitted by two healthy people to their child is probably transmitted by a _____ gene.

9. Chromosome pairs 1 through 22 are called
   a. karyotypes.
   b. autosomes.
   c. nongender chromosomes.
   d. alleles.

10. A zygote that contains a gene for brown eyes and a gene for blue eyes is said to be
    a. dominant.
    b. recessive.
    c. homozygous.
    d. heterozygous.

11. The combination of genes within a zygote and subsequent daughter cells is said to be the individual's
    a. cell type.
    b. phenotype.
    c. genotype.
    d. genetic endowment.

12. A characteristic that can occur in an individual of either gender and only when both parents have a recessive gene for that characteristic is due to
    a. a mutant gene.
    b. an autosomal, recessive gene.
    c. sex-linked inheritance.
    d. incomplete dominance of the dominant gene.

13. The tool(s) used by genetic counselors is/are
    a. Punnett squares.
    b. an individual's history.
    c. a pedigree.
    d. epidemiological data.

14. Carriers of sickle cell disease rarely contract _____.

15. Huntington's disease is an example of
    a. autosomal recessive inheritance.
    b. X-linked recessive inheritance.
    c. autosomal dominant inheritance.
    d. a mutation.

16. When everyone who inherits a particular genotype has symptoms, the alleles are _____ penetrant.

17. When individuals with the same phenotype have symptoms that vary in intensity, the phenotype is _____ expressive.

18. When the same phenotype may result from the actions of different genes, the cause may be _____ _____.

19. List two traits that are multifactorial traits.

20. Environment plays a role in determining height and skin color.
    a. True
    b. False

21. The somatic cells of a female have
    a. two Y chromosomes.
    b. an X chromosome and a Y chromosome.
    c. two X chromosomes.
    d. no sex chromosomes.

22. Y-linked characteristics are inherited only by sons.
    a. True
    b. False

23. If a male parent has the genotype AA and the female parent has the genotype aa, the offspring's genotype will be
    a. AA.
    b. aa.
    c. Aa.

24. X-linked characteristics are transmitted to
    a. sons from fathers.
    b. daughters from mothers.
    c. sons from mothers.
    d. daughters from fathers.

25. Nondisjunction, a common cause of chromosomal abnormalities, occurs during
    a. meiosis.
    b. mitosis.
    c. fertilization.
    d. cleavage.

26. A chromosomal disorder, due to an entire extra set of chromosomes, is called _____.

27. Cells missing a chromosome or having an extra one are _____.

28. Down syndrome is due to a _____ of chromosome 21.

29. When chromosome 21 exchanges parts with a different chromosome, a subsequent child is (more/less) likely to have mental developmental delays than one with a trisomy of chromosome 21.

30. A female with three X chromosomes is likely to be
    a. mentally delayed.
    b. very tall.
    c. subject to menstrual irregularities.
    d. excessively hairy.

31. A male with XXY syndrome is likely to
    a. have acne.
    b. be infertile.
    c. have speech and reading problems.
    d. have excessive facial hair.

32. Chorionic villus sampling can be performed as early as
    a. 6 weeks.
    b. 10 weeks.
    c. 12 weeks.
    d. 15 weeks.

33. Which is more informative, knowledge of the genomic sequence of a person or examination of the pattern of gene expression?

34. The field of _____ uses gene expression profiling to predict effective drugs with fewer adverse reactions on an individual basis.

STUDY ACTIVITIES

Definition of Word Parts

Define the following word parts used in this chapter.

chromo-

gen-

hetero-

hom-

karyo-

mono-

phen-

tri-

24.1 Genes and Genomes

A.   Answer the following general questions regarding the genetic material of the cell.

   1.   What is a gene?

   2.   What is the chemical make-up of DNA? Name the four chemicals.

   3.   How many nucleotides are found in somatic cells and how many chromosomes are they divided into?

   4.   Transfer of genetic information from one generation to the next occurs through the processes of
        _____ and _____.

   5.   Why are somatic cells defined as diploid?

   6.   Which cells are haploid and how many chromosomes would you find in a haploid cell?

   7.   How many genes are found in the human genome and what does the term "exome" mean?

   8.   Please explain how there can be so many more proteins than there are genes.

   9.   Why is genetic determinism a misconception?

24.2 Mode of Inheritance

A.   Answer the following regarding chromosomal and gene pairing.

   1.   What is a karyotype?

2. How do you discriminate the autosomes from the sex chromosomes?

3. How many genes are found on chromosomes?

4. What is an allele? Describe how alleles determine whether an individual is homozygous or heterozygous.

5. Compare genotype and phenotype.

6. What is the difference between wild-type and mutant alleles?

B. Answer the following concerning dominant and recessive inheritances.

1. How would you know whether an allele was dominant or recessive?

2. The terms autosomal and sex-linked are related to locations of what?

3. Genetics is a field traditionally relying upon observations of traits or illnesses in populations. In the following circumstances, explain how you would determine the mode of inheritance.
   a. An autosomal from an X-linked condition

   b. A recessive allele inheritance from a dominant allele inheritance

4. What tools do genetic counselors use to assist couples planning to conceive?

5. Which pattern do most diseases fall into and why do genetic illnesses remain in populations?

C. Answer the following about different dominance relationships.

1. Define *incomplete dominance* and give an example of a disease with this pattern of inheritance.

2. Define *codominance* and explain how this is different from incomplete dominance.

24.3 Factors That Affect Expression of Single Genes

A. Answer the following regarding expressions of genotypes and phenotypes.

　　1. Define *penetrance*. What is meant when something is incompletely penetrant compared to completely penetrant?

　　2. What does it mean to say that a phenotype is variably expressive?

B. What is pleiotropy?

C. What is genetic heterogeneity?

24.4 Multifactorial Traits

A. Define *polygenic*.

B. What are multifactorial traits? Give examples of these in the human population.

C. How do you recognize polygenic traits in a population?

24.5 Matters of Sex

A. How and when is sex determined?

B. What is "maleness" the result of?

C. Answer the following concerning genes on sex chromosomes.

　　1. What is meant by sex-linked traits?

2. What is the difference between the sex chromosomes, and why aren't they homologues?

3. What are the three groups of Y-linked genes?

4. Explain the inheritance pattern of X-linked and Y-linked traits, including why more males have X-linked traits and why only males have Y-linked traits.

D. Answer the following concerning gender effects on phenotype.

1. What is a sex-limited trait? Give an example.

2. What are sex-influenced traits?

3. Describe genomic imprinting.

24.6 Chromosome Disorders

A. Define *polyploidy* and describe its effects.

B. Answer the following regarding aneuploidy.

1. Define *aneuploidy*.

2. When does this occur and why?

3. What are the results of this and what is a determinant of the survival of the individual?

4. What is the term for an extra chromosome and what is the term for a missing chromosome?

5. Which of the conditions in #4 is more likely to result in a child that survives?

6. Name the three examples of autosomal aneuploidy and explain what happens as a result of the nondisjunction of the specific chromosome.

7. Name the four examples of sex chromosome aneuploidy and describe what happens in each.

8. Why are there more cases of sex chromosome aneuploidy in the population compared to autosomal aneuploidy?

C.   1. Fill in the following table concerning prenatal screening procedures.

Procedure	Time (in Weeks)	Source	Information Provided
Ultrasound			
Maternal Serum Markers			
CVS			
Amniocentesis			
Cell-free Fetal DNA			

2. Why are maternal serum markers being replaced by the cell-free fetal DNA analysis?

24.7 Genomics and Health Care

A.   What is the value of whole exome sequencing? Please give some examples of when it is practical.

B.   Why might examining gene expression profiles be a more practical approach?

C.   Give examples in which the gene expression profiles of certain diseases are predicting better use of pharmaceuticals.

Clinical Focus Questions

A classmate tells you she cannot marry because her mother has Huntington's chorea. How would you respond to this statement? What would you advise her to do?

When you have completed the study activities to your satisfaction, retake the mastery test and compare your performance with your initial attempt. If there are still areas you do not understand, repeat the appropriate study activities.

1 Mastery Test Answers

1. illness and injury
2. hunter-gatherer to agriculture: exposure to intestinal parasites such as pinworms, hook worms due to use of human for fertilizer urbanization: infectious disease due to crowding, decreased exercise, beginning of economic disparities
3. a
4. Latin and Greek
5. anatomy
6. physiology
7. always
8. b
9. d
10. a
11. c
12. e
13. cell
    tissue
    organ
    organ system
    organism
14. movement, responsiveness, growth, reproduction, respiration, digestion, absorption, circulation, assimilation, excretion
15. metabolism
16. pressure
17. water
18. energy living matter
19. necessary to release energy
20. increases
21. respiration
22. a
23. negative feedback
24. receptors, control center, effectors
25. a
26. d
27. are
28. illness
29. axial
30. appendicular
31. diaphragm
32. mediastinum
33. c
34. pleural cavity
35. pericardial
36. abdominopelvic

37. 1. c, 2. d, 3. b, 4. f, 5. d, 6. f, 7. b, 8. c, 9. f, 10. a, 11. e
38. b
39. c
40. a, c, d
41. b, c
42. c
43. b
44. self-assessment

2 Mastery Test Answers

1. biochemistry
2. Matter is anything that has weight and takes up space. It occurs in the forms of solids, liquids, and gases.
3. elements
4. compound
5. bulk
6. C, N, P, O, H, S
7. metabolic
8. a, b, c, d
9. 1. c, 2. a, 3. b
10. protons
11. protons, neutrons
12. number, weight
13. protons, neutrons
14. b
15. electrons
16. c
17. half-life
18. a
19. b
20. d
21. cations; anions
22. a
23. a, b, c, d
24. Yes, molecules are composed of two or more atoms. Compounds are composed of two or more different atoms.
25. molecular
26. structural
27. synthesis, decomposition
28. reversible reaction
29. catalyst
30. 1. b, 2. c, 3. a
31. 7, less than 7, more than 7
32. alkalosis
33. water
34. less
35. ether, alcohol
36. c

47. a. l, b. O, c. O, d. l, e. O, f. l, g. O
41. carbon, oxygen, hydrogen
42. fatty acids, glycerol
43. amino acids
44. a
45. conformations
46. hydrophilic

3 Mastery Test Answers

1. Cell is the basic unit of structure of multicellular organisms.
2. 50–100 trillion cells; 7.5 μm to 500 μm diameter; egg cell
3. differentiation
4. 1. d, 2. c, 3. b, 4. a
5. a, b
6. cytoplasm, nucleus, cell membrane
7. b
8. c
9. a
10. c
11. d
12. b
13. b
14. a
15. a
16. b
17. endoplasmic reticulum
18. a, d
19. d
20. modify proteins
21. powerhouses
22. more
23. d
24. b
25. a, c
26. d
27. cilia, flagella
28. c
29. microfilaments, microtubules
30. nucleolus, chromatin
31. d
32. diffusion
33. facilitated diffusion
34. osmosis
35. a
36. filtration
37. active transport
38. pinocytosis
39. phagocytosis

40. b
41. b
42. interphase
43. 1. c, 2. a, 3. d, 4. b
44. interphase
45. a
46. a. A, b. B, c. A, d. C, e. A
47. a, c, d
48. oncogenes, tumor suppressor
49. pluripotent
50. apoptosis

4 Mastery Test Answers

1. metabolism
2. b
3. anabolic metabolism
4. catabolic metabolism
5. a
6. c
7. protein
8. hydrolysis or digestion
9. balanced with
10. release, require
11. c
12. decreasing
13. b
14. b
15. coenzyme, cofactor
16. minerals, vitamins
17. b
18. a
19. cellular respiration
20. adenine, ribose, phosphates
21. phosphorylation
22. anaerobic, glycolysis
23. b
24. c
25. aerobic
26. oxygen
27. second or aerobic
28. a
29. lactic acid
30. c
31. c
32. muscle cells, liver
33. c
34. a, c
35. genome
36. DNA
37. adenine, thymine, guanine, cytosine
38. purines; pyrimidines
39. a, b
40. nucleus, cytoplasm
41. transfer, messenger, ribosomal
42. c
43. b
44. a
45. b

46. ATP
49. a, c, d
48. spontaneous, induced
49. single nucleotide polymorphism
50. enzyme

5 Mastery Test Answers

1. tissues
2. intercellular junctions
3. c
4. b
5. epithelial, connective, muscle nervous
6. b
7. a, c
8. b
9. shape, layers
10. 1. e, 2. b, 3. f, 4. c, 5. d, 6. h, 7. i, 8. g, 9. a
11. exocrine
12. b
13. a
14. a, b, d
15. fibroblast
16. macrophage
17. heparin, histamine
18. c
19. less; stretched
20. a, b, c, d
21. a, b
22. a
23. c
24. perichondrium
25. hyaline, elastic, fibrocartilage
26. a
27. diffusion
28. a
29. bone
30. plasma
31. b
32. smooth, skeletal, cardiac
33. d
34. nervous
35. neuroglial

6 Mastery Test Answers

1. An organ is two or more kinds of tissues grouped together and performing a specialized function.
2. skin
3. prevents harmful substance from entering, retards water loss, regulates temperature, houses sensory receptors, contains immune cells, synthesizes chemicals, excretes wastes

4. epidermis
5. dermis
6. subcutaneous layer
7. c
8. a, c
9. decubitus ulcer
10. a, b
11. a
12. sunlight
13. b
14. contains
15. hair, hair follicles, nails, skin glands (sebaceous glands, sweat glands)
16. papillary layer composed of loose areolar; reticular layer composed of dense irregular
17. melanin
18. c, d
19. lunula
20. b, c
21. sweat
22. a
23. c
24. a, b, c, d
25. a, d
26. a
27. b
28. granulations
29. a
30. b
31. a

7 Mastery Test Answers

1. a, b, c, d
2. long
3. c
4. b
5. b, d
6. b
7. compact
8. spongy (cancellous)
9. c
10. collagen, inorganic salts
11. sickle cell anemia
12. intramembranous bones
13. endochondral bones
14. d
15. b
16. b
17. a, d
18. nutrition, exposure to sunlight, hormonal secretions, physical exercise
19. a
20. a
21. c
22. b

23. a
24. a, b, c, d
25. red, yellow
26. a, c
27. blood clot formation, nerve impulse conduction, muscle cell contraction
28. c
29. hematopoiesis
30. b
31. 206
32. a
33. skull, hyoid, vertebral column, thoracic cage
34. pectoral girdle, arms or upper limbs, pelvic girdle, legs or lower limbs
35. b
36. a, d
37. occipital
38. sphenoid
39. cranium
40. palatine processes
41. fontanels
42. c
43. c
44. b
45. spondylolysis
46. c
47. sacrum
48. c
49. a, b, c, d
50. sternum
51. d
52. sternal angle
53. clavicles, scapulae
54. b
55. a
56. metacarpal
57. a
58. c
59. b
60. calcanus
61. a
62. pelvis, vertebrae

8 Mastery Test Answers

1. a, b, c
2. diarthrosis, amphiarthrosis, synarthrosis, fibrous, cartilaginous, synovial
3. b, c
4. fibrous
5. synchondrosis, cartilaginous
6. is
7. c
8. subchondral plate
9. b
10. c
11. b

12. synovial membrane
13. a, c
14. d
15. by location
16. covering the epiphyses
17. d
18. 1. c, 2. e, 3. b, 4. a
19. a
20. c
21. humerus, scapula
22. is not
23. dislocation
24. humerus, ulna
25. pronation and supination of the hand
26. arthroscope
27. acetabulum, hip
28. extension, flexion, abduction, adduction, rotation, and circumduction
29. knee
30. a
31. sprain
32. b

9 Mastery Test Answers

1. skeletal or voluntary
2. a
3. b
4. fasciculli or fascicles
5. epimysium
6. d
7. fasciotomy
8. actin, myosin
9. b
10. actin
11. transverse tubules
12. tropomyosin, troponin
13. muscle strain
14. c
15. does not
16. neurotransmitter
17. c
18. a
19. calcium
20. tropomyosin
21. rigor mortis
22. adenosine triphosphate or ATP
23. c
24. myasthenia gravis
25. creatine phosphate
26. myoglobin
27. a, d
28. lactic acid
29. d
30. threshold stimulus
31. twitch
32. c
33. a

34. c
35. isotonic
36. isometric
37. c
38. fast
39. b
40. more slowly
41. multiunit, visceral
42. calmodium
43. a, c
44. a, c
45. yes
46. calcium channel blockers
47. levers
48. origin, insertion
49. antagonists
50. d
51. temporomandibular joint
52. a
53. trapezius
54. b
55. d
56. linea alba
57. b
58. calcaneal, Achilles

10 Mastery Test Answers

1. neurons, neuroglia
2. a
3. b
4. synapses
5. neurotransmitters
6. central, peripheral
7. sensory
8. somatic, autonomic
9. cell body, axons, dendrites
10. chromatophilic substances, Nissl bodies
11. b
12. d
13. a
14. c
15. c
16. c
17. c
18. b
19. presynaptic
20. resting potential
21. membrane potential
22. c
23. absolute refractory
24. d
25. a
26. a
27. b
28. a
29. c
30. enkephalins
31. convergence
32. divergence

11 Mastery Test Answers

1. brain, spinal cord
2. two cerebral hemispheres, the diencephalon, the brain stem, and the cerebellum
3. d
4. a
5. c
6. a, b
7. b
8. choroid plexus
9. a, b, d
10. c
11. 31
12. b, d
13. d
14. b
15. d
16. b
17. b
18. b
19. b
20. a
21. spina bifida
22. a
23. c
24. b, c
25. 1. c, 2. d, 3. b, 4. a, 5. b, 6. a
26. pre-frontal
27. a
28. b, c
29. c
30. left
31. b
32. speak
33. b
34. a
35. b
36. c
37. b
38. d
39. c
40. d
41. b
42. limbic system
43. medulla oblongata
44. paradoxical
45. a, d
46. a
47. somatic, autonomic
48. c
49. 12, brain stem
50. b
51. c
52. a
53. brachial
54. b
55. autonomic
56. lateral horn; thoracic, lumbar
57. brainstem, sacral
58. 1. a, 2. b, 3. a, 4. b
59. a, b
60. c, d
61. brain, spinal cord, ganglia

12 Mastery Test Answers

1. a, c
2. cerebral cortex
3. a, b, c, d, e
4. sensory adaptation
5. general
6. 1. b, 2. d, 3. b, 4. b, 5. c, 6. a
7. b
8. b
9. b
10. neuropathic
11. a, d
12. d
13. d
14. referred
15. acute
16. spinal
17. endorphins
18. a
19. special
20. b
21. c
22. olfactory nerve or olfactory tracts
23. c
24. b
25. sweet, salty, sour, bitter, umami
26. smell
27. equilibrium
28. cerumen
29. c, d
30. d
31. c
32. c
33. osseous labyrinth, membranous labyrinth
34. perilymph
35. a
36. c
37. sensorineural
38. sensorineural
39. vestibule
40. b
41. c
42. a
43. cornea
44. a
45. d
46. b
47. optic nerve
48. b, c
49. a
50. cornea
51. b
52. pupil
53. melanin
54. retina
55. b
56. vitreous humor
57. refraction
58. presbyopia
59. rods, cones
60. 1. a, 2. b, 3. a, 4. b
61. rhodopsin, opsin, retinal
62. erythrolabe, chlorolabe, cyanolabe
63. color blindness
64. partial, both eyes

13 Mastery Test Answers

1. hormone
2. paracrine; autocrine
3. exocrine
4. hormones; bloodstream
5. regulate metabolic processes; control rates of chemical reactions; help transport substances across cell membranes; help regulate fluid and electrolyte balance; regulate blood pressure; play roles in reproduction, growth, and development
6. b
7. a
8. b
9. a, d
10. locally
11. d
12. nonsteroid
13. c
14. c, d
15. steroid hormones
16. b
17. b, d
18. hypothalamus
19. a, b
20. posterior
21. a, c
22. b, d
23. acromegaly
24. prolactin
25. a, d
26. a, b, d
27. a, c
28. a
29. thyroxine, triiodothyronine
30. c, d
31. iodine
32. calcitonin
33. c

34. a, b, c
35. a, d
36. epinephrine, norepinephrine
37. a
38. a, b, c
39. male
40. b, c
41. pancreatic islets
42. glucagon
43. b, d
44. diabetes mellitus
45. b
46. a
47. T lymphocytes
48. c, d
49. more
50. renin
51. c

14 Mastery Test Answers

1. nutrients, oxygen, wastes, hormones, electrolytes, erythrocytes, thrombocytes, leukocytes
2. red bone marrow
3. 4–6 liters
4. hematocrit
5. transport, regulation, defense
6. 55
7. a
8. a, b, c
9. nucleus
10. 4,200,000–5,400,000 cells/µl; 4,600,000–6,200,000 cells/µl
11. c
12. a, d
13. d
14. erythropoietin
15. yes
16. b
17. b
18. a
19. a
20. b
21. 5,000 to 10,000
22. b, c
23. platelet or thrombocyte
24. 1. c, 2. a, 3. b, 4. b, 5. c
25. a
26. sodium, magnesium, potassium, calcium, phosphates, sulfates, chlorides, bicarbonates
27. b, c, d
28. b
29. d
30. b
31. fibrinogen, fibrin
32. a, c

33. d
34. positive
35. prothrombin time, partial prothrombin time
36. b
37. streptokinase
38. d
39. a
40. hemophilia
41. b
42. a
43. c
44. erythroblastosis fetalis
45. Rhogam
46. a

15 Mastery Test Answers

1. 7,000–9,000
2. pulmonary and systemic circuits
3. mediastinum
4. d
5. a
6. c
7. atria, ventricles
8. auricles
9. a, d
10. c
11. a, b
12. d
13. aortic
14. b
15. cardiac skeleton
16. right atrium, tricuspid valve, right ventricle, pulmonary valve, pulmonary arteries; lungs; pulmonary veins, left atrium; mitral valve; left ventricle, aortic valve, aorta, coronary arteries, systemic circulation
17. coronary arteries
18. b
19. decreases
20. coronary sinus
21. cardiac cycle
22. c, d
23. b
24. a
25. AV node
26. c
27. ECG (electrocardiogram)
28. a
29. d
30. decreases
31. b, c
32. d
33. b
34. c
35. a, d
36. endothelium

37. b, d
38. a, c
39. a
40. filtration, osmosis, diffusion
41. diffusion
42. They are not lipid soluble and their molecules are too large to diffuse through the capillary wall.
43. an increase in blood pressure due to ventricular contraction
44. a
45. a
46. c
47. valves
48. d
49. varicose veins
50. b
51. stroke volume
52. heart rate, blood volume, stroke volume, viscosity, peripheral resistance
53. resistance
54. stroke volume, heart rate
55. c
56. parasympathetic
57. b
58. vasodilator
59. essential or primary
60. b, c, d
61. a, b
62. b
63. d
64. left atrium
65. b, c
66. circle of Willis
67. hepatic portal system
68. cholesterol

16 Mastery Test Answers

1. transportation of excess fluid from interstitial spaces and defend against infection and absorb fats
2. d
3. lacteals, fats
4. lymphatic capillaries,
5. b
6. b
7. b
8. c
9. c
10. a, c
11. veins
12. a
13. edema
14. a, b
15. d
16. lymphadenitis
17. Peyer's patches

291

18. b
19. b
20. b
21. b, c
22. spleen
23. b, d
24. pathogens
25. a, c
26. c
27. more rapidly
28. c
29. c
30. redness, swelling, heat, pain
31. b
32. neutrophils, monocytes
33. b
34. mononuclear phagocyte (reticuloendothelial)
35. immunity
36. thymus
37. antigens
38. d
39. d
40. cell-mediated
41. gamma globulin
42. b
43. a, b, c, d
44. complement
45. both
46. d
47. passive
48. hypersensitivity reaction
49. a
50. a, b
51. T cells
52. c
53. autoimmune
54. c, d

17 Mastery Test Answers

1. digestion
2. alimentary canal
3. accessory organs
4. mucosa, submucosa, muscular layer, serosa
5. b
6. mixing, propelling
7. no
8. b, c
9. a, c, d
10. frenulum
11. c
12. wisdom teeth
13. a
14. c
15. d
16. increase
17. b
18. peristalsis
19. Barrett's esophagus
20. b

21. hypertrophic pyloric stenosis
22. c
23. b
24. vitamin B_{12}
25. decreases
26. b
27. inhibits
28. chyme
29. a
30. a, b
31. inhibits
32. medulla oblongata
33. a
34. a
35. b
36. alkaline
37. a
38. upper right
39. c
40. ferritin
41. c
42. b, c, d
43. a, d
44. c, d
45. a, b, d
46. duodenum, jejunum, ileum
47. b
48. c
49. d
50. c
51. peristaltic rush
52. LDL; HDL
53. cecum
54. b
55. electrolytes, water
56. a, c
57. c

18 Mastery Test Answers

1. carbohydrates, proteins, fats
2. vitamins, minerals
3. essential nutrients
4. leptin
5. b
6. a, b
7. cellulose
8. oxidation or cellular respiration
9. b, d
10. d
11. b
12. triglycerides
13. linoleic acid or linolenic acid
14. b
15. d
16. cholesterol
17. too much
18. a, c, d
19. amino acids

20. complete
21. yes
22. a
23. a, c
24. calories
25. basal metabolic rate
26. a, c
27. negative
28. c
29. fat
30. a, b
31. a
32. sunlight or ultraviolet rays
33. c
34. b, d
35. b
36. a
37. a
38. a, c
39. b
40. c
41. d
42. c
43. calcium, phosphorus
44. c
45. b
46. aldosterone
47. sodium
48. d
49. oxygen
50. a, b, c, d
51. vitamin C
52. c
53. primary
54. b
55. b

19 Mastery Test Answers

1. respiration
2. c
3. energy
4. carbonic acid; decrease
5. b, d
6. 1. a, 2. b, 3. a, 4. a, 5. c
7. a, b, c, d
8. no
9. nasal cavity, larynx
10. b, c
11. thyroid cartilage
12. a
13. a
14. tracheostomy
15. c
16. alveolar ducts
17. decreases
18. fiberoptic bronchoscope
19. a
20. b
21. hilum
22. right
23. visceral pleura

292

24. parietal pleura
25. contracts, increasing, decreasing
26. c
27. pleural
28. surfactant
29. c
30. compliance
31. b
32. spirometer
33. d
34. respiratory capacities
35. trachea, bronchus, bronchioles
36. equal
37. alveolar ventilation
38. nonrespiratory air movements
39. b
40. c
41. brain stem
42. a
43. ventral respiratory group
44. a
45. carbon dioxide
46. c
47. a, c, d
48. alveolar macrophage
49. alveolus, capillary
50. pressure
51. partial pressure
52. a
53. hemoglobin
54. increase
55. hemoglobin
56. c
57. increases

20 Mastery Test Answers

1. b, c
2. a, b, c
3. renal pelvis
4. d
5. renal cortex
6. a, b, c, d
7. d
8. a, b
9. b
10. b
11. c
12. collecting duct
13. macula densa
14. d
15. urine
16. a
17. glomerular filtration rate
18. b
19. hydrostatic pressure
20. maintain
21. decrease

22. decrease
23. no
24. c
25. d
26. b
27. a
28. b
29. aldosterone
30. countercurrent
31. b
32. protein
33. d
34. b, d
35. d
36. d
37. b
38. ureters
39. b, c
40. decrease
41. trigone
42. b
43. urgency
44. 150
45. a
46. vagina, clitoris

21 Mastery Test Answers

1. equal
2. c
3. intracellular
4. extracellular
5. d
6. hydrostatic
7. osmotic
8. a
9. c
10. c
11. diuretics
12. extracellular fluid
13. c, d
14. enters
15. a
16. decreased, osmotic
17. food, beverages
18. perspiration, feces, urine
19. aldosterone
20. a, b, c
21. a, c
22. hydrogen ion
23. c
24. 7.4
25. more
26. b
27. c
28. combine with
29. c
30. a
31. rate, depth
32. c
33. hydrogen

34. a
35. b

22 Mastery Test Answers

1. a, b, c, d
2. haploid
3. 23
4. testes
5. b, c
6. b
7. spermatic cord
8. gubernaculum
9. d
10. cryptorchidism
11. b
12. a
13. spermatogonia
14. d
15. acrosome
16. continuously
17. mitochondria, midpiece
18. c
19. seminal vesicles
20. b, d
21. neutralize
22. c
23. a, d
24. dartos
25. b
26. a, b, d
27. c
28. secondary sex
29. inhibin
30. ovaries
31. c
32. one
33. primary follicle
34. b
35. d
36. ovulation
37. a, d
38. endometrium
39. a
40. b, c
41. c
42. a, c
43. estrogen, progesterone
44. b, c
45. menarche
46. a, d
47. b
48. corpus luteum
49. b
50. a, c
51. pectoralis major
52. b, c
53. b
54. vasectomy
55. c
56. c

23 Mastery Test Answers

1. growth
2. development
3. prenatal
4. postnatal
5. b
6. d
7. c
8. b, d
9. morula
10. c
11. d
12. human chorionic gonadotropin
13. inner cell mass
14. b
15. placenta
16. b
17. primary germ
18. b
19. b
20. a
21. placenta
22. amnion
23. c
24. c, d
25. 8
26. teratogens
27. neural tube
28. b
29. c
30. b, d
31. vein
32. a
33. foramen ovale, ductus arteriosus
34. surfactant
35. progesterone, oxytocin
36. c
37. prolactin
38. b
39. c, d
40. less
41. d
42. infancy
43. adolescence
44. senescence
45. a, c
46. b
47. a, b, d
48. apoptosis

24 Mastery Test Answers

1. genome; DNA
2. genetics
3. b, c
4. diploid, 46; haploid, 23
5. c
6. a
7. dominant
8. recessive
9. b
10. d
11. c
12. b
13. a, c
14. malaria
15. c
16. completely
17. variably
18. genetic heterogeneity
19. height, skin color
20. a
21. c
22. a
23. c
24. b, c, d
25. a
26. polyploidy
27. aneuploid
28. trisomy
29. more
30. b, c
31. b
32. b
33. examination of the pattern of gene expression
34. personalized medicine